Security and Global Health

Security and Global Health

Toward the Medicalization of Insecurity

STEFAN ELBE

Dear Sara,
I wish you all
the best for
your studies!

polity

First published in 2010 by Polity Press

Polity Press
65 Bridge Street
Cambridge CB2 1UR, UK

Polity Press
350 Main Street
Malden, MA 02148, USA

ISBN-13: 978-0-7456-4373-1
ISBN-13: 978-0-7456-4374-8 (paperback)

A catalogue record for this book is available from the British Library.

Typeset in 10.5 on 13 pt Minion
by Servis Filmsetting Ltd, Stockport, Cheshire
Printed and bound by MPG Books Group Ltd

The publisher has used its best endeavours to ensure that the URLs for external websites referred to in this book are correct and active at the time of going to press. However, the publisher has no responsibility for the websites and can make no guarantee that a site will remain live or that the content is or will remain appropriate.

For further information on Polity, visit our website: www.politybooks.com

To James

The health of all peoples is fundamental to the attainment of peace and security.
Constitution of the World Health Organization

Politics is nothing else but medicine on a large scale.
Rudolf Virchow

It is clear that humanity did not remain immune to medicalization.
Michel Foucault

Contents

Acknowledgements   viii

1. Health Security: The Medicalization of Security in the
   Twenty-First Century   1

2. Microbes Take to the Sky: Pandemic Threats and National
   Security   30

3. Poisoning Populations: Biosecurity and the
   Weaponization of Disease   66

4. A Global Pharmacy for the Poor? Endemics and Other
   Human Insecurities   99

5. The Lifestyle Timebombs: Panics about Cigarettes, Fat
   and Alcohol   132

6. Bodies as Battlefields: Medicalization and the Future of
   Health Security   165

References   189

Index   208

Acknowledgements

I would like to thank the many public officials and scholars who agreed to provide background interviews for this project. Although they are far too numerous to be mentioned here by name, the book could not have been written if they had not decided to take time out of their busy schedules. I am particularly grateful in that respect to Paul Gully who provided extensive help in facilitating the interviews carried out at the headquarters of the World Health Organization in Geneva just days before the outbreak of pandemic H1N1 flu in the spring of 2009.

I would also like to thank all those who, in one form or another, have commented on the wider research project that formed the basis of this book, including Emma Broughton, David Campbell, Christopher Coker, Peter Conrad, Martin Coward, Christian Enemark, Harley Feldbaum, Paul Forster, Jonathan Herrington, Mellissa Leach, Aline Leboeuf, Ronnie Lippens, Luis Lobo-Guerrero, Colin McInnes, Simon Rushton, Ian Scoones, Hakan Seckinelgin, Jan Selby, Nick Thomas, Nadine Voelkner, Maja Zehfuss and the graduate students on my Global Politics of Disease course at the University of Sussex.

The project benefited further from feedback received at the French Institute of International Affairs (IFRI), the University of Hong Kong, the STEPS Centre at the University of Sussex, the annual convention of the International Studies Association, and the general conference of the European Consortium for Political Research. I am also indebted to two anonymous reviewers of this manuscript, as well as to Louise Knight, Rachel Donnelly, Emma Hutchinson and David Winters at Polity Press, all of whom helped to improve the manuscript immeasurably.

My deepest gratitude, finally, goes to Louiza Odysseos who has been a constant intellectual companion throughout the voyage of this book. Without her copious help and encouragement it would never have come to fruition. Any errors of fact, judgment or interpretation remain, of course, entirely my own.

The research conducted for this book was supported by a British Academy Research and Development Award (BARDA-47928).

1

Health Security: The Medicalization of Security in the Twenty-First Century

The health of all peoples is fundamental to the attainment of peace and security. So, at least, argued the constitution of the World Health Organization agreed in New York on 22 July 1946. It seems that, initially, no one took this argument too seriously. For several decades the connection between health and security would be dismissed as a mere hyperbole generated amongst the frenzy of international-ist idealism arising from the ashes of the Second World War. The international management of disease would largely remain confined to the mould of 'low' politics. It was perennially overshadowed in the theatre of world politics by the more pressing concerns of avoiding renewed wars, and the ever-present spectre of a nuclear confrontation.

The twentieth century's deep addiction to war, coupled with its revolutionary advances in medicine, reinforced the view in the West that the world was moving toward a situation in which infectious dis-eases would eventually be controlled by a series of scientific, medical and pharmacological breakthroughs. How else can we explain the bold declaration made by US Secretary of State George Marshall, only two years after the creation of the World Health Organization, that the conquest of all infectious diseases was imminent? And, one by one, many of the big killer diseases of history did indeed succumb at the altar of modern medicine – from diphtheria and typhoid through to smallpox and polio. Our concept of security reflected that mood of medical optimism, becoming ever more obsessed with a narrow focus on controlling the deployment of armed force in international relations.

More than half a century later, things have changed considerably. Today there are once again high levels of international concern about a host of potentially lethal 'rogue' viruses circulating the planet. These include relatively new ones such as the pandemic H1N1 2009 influenza virus ('swine flu') and the highly pathogenic H5N1 strand of avian influenza, through to the coronavirus responsible for severe acute respiratory syndrome (SARS) and the globally much more entrenched human immunodeficiency virus (HIV) that causes AIDS. The medical optimism of the twentieth century has thus been displaced. We have entered a new era of deep microbial unease.

Nothing exemplifies that mood shift more poignantly than the growing tendency to articulate international health policy through the metaphors and vocabulary of security. Once confined to the rumblings of 'low' politics, many health issues are now advancing toward the apex of the international security agenda, as policy-makers working in international organizations and national governments grapple with a range of important links between health and security. Only now, in other words, are we truly beginning to heed the warning issued by the founders of the World Health Organization more than half a century ago – that health issues and security concerns are inextricably linked. Our concept of security is therefore in flux once more. Following its severe contraction in the course of the twentieth century, the meaning of 'security' is widening again – this time to acquire an important health dimension.

That expansion of the security agenda to incorporate a growing range of international health issues also forms the subject matter of this book. Specifically, the book wishes to analyse how those health security debates subtly transform our understanding of security. Thus the book deliberately approaches the health–security nexus from directly the opposite perspective of most prior studies. Where others have sought to probe how discussions on health security affect the international governance of particular diseases for better or for worse, this study analyses how those same debates conversely also reshape our notions of security and insecurity in contemporary world politics. The focus of this book, in short, is on security rather than on disease. Taking such a fresh approach is fruitful in that it opens up a novel perspective on the recent rise of health security. Widely understood in the existing literature as the 'securitization' of health, the pages below advance a novel conceptualization of the health–security nexus as the medicalization of security.

The Rise of Health Security

The collision between the worlds of health and security which is unfolding at the outset of the new millennium has already given rise to a new concept – 'health security'. The precise meaning of the term, which is now frequently invoked in policy debates and official documents, still remains far from settled. William Aldis (2008: 370) notes in his recent overview of the concept that 'there is no universally agreed definition. Widespread but inconsistent use of the term by global public health stakeholders with widely divergent perceptions, priorities and agendas has created confusion and mistrust.' Clearly the idea of health security still means different – even conflicting – things to many people, and usage of the concept fluctuates considerably depending upon which political groups and organizations are represented at the table. Perhaps that ambiguity is to be expected given the relative novelty of the term. It also mirrors the evolution of earlier notions whose exact meanings remain similarly contested – such as human security, environmental security or, indeed, sustainable development.

Looking back over the past decade, it is possible to detect an early appearance of the idea of health security in May 2001, when the World Health Assembly (WHA) – the Geneva-based policy-setting forum of the World Health Organization – passed a resolution on 'Global Health Security: Epidemic Alert and Response'. A background report to the meetings warned that:

> The globalization of infectious diseases is not a new phenomenon. However, increased population movements, whether through tourism or migration or as a result of disasters; growth in international trade in food and biological products; social and environmental changes linked with urbanization, deforestation and alterations in climate; and changes in methods of food processing, distribution and consumer habits have reaffirmed that infectious disease events in one country are potentially a concern for the entire world. (WHA 2001: 1)

Under the single heading of 'health security' that brief and early document thus dealt simultaneously with a broad set of diverse issues, ranging from the revision of the International Health Regulations and responses to infectious disease outbreaks through to countering rising rates of antimicrobial drug resistance throughout the world. From its genesis, the meaning of 'health security' was quite fluid, imprecise and ambiguous.

Half a year later, the idea of health security received renewed impetus in very different quarters when, on 7 November 2001, the health ministers of Canada, France, Germany, Italy, Japan, the United Kingdom, the United States and Mexico met in Ottawa to convene the first meeting of the Global Health Security Initiative (GHSI). That initiative represents one of the most prominent institutionalizations of the idea of health security to have emerged so far. The Global Health Security Initiative was established in direct response to the attacks of 11 September 2001. United States Secretary of Health and Human Services Tommy Thompson argued at the time that protecting populations against such attacks would henceforth require countries to pool more information and to increase levels of cooperation. The ministerial statement issued at the end of that inaugural meeting made the direct connection between health issues and security concerns. It referred to the importance of the 'health *and* security' of populations (emphasis added). By the time of the second meeting of the initiative, held in London in March 2002, those two areas had been conflated into the singular concept of 'health security'. The ministerial statement from that meeting thus set out the network's determination to 'improve health security globally, and to better prepare for and respond to acts of biological, chemical and radio-nuclear terrorism' (GHSI 2002).

Here usage of the health security concept was also much narrower than at the World Health Assembly. Health security effectively became part of the international effort to re-focus the security agenda around the threat of terrorism following the momentous events of 2001. Specific areas singled out by the network thus included the ability to respond to radiological or nuclear events, chemical events and biological threats (especially smallpox), as well as strategies for ensuring the safety of food and water supplies. In that vein, the Global Health Security Initiative network set out to explore greater collaboration between its members in relation to the procurement, development and rapid testing of vaccines and antibiotics, as well as setting up the necessary links between various national laboratories. The network also sought to share more information on disease surveillance and emergency response plans. All of those activities marked a very different appropriation of the concept of health security, and one that many in the international public health community felt was anathema to the broader humanitarian spirit of global health.

Responding in part to such concerns, it did not take long before the Global Health Security Initiative decided to broaden its health security remit beyond the threat of terrorism. The Mexico City meeting in December 2002 was particularly significant in that regard, in that the network there decided to expand its portfolio of issues to include as well the public health threat posed by pandemic influenza. Naturally occurring infectious diseases and bioterrorist threats were increasingly perceived as two sides of the same coin. The argument justifying this move was that countries could be harmed by infectious disease irrespective of whether such an outbreak was caused intentionally or unintentionally. That effectively combined some of the earlier usages of the term by the World Health Assembly with the efforts of the Global Health Security Initiative. Much like the initial resolution of the World Health Assembly, therefore, the GHSI too eventually found the meaning of health security to be far from settled and ended up incorporating a diverse range of policy concerns under that heading – ranging from bioterrorism through to infectious diseases with pandemic potential.

Since that time, the concept of health security has also made inroads elsewhere. The European Commission created the Health Security Committee as an informal coordinating body for exchanging information on health-related threats stemming from acts of terrorism and other deliberate releases of harmful agents. At its headquarters in Geneva, the World Health Organization established a similar Strategic Advisory Committee for Global Health Security. That group comprises more than twenty experts external to the organization who provide advice on health security matters in a personal capacity. The World Health Organization recently also changed the name of its Communicable Disease Cluster to the 'Health Security and Environment' Cluster.

Such is the importance which the World Health Organization

attaches to the notion that it also dedicated the annual commemoration of its foundation – World Health Day (7 April) – to the theme of 'International Health Security', sponsoring a series of high-level debates on the theme. According to its future plans, strengthening 'individual' and 'global' health security represents one of the core priorities for the World Health Organization for the period of 2006 to 2015. The notion of health security even featured in the title of its 2007 World Health Report, *A Safer Future: Global Public Health Security in the 21st Century*. That report defined health security as 'the activities required, both proactive and reactive, to minimize vulnerability to acute public health events that endanger the collective health of populations living across geographical regions and international boundaries' (WHO 2007a: ix). Rather than drawing a firm line between naturally occurring outbreaks and the threat of bioterrorism, this definition of health security too remained amenable to both eventualities by focusing on 'acute' events – irrespective of how they are caused.

At times, that emphasis on acute events has placed the secretariat of the World Health Organization at odds with several other groups within the wider United Nations system which are pursuing much broader global health objectives. Amongst those groups, it is often felt that the focus of health security concerns should not be restricted to the threats of bioterrorism or pandemics, as those are the health threats perceived to be most closely associated with the interests of Western states. Rather, the focus of health security should be on diseases that are endemic in the global South. Various global health groups have thus been attempting to re-adjust the priority of international health security activities around diseases that already burden large numbers of people in the developing world as they go about their daily lives. Increasingly the need to address those frequently overlooked and neglected diseases also forms an important element in the ongoing contest over the precise meaning of health security.

Irrespective of which interpretation of the health security concept one favours in the end, there is a clear sense that something important is happening in the growing association between health and security and that 'neither security nor public health policy will ever be the same again' (Fidler and Gostin 2008: 122). That alone makes the rise of health security a phenomenon worthy of further investigation and has already prompted a burgeoning literature analysing various aspects of the emerging health–security nexus. So far, that health security literature has tended to address one of two questions, both of which remain very relevant today.

Health and Security: Where are the Links?

First, several studies seek to answer the question of exactly how health issues and security concerns are linked empirically. Using both qualitative and quantitative research methodologies, these studies try to identify which health issues have, or could have, a significant impact on security concerns. Amongst the most pioneering of these are the book-length analyses carried out by Andrew Price-Smith entitled *The Health of Nations* (Price-Smith 2001) and *Contagion and Chaos* (Price-Smith 2009). Yet the literature on the links between health and security has already become too extensive to be summarized here. That literature has been produced by scholars (see Elbe 2002; Fidler 2003; Huang 2003; Ostergard, Jr, 2005; Feldbaum et al. 2006; McInnes and Lee 2006; Enemark 2007; Ingram 2007; Fidler and Gostin 2008), as well as by influential think tanks (see CBACI 2000; Ban 2001; ICG 2001; Kassalow 2001; Elbe 2003; Garrett 2005; CSIS 2006). Schematically – and mirroring the competing understandings of health security noted above – this growing body of work can be divided into four broad groups, depending on the underlying concept of security that the studies use as their analytical reference point: national security, biosecurity, human security and public health security.

Studies focusing on national security have highlighted the threat that emerging and re-emerging infectious diseases pose in the context of a globalized and interdependent world economy. As early as 1992, and amidst the shifting geopolitical tectonics of the end of the Cold War, an influential report issued by the Institute of Medicine in the United States, entitled *Emerging Infections: Microbial Threats to Health in the United States*, warned that 'some infectious diseases that now affect people in other parts of the world represent

potential threats to the United States because of global interdependence, modern transportation, trade, and changing social and cultural
patterns' (Lederberg et al. 1992: v). A national intelligence estimate
subsequently produced by the National Intelligence Council (NIC
2000) in the United States confirmed many of those fears. 'The Global
Infectious Disease Threat and Its Implications for the United States',
which was declassified in January 2000, noted that, since 1973, at
least thirty previously unknown disease agents have been identified
(including some for which there is no cure, such as HIV, Ebola, hepatitis C and the Nipah virus). The report also pointed out that during
that same period, at least twenty older infectious diseases have re-
emerged, frequently in drug-resistant form – most notably amongst
them tuberculosis (TB), malaria and cholera. Such infectious diseases
are thought to be linked to national security because of the mortality and economic disruption they could potentially cause – be it
SARS, bird flu (H5N1) or the novel pandemic H1N1 virus that began
causing human infections in 2009.

A further nexus between disease and security has been identified
by security analysts concerned about the prospects of a biological
weapons attack. Here the worlds of health and security coincide
because terrorists and other radical political groups might attempt
to release a disease-inducing biological agent deliberately in order
to stage a mass-casualty attack on a civilian population. The fear, in
short, is that disease could become a weapon for terrorists – although
expert opinion remains deeply divided about the likelihood of such
an attack. The deliberate release of sarin gas in Tokyo's subway system
by the Aum Shinrikyo cult in 1995 represented an early warning sign
in that respect. Although that was a chemical (rather than a biological) attack, the release also provoked wider fears about the possibility
of future biological attacks. Those concerns were exacerbated by the
events of 11 September 2001 in New York City and Washington, DC,
which demonstrated that terrorist groups – if capable – might not shy
away from orchestrating mass-casualty attacks on civilian populations. What is more, the following month, mysterious letters laced
with anthrax were then also mailed to various prominent addresses
in the United States. That showed just how easily biological materials
could be disseminated throughout the United States if an individual

or group gained possession of them. Here too the domains of health and security are seen to intersect in a crucial way.

Additional links between health and security have been identified by those working with the newer and broader concept of human security. As its name implies, the human security framework privileges the individual as the referent object of security. It too is concerned about the threat posed by a range of diseases. 'At the simplest level', two scholars note, 'premature and unnecessary loss of life is perhaps the greatest insecurity of human life' (Chen and Narasimhan 2003: 5). That argument renders virtually any lethal disease a human security threat, bringing even more diseases into play. Here the most pervasive threats to security are not seen to emanate from those 'acute' and highly infectious diseases that can spread rapidly between countries, or those that could be deliberately released by a terrorist group. They stem instead from a range of much less sensational illnesses that remain endemic in many low-income countries hampered by a weak public health infrastructure – such as HIV/ AIDS, malaria and tuberculosis. Collectively, those three illnesses alone are estimated to account for around 5 million deaths annually. Human security advocates thus highlight that, in many low-income countries, it is not so much the spectre of armed conflict, or indeed bioterrorism, which constitutes the greatest security threat for the majority of people – but the absence of more effective and affordable health care. That in turn has generated a third, but no less important, nexus between health and security.

Finally, a more subtle link between health and security has also been postulated by public health officials in relation to a number of non-communicable 'lifestyle' diseases that seem to be rapidly gathering pace – especially (though not exclusively) in many wealthier societies. A plethora of official reports and statements now habitually warn that several lifestyle diseases have reached 'epidemic' proportions in the West, especially problems such as smoking, obesity and excessive alcohol consumption. The word 'security' hardly ever crops up explicitly in discussions about how to respond to such challenges. Yet, implicitly, those debates and discourses too postulate links between health and security by portraying those phenomena not just as 'mere' public health issues, but as much more serious 'threats' to societies and populations. Those phenomena are routinely construed as population 'timebombs' and impending 'crises'. If nothing is done, it is only a matter of time before those phenomena will reach such high levels within the population that they will begin to have a range of deeply detrimental economic and social consequences. That too is an area where links between health and security have been implicitly asserted, and thus forms an important part of the first research trajectory on health security concerned with identifying the most important empirical relationships between health and security.

The Securitization of Health

Increasingly, scholars are also raising a second and more reflective question about health security: does the security framing of diseases actually improve or diminish international attempts to govern them more effectively? Here the primary concern is not to identify the empirical links between health and security, but to probe whether the construal of health issues as security threats is beneficial or in fact harmful when it comes to responding to the complex social, economic and political challenges they pose. These studies tend to conceptualize the health–security nexus as the 'securitization' of health – a phrase that has now become ubiquitous in the literature (Elbe 2006; McInnes 2006a, 2006b; Davies 2008). One of the most prominent writers on international health issues even argues that global health governance has already entered its 'post-securitization' phase, meaning 'the policy belief that public health can be improved by framing and approaching problems through security-related tactics and strategies has become a leading driver of public health governance' (Fidler 2007: 41).

Drawing upon securitization theory (see Buzan et al. 1998; see also Wæver 1995; M. Williams 2003), many of these studies take a broadly constructivist approach to the study of security practices, and remain sensitive to the inter-subjective nature of portraying social issues as security threats – that is of 'speaking' security. In that respect, they also form part of a growing body of literature bringing the insights of speech act theory – as pioneered by J. L. Austin (1962) at Harvard

University in the 1950s and subsequently developed by several other prominent philosophers and linguists (Searle 1969) – to bear on contemporary social and political analysis. Austin (1962: 1) had argued that the point of speech act theory was to challenge the assumption that 'the business of a "statement" can only be to "describe" some state of affairs, or to "state some fact", which it must do either truly or falsely'. Even though language certainly encodes and transmits factual information, speech act theory illustrates how language can also do much more than just convey information. Austin became particularly interested in phrases that constitute a form of action or social activity in themselves, i.e. phrases such as saying 'thank you', 'you are fired', 'I promise', 'I bet', 'I nominate', and so forth. These are instances in which a speaker is using language not just for the purposes of description, but also for actually doing something with wider social significance – hence the term speech acts. In saying 'thank you', for example, one is not making a statement that is either true or false, but is undertaking the act of thanking somebody with all of the wider social significance which that act entails.

The core conceptual innovation of securitization theory is to view the act of labelling an issue a security threat as similarly constituting such a performative speech act. Security 'is not interesting as a sign referring to something more real; it is the utterance itself that is the act. By saying the words, something is done (like betting, giving a promise, naming a ship)' (Buzan et al. 1998: 26). That security speech act has four constituent elements which must be met for a successful securitization to occur (Buzan et al. 1998: 24, 36): (1) securitizing actors (political leaders, intelligence experts, and so on) must declare (2) a referent object (such as a state, society or population) to be existentially threatened (for example by an immanent invasion), and must make a persuasive call for the adoption (3) of emergency measures to counter this threat (such as declaring war or imposing a curfew), and (4) the audience must then also accept that argument to a sufficient degree for it to become possible to do things politically that would not have otherwise been possible to do under normal or more routine political conditions.

Health security debates frequently advance arguments conforming to that linguistic grammar of the security speech act. Many officials in international organizations, governments and non-governmental organizations (securitizing actors) have insisted that beyond human-itarian and medical considerations, the very survival of communities, states, militaries, economies and individuals (referent objects) is now at stake (existentially threatened), unless drastic action (emer-gency measures) is undertaken by national and international actors to address better those urgent threats. Already some scholars have therefore begun to trace the detailed political processes involved in those speech acts (see Kelle 2005a, 2005b, 2007). They demonstrate that it is indeed possible to conceptualize health security debates as the 'securitization' of health.

Yet that perspective on health security also immediately opens up a second, crucial research question: is this securitization of health issues desirable politically? As one of the scholars who initially devel-oped securitization theory insists in this regard, 'use of the security label does not merely reflect whether a problem is a security problem, it is also a political choice, that is, a decision for conceptualization in a special way' (Wæver 1995: 65). The leader of a political party, for example, can choose whether to portray immigration as a security threat or as a human rights issue. Similarly, leaders of international organizations can choose whether they portray health issues as a public health concern, as a development concern or, as they have done more recently, as an international security concern. Because that fundamental choice cannot be avoided, it becomes necessary to reflect much more closely on how the securitization of health in various policy forums actually influences the international govern-ance of diseases for better or for worse.

Recently, a growing number of studies have been turning to that very question. For example, in the United States, David Fidler has argued that 'securitization has happened, and analysis should direct its attention to sorting out the implications of this sea change in public health governance' (Fidler 2007: 41). From the other side of the Atlantic, two French scholars have echoed that call for a more reflexive research agenda on health security – one which is no longer concerned principally with the securitization process itself, but with a more sustained analysis of 'the impacts, the consequences and the effects of this process' (Leboeuf and Broughton 2008). These are timely calls, not least because opinion amongst analysts about the political desirability of the securitization of health still remains deeply divided.

On the one hand, advocates of health security insist that the securitization of health is crucial for the security landscape of the twenty-first century. Although they prefer to use the term 'biosecurity' rather than 'health security', David Fidler and Lawrence Gostin (2008: 9) argue that security will not be possible without the closer integration of the health and security communities: 'the integration of security and public health is not only practically but also normatively necessary in seeking better biosecurity'. From the Asian perspective, Mely Caballero-Anthony echoes that 'the threats of infectious diseases require urgent responses. The regional community and states need not wait for the worst-case scenario of state failure before infectious diseases can be considered as a matter of national security. Hence, there is a need to "securitize"' (2005: 489). Some have also viewed the elevation of health issues to the status of a security concern as a way of mobilizing greater political momentum and crucial resources for addressing a range of health issues throughout the world.

However, others have been far more sceptical about the persuasiveness and utility of conflating health issues and security concerns. Reviewing the influential report by the US National Intelligence Council on the global infectious disease threat in the pages of *Foreign Affairs*, Philip Zelikow (2000: 154) argued at the time that '[t]he analysis is fascinating, and the case for international humanitarian action is compelling. But why invoke the "national security" justification for intervention? The case for direct effects on US security is thin. Do the officials have so little faith in the altruism of their fellow citizens?' That echoes a wider concern about how the idea of health security could detract from and diminish the humanitarian case for addressing health inequalities in the world. Does the notion of health security not risk simply transforming health into yet another foreign policy or diplomatic 'tool' that governments can use and manipulate for pursuing wider political objectives?

Focusing specifically on security debates about the AIDS pandemic, Susan Peterson is also concerned that responding to health issues as national security threats transforms the logic of international action on health into one based on narrow self-interest, which historically has not proved very effective in terms of addressing global health issues. Peterson warns therefore that 'if well-intentioned people seek to rally support among western governments for anti-AIDS efforts in Africa, portraying disease as a security issue may be exactly the wrong strategy to employ' (2002/3: 81). Many non-governmental organizations and public health institutions have also become worried about how the idea of health security might undermine the political neutrality of their efforts, especially as military and security organizations become more closely involved in a range of health matters (CSIS 2009: 14). Such persisting scepticism regarding the appropriateness of merging the worlds of health and security shows that the second question, about whether the securitization of health is actually improving international health policy, also remains highly pertinent.

Security and Medicalization

Rather than advancing those debates further, the purpose of this book is to raise yet a third question about health security: how do health security debates also begin subtly to reshape our understandings of security and insecurity in international relations? Despite the growing number of both empirical and more reflexive studies on health security, that question remains almost completely overlooked in the health security literature. As we have just seen, many studies ask how health issues and security concerns are linked empirically. Other studies inquire into whether the securitization of health issues improves or diminishes the ability to govern them nationally and internationally. Yet no one, to the author's knowledge, has directly raised the opposite question of how security practices also change, if at all, as a result of their growing concern with a wide range of contemporary international health issues. That question is tackled in the pages that follow.

Undertaking such an analysis of the changing nature of security practices will require conceptual resources that are quite different from the ones conventionally used in security studies, and indeed the health security literature. Securitization theory, in particular, is of little help when it comes to this question because the theory does not advance a transformative account of security. Its constructivist orientation notwithstanding, securitization theory ultimately posits a fairly static understanding of security, which consists of the formal security speech act grammar that was outlined above. Securitization theory thus advances a very innovative and even radical re-conceptualization of security, and one that is significantly broader than the traditional understanding of security. Yet it also tends to assume that, when the security agenda is broadened to include wider social issues, this security logic remains fairly unchanged and indeed dominates in terms of producing a range of (often undesirable) political effects. Securitization theory therefore offers us no account of how the practice of security may itself also become transformed as a result of a growing association with non-military issues. In the specific case of health security, the 'securitization of health' perspective does not encourage us to ask how our understanding of security might also be affected or shaped by this 'marriage' to a growing set of global health and medical issues.

Fortunately, other conceptual resources exist beyond the disciplinary boundaries of International Relations and Security Studies that are better suited to this task. Long before the birth of securitization theory, a number of theoretically diverse sociologists had already been arguing that the practice of medicine too possesses a distinct logic. As early as the 1960s they were advancing the concept of 'medicalization' within the context of their research into deviance. Their studies were showing a broader trend within American society in which designations of deviant behaviour were increasingly shifting from notions of 'badness' to notions of 'sickness' (Conrad and Schneider 1992: xi). As the wider social influence of medical categories and vocabularies became apparent, the concept of medicalization was also adopted by a number of scholars working outside the discipline of sociology – including anthropologists, physicians and historians (Conrad 2007: 4). For decades, scholars working in different disciplines have thus been analysing a plethora of medicalization processes through which more and more social issues become framed as medical problems and are responded to through medical frameworks. Their research has revealed that, among other things, medicalization processes usually consist of three interrelated elements.

Defining social issues as medical problems

According to one leading scholar, the crux of medicalization lies in the process of definition. Peter Conrad (2007: 4) describes medicalization as 'a process by which non-medical problems become defined and treated as medical problems, usually in terms of illnesses or disorders'. In his view, 'the key to medicalization is the definitional issue. Medicalization consists of defining a problem in medical terms, using medical language to describe a problem, adopting a medical framework to understand a problem, or using a medical intervention to "treat" it' (Conrad 1992: 211). Scholars have already traced such processes of medical redefinition in relation to a diverse set of phenomena ranging from addiction, alcoholism, childbirth, ageing and baldness, all the way through to homosexuality, compulsive gambling, menopause, hyperactivity, post-traumatic stress disorder and obesity. Their studies identify the main actors driving that process of medical redefinition, trace the implications of that medicalization for medical practitioners as well as laypersons, and evaluate the wider social consequences of redefining such issues in medical terms.

These studies also reveal that there can be different degrees to which phenomena are redefined in medical terms. The process of medical redefinition is not always all-encompassing: 'often medicalization is not complete: some aspects or instances of a condition may be medicalized while others are defined non-medically, or remnants of older definitions may linger and make meanings equivocal' (Conrad and Schneider 1992: 278). Several competing definitions for understanding and responding to the same problem can thus exist simultaneously, and some issues are not redefined in medical terms at all (Conrad 2007: 6). It is even possible for the process of medical redefinition to be reversed. De-medicalization occurs 'when a problem is no longer defined as medical, and medical treatments are no longer deemed appropriate' (Conrad 2007: 210). Homosexuality, which was described as an illness by the American Psychiatric Association until 1973, and masturbation are frequently cited examples in that respect. In either case, the process of redefining wider social issues as medical problems marks the first and perhaps most crucial dimension of medicalization.

Expanding the societal jurisdiction of medical professionals

Medicalization processes also tend to augment the societal influence and standing of the medical professions. Williams and Calnan (1996: 1609) advance a similar but distinct understanding of medicalization when they define it as 'the ways in which medical jurisdiction has expanded in recent years and now encompasses many problems which hitherto were not defined as medical issues'. Here the concern is more explicitly with medical 'jurisdiction' and the growing social influence of the medical professions, in a way that echoes the earlier and influential definition advanced by Irving Zola. He had famously argued that:

> Medicine is becoming a major institution of social control, nudging aside, if not incorporating, the more traditional institutions of religion and law. It is becoming the new repository of truth, the place where absolute and often final judgments are made by supposedly morally neutral and objective experts. And these judgments are made, not in the name of virtue and legitimacy, but in the name of health. Moreover, this is not occurring through the political power physicians hold or can influence, but is largely an insidious and often undramatic phenomenon accomplished by 'medicalizing' much of daily living, by making medicine and the labels 'healthy' and 'ill' relevant to an ever increasing part of human existence. (Zola 1972: 487)

According to Zola (1972), that medicalization of society did not just entail a growing proportion of social life becoming understood as illness. More significantly, it also consisted of doctors acquiring an expanded role in making moral decisions – not least because only they can carry out what are often complex and highly technical medical procedures. Compared to the definitional account of medicalization advanced by Conrad, scholars like Zola have thus placed greater emphasis on how medicalization processes also tend to enhance the social standing and power of the medical professions.

Yet here too the normative impetus is against accepting the power exerted by medical institutions uncritically. That power is seen to circumscribe the autonomous capacities of individuals – both in terms of individuals being able to manage their own health, and in terms of them being able to challenge the principles, assumptions and methods embodied in modern medical practice. All too rarely are patients found to be in a position to examine critically the recommendations of doctors. Because patients lack the relevant knowledge and experience, the medical professions end up having a considerable degree of power and influence over decisions. Medicine can thus also become seen as an essentially oppressive and socially dominating force, with the medicalization critique aspiring to re-empower patients, reducing their dependency on medical professionals, and reversing the ever expanding jurisdiction of the medical professions (Lupton 1997: 96–7).

Within this broad strand of medicalization theory there are different accounts of the detailed factors driving the medicalization of society (S. J. Williams and Calnan 1996: 1610–11). Some trace that process directly to the activities of the medical professions and pharmaceutical industries, which are seen to be actively trying to gain a higher social standing and to influence a wider range of social activity. Others (like Zola above) assign the medical professions a more passive role within this history, and contextualize their activities within wider social processes of rationalization and bureaucratization. Marxist accounts have in turn located the medicalization of society within the broader rise of capitalist economies, showing how medicalization also serves dominant class interests, including the commercial interests of medical practitioners and pharmaceutical companies. Feminist accounts further highlight the ways in which the influence of the medical professionals is also facilitated by underlying gender dynamics within society. They point to the patriarchic nature of the medical profession and show how women's bodies have been integrated into a range of medical practices, especially (but not exclusively) surrounding the area of childbirth.

Such differences notwithstanding, this broad strand of medicalization theory highlights a second significant dimension of medicalization: it tends to expand the societal jurisdiction of medical professionals who then find themselves in a position of influencing a growing proportion of social life. Medicalization thus helps to elevate medicine to the status of a powerful social institution – much like religion has been in the past. That also has important ramifications for any analysis of medicalization processes. It implies that the task of tracing the medicalization of wider social issues cannot be delimited to an examination of definitional processes alone. It must also remain sensitive to the ways in which such processes of medical redefinition have wider social consequences in terms of further expanding the societal jurisdiction of medical professionals.

Medicine, the body and the population

Scholars influenced by Michel Foucault's genealogical studies of medicine highlight a final element of medicalization. In comparison to Conrad's definitional perspective, and sociological approaches focusing on the power of the medical professions, Foucauldian accounts understand medicalization at a wider discursive level. Here medicine is conceptualized not just as a set of complex technical procedures, but as a broad system of knowledge used to understand and experience our bodies. This approach to medicalization differs from the above accounts in several respects (Lupton 1997: 98–9).

First, Foucault's understanding of medicine – and therefore also of the medicalization phenomenon – is considerably broader. In his view, it is not possible to reduce the practice of modern medicine to the 'private' interactions of doctors and patients that occur in clinical settings. It is, he argued, 'inadequate to posit, at the threshold of modern medicine, the existence of a singular, private, individual medical relation' (Foucault 2000a: 90). In fact modern medicine has long consisted of a broad spectrum of strategies for managing disease. Those strategies certainly include the activities of doctors treating patients in hospitals and surgeries; but they also extend all the way through to much wider preventative interventions occurring at the population level and designed to improve public health. Foucault referred to the latter as 'social' medicine – as did many others before him.

Much of the conventional medicalization literature tends to focus only on the first of those two dimensions – analysing the doctor–patient relationship, the clinical setting, and the wider socioeconomic forces shaping those interactions. In fact, that bias in the existing medicalization literature is so pervasive that, when we think of the problem of medicalization today, we also tend to think immediately of those settings. Yet Foucault highlighted how, at least in the European context (rather than the American one that informs much contemporary research on medicalization), the rise of private medical practices in the eighteenth century also 'cannot be divorced from the concurrent organization of a politics of health', and that '"private" and "socialized" medicine, in their reciprocal support and opposition, both derive from a common global strategy' (Foucault 2000a: 91). Modern medicine, in other words, has always been a double-sided phenomenon incorporating measures aimed at both the individual and the population.

A second difference in the Foucauldian approach to medicalization is that it also does not understand power in the same negative or coercive way as those who view medical knowledge and institutions as essentially repressive. Instead, power was thought of by Foucault as something that is 'productive' in that it also gives rise to particular understandings of the self, of the body and, indeed, of health. Those understandings in turn shape modern subjectivity and identity in crucial respects. Precisely because of its concurrently 'private' and 'social' manifestations, Foucault understood the practice of modern medicine to stand at the intersection of two crucial networks of power: one disciplinary and one biopolitical. The former shapes conceptions of health and subjectivity through working at the level of the individual human body, the latter through interventions carried out at the aggregate level of the population. Foucault even once characterized the entire enterprise of modern medicine as 'a power-knowledge that can be applied to both the body and the population, both the organism and biopolitical processes, and it will therefore have both disciplinary effects and regulatory effects' (Foucault 2003: 252). Here it becomes necessary to trace how modern medicine, in both its individuating and collective manifestations, also has a range of subjectifying tendencies.

A final, and related, difference of the Foucauldian approach to medicalization is that it remains far more sceptical about the possibility of 'liberating' individuals in the way assumed by many of the orthodox medicalization critics. It challenges the assumption that there is such a thing as an authentic human body which exists independently of wider medical discourses and practices (Lupton 1997: 106, 99). Instead, medical discourses and practices are seen to shape our very understanding of who we are and how our lives ought to be lived. Today, Nikolas Rose observes in this vein:

> we relate to ourselves and others, individually and collectively, through an ethic and in a form of life that is inextricably associated with medicine in all its incarnations. In this sense, medicine has done much more than define, diagnose and treat diseases – it has helped make us the kinds of living creatures that we have become at the start of the 21st century. (Rose 2007: 701)

Because the modern subject is itself constituted through medical discourses, it is not actually possible simply to free the individual from the 'oppressive' forces of medicine. Here the nature of the critique in relation to medicalization processes becomes much more genealogical. It consists of exposing some of the contingent ways modern individuals have come to understand themselves and their existence through a range of medical categories.

Foucault's intervention into the medicalization debate is thus quite a pertinent one. It marks a useful reminder that the medicalization of life has never been confined to the clinical setting alone. Medicine is also 'a social practice, and only one of its aspects is individualistic and valorizes the relations between the doctor and the patient' (Foucault 2000b: 136). For centuries, modern medicine has simultaneously made concerted efforts to manage disease at the societal level via targeted public health interventions. That renders medicalization an even broader and more pervasive social force than has hitherto been assumed in much of the classical canon on medicalization. The latter has not cast its net wide enough. A comprehensive analysis of the medicalization of social life, by contrast, will not restrict itself solely to the clinical setting and the doctor–patient relationship: it will also account for those wider public health dimensions of 'social' medicine.

Significant differences remain, then, within the field of medicalization theory. Yet all three strands continue to be utilized by scholars working in the sociology and history of medicine today. All three strands also highlight significant dimensions of medicalization. The first emphasizes the crucial, definitional component of medicalization. The second draws attention to the social effects of such definitional processes in terms of expanding the societal jurisdiction of medical professionals. The third strand takes the analysis of those two phenomena and extends it beyond the narrow clinical setting by also bringing it to bear on much wider strategies for managing the problem of disease at the level of population.

The Medicalization of Security

What does medicalization theory have to do with the recent rise of 'health security'? It is true that scholars of medicalization have so far not directed their attention to ongoing discussions about health security. That oversight is certainly understandable. There are the usual disciplinary divisions between Sociology and the study of International Relations that would first need to be overcome – although such barriers have already been breached in relation to other areas that are of joint interest to both disciplines. Those barriers have also been transgressed in relation to other disciplines like Anthropology and History, in which medicalization theory has long figured prominently. Even if those disciplinary obstacles could be overcome, however, there is still a more intractable problem to be reckoned with: contemporary practices of security simply appear, at least on the surface of things, to have very little to do with the shifting ways in which problems like baldness, attention deficit disorder, menopause and so forth are understood and responded to by medical experts. In that respect, it is not surprising that the insights of medicalization theory have not so far been brought to bear on the field of health security.

Yet, on a deeper level, those phenomena may be much more closely related than initially meets the eye. Does the rise of health security not also constitute – from a much broader perspective – precisely such a subtle process through which our understanding of insecurity in international relations is similarly becoming redefined as a medical problem, and is now understood as a predicament also brought about by the onset and spread of disease? Likewise, are health security debates in contemporary world politics not also important sites where the societal jurisdiction of the medical professions is gradually expanding further, as a broad range of medical experts now become much more closely involved in the analysis and formulation of security policy? If that is true, then medicalization theory may have much more to say to those interested in health security than is immediately apparent. Indeed, it may well turn out that the logic of medicalization is not only redefining wider social problems and deviant behaviours as chronicled in the existing sociological literature on medicalization. That logic may also be permeating the political sphere – including the more restricted domain of security.

In order to determine whether that is in fact the case, we will first need to wrest medicalization theory away from its sociological moorings and its narrower focus on the clinical management of disease – much as Foucault urged. Then we will be at liberty to unleash medicalization theory upon the 'high' politics of contemporary national and international security policy as well – illustrating how those domains too are becoming infused with the logic of medicalization. Taking that conceptual plunge will show that, just as securitization theory encourages us to think about the advantages and drawbacks of securitizing international health issues, so too medicalization theory can help us reflect on how our underlying practices of security begin to change as a result of their growing association with international health issues. That transformation marks nothing short of the medicalization of security. Echoing the multiple dimensions of medicalization noted above, the medicalization of security will be shown to consist of three interrelated developments.

Insecurity as a medical problem in international relations

The medicalization of security entails a definitional process in which our conception of insecurity in international politics is becoming partially redefined as a medical problem. Put differently, insecurity too is now understood as a problem caused by the presence of disease. Health security debates thus begin to construe insecurity in world politics as something that no longer stems solely from the military capabilities and hostile political intentions of other states. It is also brought about by a range of underlying medical conditions presenting in the population. That could take the shape of a rapidly emerging lethal infectious disease like H5N1 influenza, a disease intentionally unleashed by terrorists such as anthrax, a disease that is already endemic in many developing countries like malaria, or even a new lifestyle disease such as obesity that is taking on epidemic proportions.

Of course, insecurity is not understood in those health security discussions as constituting a medical condition in the narrow sense of the term. 'Insecurity' has not become a new clinical diagnosis. But, much as baldness, hyperactivity and even shyness have become medicalized by the suggestion that they are ultimately caused by underlying physiological processes and dysfunctions, so too health security debates begin partially to redefine our understanding of insecurity in world politics as something prompted by medical problems presenting within the bodies of citizens. Health security debates too are thus instances in which a previously non-medical issue – insecurity – now comes to be partially understood as a problem having a medical origin. Insecurity too becomes seen as a 'disorder' caused by disease.

That, to be clear, is not to argue that the medical redefinition of insecurity in world politics is total and complete. Clearly, more conventional conceptions of insecurity still remain highly influential in international relations. There also continues to be formidable concern about military developments across the globe, and all the while war remains a perennial activity in the international system. Yet we already noted how other scholars have long pointed out that medicalization processes exist along a spectrum. Different degrees of medicalization can usually be found to exist, and such processes are frequently partial – especially when important social phenomena are simultaneously handled through competing frameworks. Insecurity is a case in point. Here we have a phenomenon that has not been completely medicalized in all of its manifestations; but we will encounter at least four significant sites in international relations where insecurity too is becoming redefined as a medical problem caused by the onset of disease. The partial nature of that redefinition of insecurity thus does not invalidate the underlying thesis about the medicalization of security.

Nor is the claim about the medical redefinition of insecurity meant to imply that the diseases addressed in the context of health security discussions are in any way 'bogus' diseases. There is now an extensive medicalization literature devoted to exposing how pharmaceutical companies and other interested parties have been busy 'inventing' and advertising new diseases to create larger consumer markets for their pills. Determining whether all of the phenomena discussed under the heading of health security really constitute diseases is beyond the scope of this book. Attempting to make such a determination would necessitate delineating fairly steadfast criteria about what makes something a 'disease'. 'Unless we agree on clearly defined criteria that define membership in the class called "disease" or "medical problem"', Thomas Szasz insists, 'it is fruitless to debate whether any particular act of medicalization is "valid" or not' (Szasz 2007: xiii).

Determining what does, and what does not, count as a proper disease would ultimately require a book in itself. Even then it is unlikely to end in a neat resolution. It is a question littered with methodological difficulties and laden with too many vested interests. Suffice it to say, as Nietzsche once did, that only that which has no history can be defined. This book is therefore devoted to the more modest task of focusing on ongoing health security debates, and tracing the multiple ways in which they themselves begin partially to redefine insecurity as a medical problem caused by the onset of disease.

A greater role for medical professionals in world politics

The medicalization of security also turns the provision of security into an activity which requires the closer involvement of many different kinds of medical professionals. Health security discussions thus pry open this additional, and some would say paramount, domain of politics to the growing influence of a range of medical experts. As a result, their societal jurisdiction is augmented further. This can certainly be seen in the way that health security debates are frequently accompanied by calls for the greater involvement of doctors and physicians (as well as other experts with a medical background) in the analysis and formulation of security policy. That occurs, for example, through the closer involvement of such persons in various foreign policy and security think tanks, through them being invited to attend meetings held by prominent security institutions, and also through their participation in human security initiatives on global health. That expansion in the societal influence and jurisdiction of doctors and physicians echoes many earlier medicalization processes.

Yet those are not the only medical professions whose societal jurisdiction is expanding due to the rise of health security. Health security discussions also facilitate a greater political role for a much wider range of institutions involved in the management of disease outside of a hospital or clinical setting. That extended list of medical actors includes public health institutions such as the Centers for Disease Control and Prevention in the United States, various national health ministries around the world and international initiatives like the Global Health Security Initiative, as well as intergovernmental institutions such as the World Health Organization. It also includes non-governmental organizations such as Médecins Sans Frontières and philanthropic institutions devoted to global health like the Gates Foundation. So far, these wider groups have received far less attention in the existing literature on medicalization because the latter has tended to focus on the 'private' arm of medicine and the doctor–patient relationship. Yet these too represent pertinent 'medical' actors in the broader sense of being similarly engaged in the modern prevention and treatment of disease. They are the institutions of what Foucault earlier referred to as 'social' medicine. The fact that their societal and political role too is enhanced by the rise of health security constitutes additional evidence of how health security discussions are today extending the societal jurisdiction of a wide range of different medical professionals.

None of this is meant to imply that the concept of health security is driven solely by the narrow and selfish interests of all those medical professionals, who are somehow trying aggressively to take over the 'turf' of security analysts. When it comes to discussions on health security that is often far from the case. We will see that many health professionals also express considerable reservations about the whole idea of health security. Nor, for that matter, are the interests of doctors and public health officials necessarily always aligned. It would therefore be incorrect simply to assume that the interests of medical professionals are always, or even inherently, selfish in the way that some of the medicalization literature tends to do. In fact, the entire question about who is driving the medicalization of security is not really that decisive in the end. Because medicalization is understood primarily as a definitional process, it can be driven by other social groups as well. It can even occur without the direct involvement of the medical professions: medicalization is 'a broad definitional process, which may or may not directly include physicians' (Cornwell 1984, cited in Conrad 1992: 211).

What is decisive from the medicalization perspective, however, is the overall social and political effect that such processes of medical redefinition have. We will see that, in the case of health security debates, this effect is to augment further the societal jurisdiction of a range of medical professionals working in both clinical and wider settings. The rise of health security thus adds the analysis and provision of security to the long list of activities that a broad range of different medical professionals can legitimately be seen to be engaged in today. That observation – to avoid any misunderstanding – is not intended to be pejorative. Nor is it meant to deny that the medicalization of security can yield beneficial consequences for people's health. Rather, it is meant to insist (more modestly) that 'there are certain social consequences of medicalization irrespective of any attendant medical or social benefit' which need to be analysed (Conrad 2007: 147).

Securing populations through medical interventions

A final element of the medicalization of security that will also emerge is how it partially transforms the way in which security is practised. Enhancing the security of populations against these new sources of insecurity entails recourse to an extensive range of medical interventions as well. Such medical interventions can consist, on the one hand, of new pharmacological treatments. Here health security debates expand the available arsenal of security policy and strategy to include not just the amassing of military capabilities, but also the development, procurement and stockpiling of medical equipment and new pharmacological products – what is referred to in the health security literature as 'medical countermeasures'. Those measures range from new anti-viral medications, antibiotics and medical equipment through to various medicines for treating HIV/AIDS, malaria, tuberculosis and so forth. The tendency of modern medicine to prescribe a 'pill for every ill' – so widely noted in the existing medicalization literature – is also at play in health security debates.

Yet here too we must be careful not to overlook other types of medical intervention simultaneously pursued by the 'social' arm of modern medicine at the population level. Vaccines in particular continue to be particularly important medical interventions that repeatedly surface in a variety of different health security deliberations. Strictly speaking, vaccines are not medicines because they consist of small concentrations of disease-causing microbes (or their derivatives) used to enhance a person's immuno-response to a future infection. As a public health measure, vaccines have therefore also been largely sidelined in the existing medicalization literature. Yet, generally speaking, vaccines too can be considered as medical interventions. That is certainly how the World Health Organization views them, pointing out that 'vaccines are among the most important medical interventions for reducing illness and deaths' available today (WHO 2009a). Whereas pills and other therapies mark the tools of clinical medicine, vaccines play a crucial part in the arsenal of 'social' medicine and public health. Developing and rolling out of new vaccines against a range of current (and future) diseases therefore represents further evidence of how the rise of health security is also encouraging security to be practised through the introduction of new medical interventions in society.

Strictly speaking, such recourse to medical interventions is not actually a necessary prerequisite for an issue to become medicalized – although it is a frequently noted accompaniment of medicalization processes (Conrad 2007: 6). Because medicalization is principally understood as a definitional process, the issue of taking recourse to medical interventions is again only of secondary importance. Yet it is true that, historically, medicalization processes have frequently been marked by recourse to medical measures; and, as we will see in the case studies below, that is also a prominent feature of ongoing health security debates. Here, too, there is growing pressure to develop and implement a range of medical interventions – at both the individual and population levels – to enhance the security of populations.

The next four chapters explore the three elements of the medicalization of security in greater detail and will illustrate them in relation to a number of current health security discussions. Chapter 2 turns first to national security debates about the threat posed by lethal infectious diseases with pandemic potential. Chapter 3 focuses on biosecurity policies concerned with averting the prospect of a biological weapons attack on civilian populations. Chapter 4 examines the health–security nexus that has emerged within the context of human security concerns about a number of global health issues. Chapter 5 analyses the growing anxiety prompted by a range of contemporary lifestyle diseases such as smoking, obesity and excessive alcohol consumption. Chapter 6, finally, considers the wider implications of the medicalization of security for practising security in the twenty-first century.

Collectively, the chapters that follow will show that – beyond its more conventional application in sociology – medicalization theory also constitutes a very fruitful theoretical resource for trying to understand the changing character of security practices that is unfolding within the context of ongoing health security debates. If nothing else, medicalization theory can provide us with a concise answer to the question of how security practices in international relations are being subtly transformed today by the rise of health security: they are becoming medicalized.

2

Microbes Take to the Sky: Pandemic Threats and National Security

National security discussions about the threat posed by pandemic infectious diseases mark an exemplary entry point for exploring the medicalization of security in greater depth. These debates construe a range of infectious diseases as threats to national security. During that process the meaning of insecurity in international relations begins to undergo a subtle but significant change. Insecurity is no longer seen to emanate solely from the military capabilities and hostile intentions of other states; it is now also seen to stem from the proliferation of medical conditions brought about by the rapid spread of potentially lethal infectious diseases within the population. National security discussions about pandemic threats thus begin partially to redefine insecurity in world politics as a medical problem brought about by the onset and spread of disease.

That medical redefinition of insecurity, in turn, also augments the societal jurisdiction of many different medical professionals. It does so by prompting a much closer involvement of medical experts in the formulation of national security policy. It has also already culminated in expanded powers being granted to various government and international agencies tasked with meeting the threat posed by infectious diseases. National security debates on infectious diseases have even prompted attempts to manage these new sources of insecurity through extensive recourse to new medical interventions. Governments are seeking to enhance the security of their populations by developing and stockpiling a growing range of vaccines, treatments and medical equipment. National security concerns about pandemic threats in the era of globalization thus emerge as a paradigmatic manifestation of the medicalization of security unfolding today.

Pandemics on the Radar Screen of Security Analysts

In the past, national security threats have revolved mostly (though certainly not exclusively) around the use of armed force in international relations – militaries, arms races, nuclear weapons, great-power rivalries, security dilemmas, armed conflict, border security and so forth. Medical issues were seen to bear on such issues only in a very indirect manner, for example when diseases got in the way of imperial and colonial expansion, or when soldiers were deployed to territories where infectious diseases were present (Arnold 1988; Curtin 1998; Macleod and Lewis 1988; Bashford 2004). For centuries, the institutions of military medicine have thus advised and prepared militaries for dealing with a range of diseases that may be prevalent in theatres of operation, and have even pioneered many of the medical therapies that enjoy much wider civilian application today (Gabriel and Metz 1992; Berry and Greenwood 2005). Yet historically these relationships alone have not proved sufficient to merit the designation of infectious diseases as wider threats to national security.

That perception began to change in the 1990s as arguments about the national security implications of infectious disease gradually acquired greater resonance and credence amongst policy-makers within the context of globalization. One of the most significant culprits for this renewed microbial anxiety is the substantial expansion in civilian air travel around the world that has occurred in the second half of the twentieth century, and that shows very little sign of abating at the outset of the twenty-first. The growth in air travel compresses both space and time in a way that makes many Western governments feel more vulnerable to the spread of infectious disease.

Air travel reduces the significance of geographical space in that it creates connections between places, populations and microbes that would previously only rarely, if ever, come into direct physical contact with one another because they are located in different countries or even on different continents. Aircraft thus generate what is an increasingly global epidemiological space, making even geographically distant infectious diseases a matter of concern. The reason this creates a renewed sense of vulnerability in the minds of many Western policy-makers, in particular, is that, even if their countries have comparatively sound public health infrastructures, it is still possible to import such diseases inadvertently from distant places where such an infrastructure is not present. In states where medical surveillance systems are patchy, an outbreak could initially go undetected, allowing infectious microbes sufficient time to spread to other countries around the world on the back of a modern transport infrastructure that today includes not just ships and railways (the older conduits of infectious disease), but also a range of aircraft that travel at much faster speeds.

This second factor of speed raises the level of concern higher still. It means that, in the age of globalization, a new infectious microorganism not only could circumnavigate the planet, it could do so in just a matter of hours. At any given point in time, according to the cliché, it is possibly only a plane ride away. For this reason too, infectious diseases have been added to the list of things that can threaten a nation's security. As Gro Harlem Brundtland, the former Director General of the World Health Organization, put it in an article on global health and security: 'today, in an interconnected world, bacteria and viruses travel almost as fast as e-mail and financial flows. Globalization has connected Bujumbura to Bombay and Bangkok to Boston. There are no health sanctuaries. . . . Problems halfway around the world become everyone's problem' (Brundtland 2003: 417).

As a result of these growing concerns, infectious diseases are no longer seen merely as important public health issues; they are also becoming construed as deeper and more pervasive threats to national security. The most recent National Security Strategy of the United States (NSS 2006) explicitly acknowledges the threat posed by 'public health challenges like pandemics (HIV/AIDS, avian influenza) that recognize no borders'. Pandemic threats have also been incorporated into the United Kingdom's 2008 National Security Strategy, both because of their ability to affect the country directly and because they could potentially undermine international stability more generally (Cabinet Office 2008: 3). On both sides of the Atlantic, there is a recognition now that infectious diseases also constitute threats to national security – a view confirmed more recently by the anxious international reaction that initially met the rapid and unexpected outbreak of the pandemic H1N1 influenza virus in the spring of 2009.

That process of elevating infectious diseases to the status of a national and international security threat has animated an inconspicuous but nonetheless very pertinent process of redefinition. If it is true that infectious diseases with pandemic potential are threats to national security, then our underlying understanding of what constitutes insecurity in international relations must also change. Whereas we used to think of insecurity in world politics as being a fundamentally military and political problem, national security discussions about pandemic threats suggest to us that insecurity has also become a medical problem caused by diseases presenting within the population. National security discussions about pandemic threats thus encourage a critical process of medical redefinition whereby insecurity (which was previously understood largely as a non-medical problem) is now also considered to be a problem caused by disease – at least in part. By encouraging that underlying process of medical redefinition, national security discussions emerge as one of the principal contemporary manifestations of the medicalization of security.

This process of partially redefining insecurity as a medical problem did not just begin recently with the rapid international dissemination of the novel H1N1 virus in 2009. In fact the three microbes that have done most to provoke the medical redefinition of insecurity are, in chronological succession: (1) the human immunodeficiency virus (HIV) that causes AIDS and which emerged in the late 1980s; (2) the new coronavirus that caused severe acute respiratory syndrome (SARS) and which erupted in 2002 and 2003; and (3) the highly pathogenic H5N1 avian influenza virus which has repeatedly emerged since the turn of the century – albeit without yet achieving the efficient human-to-human transmission required for a human pandemic to unfold. All three viruses have played a crucial and also distinct role in the medical redefinition of insecurity.

Virus alert: the AIDS pandemic as a security threat

In more recent history, the concept of national security first acquired an explicitly medical dimension through concerns about the wider social effects that could be triggered by the international spread of HIV/AIDS (Ostergard 2005). As early as 1990 a few pioneering analysts at the US Central Intelligence Agency began to analyse systematically the likely impact of the AIDS pandemic on the political stability of foreign countries and US interests abroad. Yet it was not until the end of that decade that the discussions on HIV/AIDS and national security really began to gather momentum.

At that point, national security arguments about HIV/AIDS were advanced by a range of interested actors who also saw this as a useful way of raising the profile of, and resources devoted to, fighting the pandemic. National security arguments about the AIDS pandemic thus formed part of a deliberate attempt by international policy-makers to move beyond the prior 'health' and 'development' frameworks that had been used to address HIV/AIDS, and to re-position the disease as a much more urgent matter of security. By early May 2000, the Clinton administration even went so far as to announce that HIV/AIDS was a threat to the national security of the United States.

How could security analysts be persuaded that a medical syndrome such as AIDS was also a deeper threat to national security? It was made possible by drawing what were, at least initially, quite plausible links between the spread of HIV/AIDS and the core traditional concerns of national security policy – such as the military, armed conflict and even peacekeeping operations. For example, international institutions like the United Nations Program on HIV/AIDS (UNAIDS) claimed that HIV prevalence rates in many of the world's armed forces substantially exceeded those in the civilian population, giving the disease an important military, and thus also a national security, dimension.

Amongst the most influential estimates of military HIV prevalence rates were undoubtedly those published in the declassified National Intelligence Estimate (NIC 2000), which drew upon figures supplied by the Armed Forces Medical Intelligence Center (AFMIC), which in turn is part of the Defense Intelligence Agency of the United States. Those estimates pointed to staggering levels of HIV-prevalence in some African armed forces in 1999: Angola (40–60%), Congo-Brazzaville (10–25%), Cote d'Ivoire (10–20%), Democratic Republic of Congo (40–60%), Eritrea (10%), Nigeria (10–20%), Tanzania (15–

30%) (NIC 2000). Those figures have since become contested and disputed, but they were widely cited at the time and formed one of the main arguments for establishing that national security could be threatened by the spread of a new infectious disease. Those estimates thus proved crucial for initiating the much wider medical redefinition of security that would subsequently unfold.

Additional links were also identified between HIV/AIDS and other traditional concerns of national security. Some analysts claimed that national security was further threatened by the spread of HIV/AIDS because of the possible longer-term ramifications for social and political stability that the disease could have in the worst-affected countries. 'Declining health, particularly in the form of the spread of infectious diseases', one report (CBACI 2000: 13) concluded, 'will work in combination with other factors to promote instability'. By that time the CIA had added AIDS incidence to the list of variables that should be considered when analysing which states were likely to become unstable or collapse in future (Gellman 2000). UNAIDS similarly warned at the turn of the century, with reference to sub-Saharan Africa that '[t]he risks of social unrest and even socio-political instability should not be under-estimated' (UNAIDS 2001: 18).

As with the arguments about the impact of HIV/AIDS on the armed forces, subsequent analysis has raised considerable doubts about the likelihood of such scenarios emerging (Elbe 2003, 2009; de Waal 2006). The macro-economic effects of HIV/AIDS are not yet properly established, with different studies, conducted even in the same country, generating very different projections. Nor, for that matter, have conflicts broken out over access to life-prolonging medicines. All the while, such medicines have become more widely available in many low-income countries, and this too serves to mitigate any potentially detrimental impact that the AIDS pandemic could have on state stability. Increasingly, it is therefore thought that HIV/AIDS is rather unlikely to generate political instability in the absence of other causes. Yet initially such arguments that HIV/AIDS can cause, exacerbate or intensify processes of state failure were instrumental in establishing the view that national security of African governments could also be threatened by a disease such as HIV/AIDS, possibly leading to regional instability and perhaps even conflict.

A final security dimension of the AIDS pandemic was also identified in relation to international peacekeeping operations. 'Here', Richard Holbrooke (2000) argued at the time, in his capacity as the United States ambassador to the United Nations, 'we get into one of the ugliest secret truths . . . about AIDS: it is spread by UN peacekeepers'. By that time the composition of international peacekeeping forces had already changed from a majority contribution by European and North American armed forces, to a majority contribution by various armed forces from Asia, Africa and the Middle East. Christian Halle, of the United Nations Department of Peacekeeping Operations (DPKO), reported at the time that HIV/AIDS was spreading rapidly through several of these newer contributor countries, leading to the possibility that they could be a vector for transmitting HIV internationally (Halle 2002: 17–18). In 2001, according to the US General Accounting Office (which has since been renamed the Government Accountability Office (GAO)), roughly 14 per cent of peacekeepers were drawn from countries where prevalence in the general population was estimated to be over 5 per cent (GAO 2001).

Of course, peacekeepers are rarely the only source of the spreading infection. Moreover, it is in fact very difficult to quantify this problem. Many of the epidemiological preconditions cannot be properly met in areas experiencing complex emergencies in which peacekeepers are deployed. According to one report, however, there were at least six confirmed HIV-positive peacekeepers deployed in East Timor and six in Kosovo. Yet even in those cases it remained unclear whether the peacekeepers were already HIV-positive prior to deployment (GAO 2001: 24).

In any event the United Nations Security Council took the issue sufficiently seriously to address it formally by passing Resolution 1308, with the result that UNAIDS now encourages member states to provide pre-deployment voluntary counselling and testing for peacekeepers, and has developed training modules to communicate key information about HIV/AIDS to troop-contributing countries (Rushton 2007). UNAIDS also provides financial and technical support to various AIDS programs in the uniformed services, allocates AIDS advisers to peacekeeping operations, and distributes AIDS awareness cards which contain the basic information about

HIV/AIDS. Even today, however, the United Nations is not in a position to discern exactly how many peacekeepers deployed in its name are HIV-positive. Because it has a policy of voluntary testing, and makes testing the responsibility of individual troop-contributing countries, it is simply impossible at present to establish the extent to which the impact of HIV/AIDS on peacekeeping operations does in fact pose a threat to international security. There is no official record publicly available (UNAIDS 2003: 6).

Notwithstanding such persisting concerns about the accuracy of claims about the links between AIDS and national security, those arguments were widely (though not universally) accepted for several years. Thus HIV/AIDS became the first infectious disease to be singled out in the twenty-first century as representing more than just an important international public health or development problem. The AIDS pandemic was also a threat to national security because it could threaten vital organs of the state, such as the military, and in the worst-case scenario might even cause some states to collapse.

More importantly, those arguments also had another effect. They created a crucial precedent by establishing that the national security of a country could be threatened by the spread of a new and lethal infectious disease. In retrospect, it was thus the AIDS pandemic, and not swine flu, that first prompted policy-makers to construe insecurity as something caused by the spread of disease within populations. AIDS tore down the barrier between the worlds of health and security. It marked the first salvo in the medicalization of security. Yet it would not be the last infectious disease to encourage the medical redefinition of insecurity.

SARS: the health security message sinks in

Any lingering doubts about the national security threat posed by infectious diseases were dispelled in 2002 when a new such disease began to emerge rapidly, not out of Africa, but out of Asia. The first known cases of SARS are believed to have occurred in the Guangdong province of China in November 2002. The region was known at the time for its lively markets where livestock mingled and were slaughtered in close proximity to the human population. That was an important feature of the region given that SARS is thought to have emerged by 'jumping' from the animal species to the human species, as has happened repeatedly throughout human history. Evidence of infection with the coronavirus could later be found in several animal groups, including Himalayan masked palm civets, Chinese ferret badgers, raccoon dogs and domestic cats. The symptoms of this new 'atypical pneumonia' – as it was initially referred to – included a high fever, a dry cough and shortness of breath or other breathing difficulties.

Yet it was not until February 2003 that the Chinese Ministry of Health officially forwarded reports of severe acute respiratory syndrome to the World Health Organization. By that time at least five deaths had already been reported in Guangdong province. At around the same time a local Chinese doctor by the name of Dr Liu Jianlun travelled from Guangdong province to Hong Kong. He had earlier treated some of the initial cases of atypical pneumonia in China. Upon arriving in Hong Kong, he stayed in room 911 on the ninth floor of the four-star Metropole Hotel (now renamed the Metropark Hotel), spreading the infection to other guests residing on the same floor of that hotel. Dr Jianlun would later become identified by public health officials as a 'super-spreader', in that those who become infected by him subsequently travelled as far as Singapore, Vietnam, Ireland, Canada and the United States. The World Health Organization ultimately attributed more than 4,000 worldwide cases of SARS to this doctor alone (NIC 2003: 10). If any one person's fate exemplifies the links between infectious diseases and security in the era of international tourism and air travel, it is his.

Nor was his an isolated experience. Another doctor who had treated the first cases of SARS in Singapore too reported symptoms before boarding a flight from New York back to Singapore on 14 March 2003. He had to disembark prematurely in Frankfurt for hospitalization. All the while, the virus was also spreading in other parts of Asia, including Hong Kong, Vietnam and Singapore. It was even beginning to spread beyond Asia, via airline routes to places where medical professionals who had come into contact with SARS patients had travelled. Through many of these cases, SARS proved that a newly emerging infectious disease outbreak can indeed only be a plane ride away. The cliché was true after all.

In March 2003 the World Health Organization began to take strong, even unprecedented, action in response to the outbreak. The most controversial of these measures was undoubtedly its decision to issue travel advisories independently. The organization warned against non-essential travel to Hong Kong and the Guangdong province of China. In April 2003 such travel advisories were extended to cover Beijing and Shanxi province in China, as well as Toronto in Canada (Fidler 2004: 91). The World Health Organization pointed out at the time: '[t]his is the first time in the history of WHO that such travel advice has been issued for specific geographical areas because of an outbreak of an infectious disease' (WHO 2003; cited in Fidler 2004: 90).

In fact officials in Canada were furious with this decision, given its predictable economic impact on tourism and trade. Yet they could do little else but make their anger known. Nor did those advisories prevent the initial SARS 'hot zones' in Hanoi, Hong Kong, Singapore and Toronto from generating secondary lines of infection as the virus began to take hold amongst health care workers who had been exposed to the virus and were unaware of the new illness. At the time there was no treatment or vaccine readily available, and so the coronavirus made inroads into two dozen countries in North America, South America, Europe and Asia before being contained.

How did governments respond to the threatening spread of SARS? Much has been made of the novelty of the international response to it. There was certainly immense scientific cooperation in terms of identifying the new coronavirus responsible for SARS, which was achieved on 17 April 2003. When it came to responding to the outbreak, however, many of the measures introduced were decidedly more medieval and relied in part on the security forces. In the end, it was mostly isolation and quarantine practices, backed by the rapid dissemination of information through the news media, which enabled a rapid and successful response to SARS. Patients and health care workers in Beijing were sometimes forcibly locked inside hospitals. Shanghai officials had quarantined more than 29,000 people by late May, threatening violators with fines (NIC 2003: 20). By the end of the outbreak in Hong Kong alone, 1,262 persons from 493 different households were subject to an isolation order (34 of whom developed SARS). Those people were not compensated financially and were subject to periodic visits by police (Siu and Wong 2004: 65). Canada similarly threatened those who violated isolation orders with fines and court-orders (NIC 2003: 20).

In a way that foreshadowed later responses to the emergence of human infections with a new H1N1 influenza virus in 2009, Singapore also deployed thermal scanners at its international borders. During the SARS outbreak, the government acquired more than 160 such scanning systems, at a cost of around $90,000 (Menon 2006: 264). Hong Kong would later follow suit, introducing temperature checks for all arriving, departing and transit passengers at the airport in mid-April 2003 (Siu and Wong 2004: 65). Japan too introduced such infrared thermometers in order to screen passengers at Tokyo's international airport – although they reportedly struggled to keep up with the volume of peak-time travellers (NIC 2003). Singapore even went so far as to launch a new television station dedicated solely to the SARS outbreak.

The final ingredient accounting for the success of the international response to SARS, however, was undoubtedly luck. Luck was decisive because many of the quarantine measures were in fact only partial successes. When, for example, the Hong Kong Department of Health realized that many of the new cases being reported in Hong Kong were residents of Block E of the Amoy Gardens residential complex in Kowloon, they decided to place a quarantine order on the block of 264 apartments that was due to last for ten days. Yet by the time the police arrived in order to enforce the measure, more than half of the apartments were already empty as residents had fled the complex. The impact of such quarantine measures could thus only be limited.

The usefulness of scanners at international airports has similarly been subject to considerable debate. In the end they are more likely to be of psychological use, giving reassurance to international travellers. Mostly, the various measures introduced by governments worked only because, in the case of SARS, people become infectious only after symptoms emerge, and not before. This meant that isolation and social distancing measures could be effective when introduced, as long as people adhered to them and also reported their symptoms promptly.

By late April 2003 new cases finally seemed to be peaking, and on 5 July 2003 the World Health Organization could report that the last human chain of transmission had been broken. Less well known is that, since 2003, there have been several occasions in which SARS has temporarily reappeared as a result of poor bio-safety at various laboratories in Singapore, Taipei and Beijing (WHO 2004b: 6). By the end of the SARS outbreak, there had been a total of 8,098 reported cases in twenty-six countries, causing 774 deaths.

The vast majority of these cases and deaths occurred in just six countries and territories: China (5,327 cases and 349 deaths), Hong Kong (1,755 cases and 299 deaths), Taiwan (346 cases and 37 deaths), Canada (251 cases and 43 deaths), Singapore (238 cases and 33 deaths) and Vietnam (63 cases and 5 deaths) (WHO 2004e). In the United Kingdom, 368 reports of suspected SARS cases were lodged at the Health Protection Agency between March and July 2003. However, only 9 of these were deemed probable cases, and only 1 patient tested positive for the SARS coronavirus (Goddard et al. 2006: 27). Other European Union countries affected by SARS included France, Germany, Italy, Ireland, Romania, Spain, Sweden and Switzerland. A total of 33 persons became infected in the European Union, of whom all but 1 recovered.

Looking back with the benefit of hindsight, one of the most striking aspects of those SARS figures is that they were actually comparatively 'low'. That, of course, is not to diminish the individual tragedies of those who lost their lives or family members. Yet with a case fatality rate of just under 10 per cent of reported cases, SARS is not nearly as lethal as HIV, which – for those without access to life-prolonging medicines – has a mortality rate approximating 100 per cent (albeit with a much longer incubation time that can run into several years). Moreover, the fatality rate of SARS is also heavily dependent upon the age of the person infected. For example, the estimated fatality rate was less than 1 per cent in persons 24 years or younger, up to 6 per cent in persons 25 to 44 years old, and up to 15 per cent in persons 44 to 64 years old. The greatest risk group was those over the age of 65 years, where the fatality rate is in excess of 55 per cent (NIC 2003: 16).

That level of mortality nevertheless proved sufficient for the disease to become widely elevated to the status of a national security threat. This was particularly true in Asia where the epicentre of the outbreak was located. In an account of his first-hand experiences with SARS in Hong Kong, Thomas Abraham describes how SARS quickly became understood as a threat to national security. Noting that the outbreak of SARS occurred at around the same time as the war in Iraq, he observed how 'the juxtaposition of these two forms of warfare awakened governments to the fact that microbial disease is as great a threat to national security as an invasion by a foreign army' (2005:2). A national security adviser from the Philippines similarly brought the disease into the realm of national security by arguing that the 'SARS threat . . . was greater than any threat of terrorism in the country' (cited in Caballero-Anthony 2006: 112). That link between SARS and national security was also picked up in the media. 'SARS outbreak is like Singapore's 9/11' read a headline from the *Singapore Straits Times* in May 2003 (Mongoven 2006: 403).

The need to reconsider infectious diseases as national security threats was also a lesson that many security analysts would take away from the SARS episode after the dust had settled. Mely Caballero-Anthony made the case particularly persuasively in relation to the future security landscape of Asia:

> given the multidimensional threats to national security posed by infectious diseases such as SARS, it is imperative that states treat these diseases within a security framework. Although the concept of security, particularly in Southeast Asia, has been expanded to include both conventional and non-conventional threats – hence the prevailing notion of comprehensive security – the idea of health security has not been included in the region's security lexicon. The recent episode should be seen as a wake-up call for how security should be reconceptualized to account for new and serious threats. By framing infectious diseases as a matter of national security, governments and their people would be better prepared to handle sudden outbreaks that endanger human lives and threaten the existence and survival of nation-states. (2005: 476)

Indeed the consensus view to emerge after the SARS episode was that it had marked a 'lucky escape', and that henceforth national security policy and strategy would have to become much more attuned to the threat posed by infectious diseases. Like AIDS before it, SARS too thus became elevated to the status of a national security threat. It similarly contributed to the medical redefinition of insecurity as something caused by the spread of disease.

That said, SARS also played a distinct role in the history of the medical redefinition of insecurity because of the particular ways in which it was construed as a national security threat. The case for considering the AIDS pandemic as a threat to national security had initially been made by tracing the impact on the more conventional and narrow national security concerns – such as the military and armed conflict. Thus AIDS was essentially construed as a pathology of the state, affecting its core institutions. In the case of SARS, by contrast, those arguments were not made very frequently and were certainly not paramount. Instead, SARS was widely considered as a national security threat primarily because of the mortality it caused and because of its potentially very serious economic repercussions. The latter in particular was of immense concern.

The economic impact of SARS

One of the most elementary effects of the SARS outbreak was that it caused a great amount of fear. By their very nature infectious diseases tend to inspire anxiety. The micro-organisms that cause these potentially lethal diseases are imperceptible to the human eye. Consisting, in the case of viruses, merely of a piece of nucleic acid (DNA or RNA) wrapped in a thin coat of protein, they exist at the very margins of our conceptions of life. Human beings could thus be exposed to them at any time without knowing it, and yet suffer a quick and violent death not long thereafter. They are, in this respect, 'silent' and 'invisible' killers. To many people, nothing is more frightening than a lethal danger they have no way of detecting.

In the case of SARS, media outlets also deliberately played on that fear by making the outbreak their main focus of attention. They continuously reminded viewers in the early stages of the outbreak that the cause of this potentially lethal disease was unknown and there was no cure available. Fuelled by this panic, people began to avoid public spaces and minimized the time they spent outside of their homes, and many families had to stay at home because schools were shut. Many people also began to wear face masks in public, spreading yet further fear and panic.

That sudden change in people's behaviour began to have negative economic effects. People, for instance, began to avoid travel. In China, year-on-year tourist arrivals in April and May 2003 dropped by 30 per cent. The value of retail sales grew 5 per cent less in May than the first quarter trend, despite the fact that during this month the week-long May Day holiday takes place in China and usually brings increased levels of economic activity compared to the first quarter trend (Hanna and Huang 2004: 109–10). Further economic ramifications of SARS included diminishing the Canton Export Exhibition where Chinese producers sign sizeable and lucrative contracts with foreign businesspeople. In 2003, the exhibition only attracted 22,670 visitors, compared to the 120,576 the previous year, and the total value of contracts signed was only US$3.9 billion compared to the US$16.86 billion agreed the previous year. That is a reduction by 81 per cent and 77 per cent, respectively (Hanna and Huang 2004: 110).

Using a forecasting model, Hanna and Huang initially calculated further that – if no additional fiscal stimulus were implemented – the overall economic impact of SARS on the Chinese economy would be a decrease of around 1.5 per cent in gross domestic product (GDP). This would be reduced to 0.9 per cent if additional measures to stimulate the economy were introduced (Hanna and Huang 2004: 111). In the end those estimates proved excessively pessimistic, but only because of the unexpected speed with which it was possible to halt the spread of SARS. Had these measures failed, the economic fallout of SARS could have been far worse. Indeed, despite the unprecedented response to SARS, China's seasonally adjusted second quarter GDP in 2003 still contracted 5 per cent on an annualized basis, largely due to the disease (Hanna and Huang 2004: 111).

A geographically more narrow survey of the economic impact of SARS on the city of Beijing looked at hotels, travel agencies, tourist attractions, airlines, railway stations, restaurants, retailers, exhibitions and taxi companies. It too found that all of those sectors had suffered a SARS-attributable decline when compared to the same period in 2002. The only exception to this trend was retail chain stores (Hei et al. 2004: 58). Bookings at hotels were down 80 per cent, which was particularly difficult as March and April are usually very busy periods for hotels in Beijing. Travel agency revenues were down 50–60 per cent. Foreign visitor numbers at tourist attractions in Beijing were down 80 per cent, while the volume of both domestic visitors and air travellers dropped by half. Customer numbers at Beijing restaurants were down 30–40 per cent (Hei et al. 2004: 58). Those are substantial declines.

In Hong Kong, on the other hand, the economic impact of SARS appeared more differentiated. There is evidence that SARS had important negative effects on the 'demand' side of Hong Kong's economy. Consumption decreased, and the travel and tourist sectors were again hit particularly hard, with anecdotal evidence suggesting a drop in sales of 10–50 per cent in restaurants and retail outlets. Yet the 'supply' side of the economy largely presented a very different picture. Here, cross-border manufacturing in the province of Guangdong remained largely unaffected, even as the SARS crisis raged (Siu and Wong 2004: 70). In Hong Kong the demand-side shock also quickly dissipated once the initial fear surrounding SARS faded away.

In terms of the aggregate economic impact of these behaviour changes for the Asian region as a whole, early estimates calculated that the ASEAN countries (Brunei, Cambodia, Indonesia, Laos, Malaysia, Myanmar, the Philippines, Singapore, Thailand and Vietnam) would lose US$25–30 billion. Those losses would be concentrated mostly in the four sectors of tourism, services, aviation and restaurants (NIC 2003: 12–13). Estimates by the Asian Development Bank in turn put the economic impact of SARS at US$18 billion in East Asia, which amounts to around 0.6 per cent of GDP (Fan 2003). Again, those initial estimates may have been too pessimistic in retrospect, as the economic consequences of SARS were mostly confined to the second quarter of 2003.

Such estimates do also indicate, however, that the economic picture could have been much worse if the virus had not been successfully contained, and if the world had witnessed a much wider and longer pandemic. Indeed, the main lesson that many took away from the SARS experience was that the writing was now clearly on the wall for all to see in terms of how a newly emerging infectious disease could rapidly appear, spread internationally and wreak havoc on the world economy. That economic impact was thus a crucial consideration in designating SARS as a national security threat. It certainly played a much more prominent role than in security discussions about the AIDS pandemic. Whereas the latter had been construed as a national security threat mostly by virtue of being a pathology of the state, SARS emerged as a pathology of the population that caused people to die and that sapped a country's economic wealth.

In the end, SARS was therefore also able to advance the scope of the medical redefinition of insecurity beyond where the AIDS pandemic had initially taken it. SARS showed that national security could also be threatened by an infectious disease other than HIV/ AIDS. It was therefore unlikely that the national security implications of infectious disease would be confined to the singular case of the AIDS pandemic. SARS also demonstrated that those threats were relevant beyond the African continent, and certainly beyond the borders of developing countries with comparatively weak public health infrastructures. The national security threat posed by infectious disease thus emerged as a geographically much wider – if not planetary – phenomenon.

Perhaps most significantly, the SARS episode also represented a medical redefinition of insecurity which no longer had to take recourse to the more conventional elements of national security policy – such as the armed forces or state stability – in order to be persuasive. The case of SARS established for all to see that a country's national security could be threatened by lethal infectious diseases presenting in the population, solely by virtue of the mortality and serious economic disruptions they cause. That last aspect gave the medicalization of security even greater scope in that it now became possible legitimately to view any infectious disease with the potential to cause significant mortality and economic damage as a national security threat. Other lethal microbes with such pandemic potential were not hard to find, and it therefore also did not take long for international concern to turn to the threat of bird flu.

H5N1 flu: the pandemic lying in wait?

Writing in the *New York Times* only two years later in 2005, two senators from the US Senate Foreign Relations Committee argued that 'when we think of the major threats to our national security, the first to come to mind are nuclear proliferation, rogue states and global terrorism. But another kind of threat lurks beyond our shores, one from nature, not humans – an avian influenza pandemic. An outbreak could cause millions of deaths, destabilize South-East Asia (its likely place of origin), and threaten the security of governments around the world' (NYT 2005). The first of those two congressmen sounding the alarm was Richard Lugar, an experienced Republican senator from Indiana who was also at the time serving as Chairman of the Senate Foreign Relations Committee. The second was a much more junior Democrat from the state of Illinois, who had just been elected to Senate the previous year, and who would later go on to become elected President of the United States – Barack Obama.

Although they sat on different sides of the aisle in Washington, both senators agreed on one fundamental point: the prospect of a renewed human influenza pandemic was a sufficiently serious matter to be considered a threat to national security. That same link between avian influenza and security has also been made in the United Kingdom. The British Civil Contingency Secretariat, for instance, warned in 2005 that avian influenza is 'as serious a threat as terrorism' to the British population (Lean 2005). It continues to rank amongst the most serious threats in the UK National Risk Register. More recently, the World Bank has similarly warned that 'the virus remains a substantial threat to global public health security' (World Bank 2008: 10), whilst the World Health Organization refers to avian influenza as 'the most feared security threat' (WHO 2007a: 45).

Literally, influenza means 'influence'. The name emerged in fifteenth-century Italy because of the widespread belief prevalent at the time that the condition resulted from a malevolent supernatural influence (Crawford 2000: 91). Today our understanding of what causes influenza has moved on, but our name for the disease remains rooted in that history. As the name implies, avian influenza refers more narrowly to influenza viruses that infect birds, which shed the virus through their saliva, faeces and nasal secretions. That in turn infects other birds which come into contact with these secretions and excretions. The low pathogenic forms of avian influenza usually only produce mild symptoms in birds (ruffled feathers, decline in egg production) and can easily go undetected. However, the highly pathogenic subtypes can rapidly affect multiple organs and have a mortality rate close to 100 per cent, usually leading to death within forty-eight hours.

In human populations, by contrast, influenza viruses predominantly attack the upper respiratory tract, including the nose and throat, causing symptoms such as fever, headaches, coughing and sore throats. In both the northern and southern hemispheres, influenza outbreaks amongst human populations occur every winter, which is why they are referred to as 'seasonal' influenza. Larger epidemics do also occur around every eight to ten years. When this happens, in the United Kingdom alone, 10 per cent of the population becomes infected and around 25,000 people die.

Human influenza pandemics, on the other hand, are much rarer events. Only three major pandemics were recorded in the twentieth century – in 1918, 1957 and 1968 (Crawford 2000: 91). The Spanish flu of 1918 was the worst of those in terms of its death toll. It was called 'the Spanish flu' because of an outbreak in Spain, but today it is thought that the pandemic probably originated in the military Camp Funston in Kansas in March 1918. From there it quickly spread throughout the United States and crossed the Atlantic to spread to Europe, China, Japan, Africa and South America.

The first wave of the Spanish flu pandemic was comparatively the lesser threat in terms of its lethality. It is nevertheless estimated to have claimed more than 800,000 lives. Later, a second, larger wave emerged in August 1918, and raged worldwide for six months. Together, the two waves are estimated to have claimed the lives of more than 20 million people during an eighteen-month period – more than the 9 million fatalities estimated to have been caused by the First World War (Zubay et al. 2005: 80–1). Yet the severity of that pandemic (which some estimates claim caused as many as 50 million deaths) was due in part to the peculiar historical factors prevailing at the time. These included the harsh and unsanitary conditions of the First World War, widespread undernourishment, as well as the lack of key instruments for medical intervention such as anti-microbial drugs, mechanical respirators and supplemental oxygen (Kilbourne 2006: 12). In the second half of the twentieth century, two smaller and lesser-known influenza pandemics also occurred: the 'Asian influenza' pandemic of 1957 which killed around 2 million people, and the 'Hong Kong influenza' pandemic of 1968 which killed approximately 1 million.

Because flu is a recurrent phenomenon in human populations, the World Health Organization established a Global Influenza Surveillance Network in 1952, for tracking the spread and evolution of influenza viruses. This network consists of around 110 laboratories in eighty-five countries. Most of those countries possess a National Influenza Monitoring Laboratory which in turn is connected to many smaller, regional contacts, thus creating a vast surveillance net that monitors which influenza strains are circulating in their areas. This information is then fed back to one of four international laboratories located in London, Atlanta, Tokyo and Melbourne. In February of each year a meeting of scientists takes place in Geneva in order to decide which flu strains should be targeted in the vaccine for the following winter in the northern hemisphere. Then it usually takes a further six to eight months to develop and produce the vaccine before it is delivered to doctors in the northern hemisphere in October; and approximately half a year later for the southern hemisphere (Crawford 2000: 99–100).

Those same international tracking mechanisms have led to the identification of highly pathogenic H5N1 avian influenza virus as a potential source of a renewed human pandemic. The H5N1 virus is not actually that novel, having already been detected in Scottish chickens in 1959 (Crawford 2007: 206). The H5N1 virus was also isolated in 1996 amongst farmed geese in Guangdong province in China. As a bird (rather than a human) influenza virus, the primary risk to the human population posed by H5N1 is that a zoonic (animal-to-human) transmission could occur, which subsequently recombines or mutates to create efficient human-to-human transmission. If this virus achieves such efficient human-to-human transmission, it would then be spread through coughing and sneezing. In contrast to SARS, moreover, people would become infectious before they display any symptoms.

Already there have been cases of human infection with H5N1 among people who have been in close contact with infected birds. The first known instances of human infections with the H5N1 avian influenza virus were documented in Hong Kong in 1997, when there were eighteen reported cases. In response to that outbreak, virtually the entire poultry population of Hong Kong was destroyed. Further cases of human infection with the virus were nevertheless detected in February of 2003, again in Hong Kong, where two cases were confirmed in a family. On 25 November 2003, a fatal case of influenza also occurred in a 24–year-old Chinese man from Beijing. In the meantime, the avian influenza virus was spreading to poultry in the Republic of Korea, Vietnam, Japan, Thailand and Hong Kong. In 2004 both Vietnam and Thailand then also identified additional cases of human infection. In late July 2005, the first poultry outbreaks were reported as far away as Russia, and by October 2005 Turkey and Romania had joined the list. So far, confirmed human cases and deaths outside of South-East Asia have occurred in Pakistan, Azerbaijan, Iraq, Djibouti, Turkey, Egypt and Nigeria (World Bank 2008: 7).

Given that those numbers are still comparatively low, why is H5N1 deemed to be a threat to national security? Arguments about the national security implications of H5N1 largely mirror those made in relation to SARS. Again, it is the combined potential impact on human mortality and economic systems that is considered paramount. In terms of mortality, there had been a total of 391 confirmed human cases of bird flu by December 2008, according to the World Health Organization. Of those, 247 died. The majority of cases and deaths have occurred in Indonesia (139 cases and 113 deaths), Vietnam (106 cases and 52 deaths), Egypt (51 cases and 23 deaths), China (30 cases and 20 deaths) and Thailand (25 cases and 17 deaths) (WHO 2008c). The fatality rate for human cases of avian influenza is thus much higher than in the case of SARS, with just under two-thirds of infected persons dying. The official mortality rate may be slightly exaggerated, however, given that many weaker forms of infection producing milder symptoms may never present at health facilities and therefore are not included in these figures (Leboeuf 2009: 57–8).

What is more worrying to policy-makers than the number of existing human infections is the fact that, in exceptional circumstances, it has been possible for H5N1 to become transmitted between people – though so far only in situations of very close contact with an infected person during the acute phase of the illness. Even when this spread has occurred, it has so far not gone beyond one generation of close contacts and has thus appeared to be non-sustainable. It could thus be years before a renewed human H5N1 influenza pandemic emerges, and it may never emerge. If the H5N1 avian influenza virus does achieve efficient and sustained human-to-human transmission, however, the United States Centers for Disease Control and Prevention (CDC) estimate that the deaths would be in the range of 2 to 7.4 million people worldwide. Many more would require hospitalization, or other forms of medical attention (World Bank 2005: 1). That is one reason why H5N1 has been considered a national security threat.

As in the case of SARS, it is also expected that the social effects of such a human H5N1 influenza pandemic would not be confined to increased morbidity and mortality. Such a pandemic would also have further economic effects. Indeed it is worth bearing in mind that avian influenza is already having economic effects due to the serious impact on the poultry population. Modelling and forecasting that potential economic impact in the event of a human pandemic is fraught with methodological difficulties. That is because of the considerable uncertainty about how many people would become infected in such a scenario. There is also uncertainty about exactly how this will affect economic activity.

According to the British Financial Services authority (FSA 2007: 22–3) the list of risks to firms and markets includes a fall in consumption, possibly triggering a recession. It also includes losses and defaults for insurance and tourism companies, as well as for other businesses relying on 'face-to-face' contact. Still further risks include increased absenteeism amongst the workforce, a decrease in investor confidence and a decreasing market liquidity which, in turn, would increase the cost of capital. At the consumer level, the report (FSA 2007: 23) also anticipated the following, additional risks for consumers: increased pressure on household finances due to absenteeism from work; difficulty in accessing financial services; and a decrease in the value of pensions and investments. More recently, an internal report by the World Bank leaked to the media (Gale 2008) estimated that, in the 'worst-case' scenario, a human influenza pandemic could cause 71 million deaths, and cost the world economy some US$3 trillion.

The prospect of such a pandemic arising, and causing economic damage, has led to links being drawn between security and an influenza pandemic. In its *Global Risks 2006* report, the World Economic Forum again noted that the threat from an influenza pandemic was on a par with that from terrorism. At the beginning of 2006, it observed that 'the global risk most preoccupying global business and political leaders is the H5N1 avian flu virus' (WEF 2006: 2). The report warned that people have little or no immunity to the virus, that there is no vaccine, and that supplies of anti-viral drugs are limited. If the virus were to establish efficient human-to-human transmission, 'the vulnerabilities of our interconnected global systems would intensify the human and economic impact. A lethal flu, its spread facilitated by global travel patterns and uncontained by insufficient warning mechanisms, would present an acute threat' (WEF 2006: 4). The construction of H5N1 as a threat thus mirrors the case of SARS rather than that of AIDS, in that it was again the arguments about mortality and economic disruption that proved to be paramount considerations.

However, there is also one obvious but crucial difference between SARS and H5N1. As we have just seen, H5N1 has not yet been able to achieve more sustained human-to-human transmission. Therefore, it has also not yet reached the levels of SARS in terms of the number of infections and deaths. The World Health Organization uses three broad stages to characterize the international situation with respect to the prospect of a human H5N1 influenza pandemic. First is the inter-pandemic stage during which there may be new viruses emerging in animals, but not in human beings. Second, there is the pandemic alert stage when a virus begins to cause new human cases. This is followed by the final, pandemic stage characterized by efficient and sustained human-to-human transmission.

According to the World Health Organization, the world is at present 'only' in the second stage in relation to avian flu, and nobody can predict if and when a human H5N1 pandemic will emerge. Indeed, there are even some signs that the overall situation with regards to avian influenza appears to be improving slightly. No countries had new infections between January and September 2008 (World Bank 2008: 9). Scientists have discovered a possible reason why the current form of H5N1 may not be spreading quickly between humans. In human beings the virus appears to be attaching itself too far down the respiratory system to be spread by coughs and sneezing, in the way more common cold viruses that are present in the upper respiratory system are (Shinya et al. 2006).

This crucial difference also means that, in the end, H5N1 too has played a distinct role in the history of the medical redefinition of insecurity. Whereas SARS was the epidemic that made the national security implications of infectious diseases evident for all to see, H5N1 is the pandemic 'lying in wait'. After the threat of SARS had dissipated by the end of 2003, it was the continuing threat of an unpredictable but possible H5N1 pandemic that ensured that governments did not forget about the security threat posed by infectious diseases. It was the threat of an imminent H5N1 pandemic that compelled them to remain vigilant about the prospect of a new pandemic erupting unexpectedly at any moment.

All of that widened the scope of the medicalization of security further still. SARS had already extended that scope to include infectious diseases outside of Africa, as well as ones which did not directly threaten the more traditional institutions of national security such as the military. H5N1 broadened that scope even further by also including infectious diseases that had not yet even taken on epidemic or pandemic human form. The experience of H5N1 showed that the mere possibility of such a future outbreak was now sufficient for an infectious disease to be considered a threat to national security and required governments to invest continually in pandemic preparedness measures. Those preparations, in turn, would require extensive input from a wide range of different medical professionals.

Muscling In: The Medical Professions at the Heart of Power

National security debates about infectious disease threats have not just begun to redefine insecurity as a medical problem. They have frequently also extended calls for the greater involvement of a broad array of medical professionals in the analysis and formulation of national security policy – ranging from physicians all the way through to government health officials and international public health experts. That represents a further augmentation of the societal influence of medical professionals and is another important hallmark of medicalization. There are several different ways in which medical professionals have recently come to play a much greater role in security policy.

Medical professionals with a variety of expertise in clinical practice, epidemiology and microbiology increasingly form part of the new health security programmes established over the past decade by influential foreign policy and security think tanks. The list of such programmes is already quite long. It includes the Global Health Program at the Council on Foreign Relations in New York, the HIV/AIDS Task Force and the Global Health Policy Center at the Center for Strategic and International Studies in Washington, DC, and both the Global Health Center and the Center for Domestic and International Health Security at the RAND Corporation in Arlington, Virginia. It further includes the Global Health Security programme at the Henry L. Stimson Center, the Global Health and Security Initiative at the Nuclear Threat Initiative, both of which are also located in Washington, DC. In the United Kingdom, it also includes the Centre on Global Health Security housed at the Royal Institute of International Affairs in London (Chatham House). These programmes analyse the ways in which infectious disease, and other global health issues, impact upon security and foreign policy. Many of the programs are run by, or at lest rely upon the close involvement of, people trained in the medical and related professions. These programmes thus mark one area where the societal jurisdiction of medical professionals is expanding through their more intimate involvement in discussion of security and foreign policy.

Medical professionals are also becoming more closely involved in the formulation of national security policy. The growing political influence of medical professionals in the United States government has been highlighted by Harley Feldbaum (2009) whose research has traced how, in the late 1990s, Kenneth Bernard – a former physician who graduated from medical school – lobbied the political leadership in the White House to create a new post at the National Security Council for a 'Senior Advisor for International Health'. Establishing such a post would mark a quite radical departure in that it would, for the first time, institutionalize international health concerns within the key forum for articulating national security and foreign policy within the United States government.

Not surprisingly, perhaps, that process of introducing medical professionals into national security circles initially proved an uphill struggle. Bernard describes his arrival as the US Special Advisor for International Health Affairs at the National Security Council in 1998 in the following, almost comical, terms:

> Nobody was here, I didn't have anything to do for six months. No one could figure out why I was here. They'd come up the hallway and say, I understand you're a doctor and you're working with Sandy Berger [the US National Security Advisor], are you like, you know, going on trips and taking care of the health issues that come up, you know when people get sick . . . Speaking of which, you know, I've been running and my knees have been hurting, do you mind taking a look at it? And there was just no sense in the public, in the national security community that health had a seat. (Cited in Feldbaum 2009: 128)

Yet, since those early days, the institutionalization of health concerns at the highest levels of government has advanced considerably. Today, political agencies devoted to the provision of national security are increasingly reliant upon the advice of a number of different medical professionals and are reaching out to them.

A key turning point in this process was President Bill Clinton's Presidential Decision Directive on Emerging Infectious Diseases, issued in 1996 (NSTC-7), which called for a coordinated effort to improve the protection of the American population against a range of infectious diseases. The directive pointed out that a variety of organizations would have to be tasked with assisting in this urgent effort. Those agencies included public health institutions such as the National Institutes of Health and the Centers for Disease Control and Prevention. Yet it also included the Department of Defense (DoD), which would henceforth have to contribute to the goal of defending the US population against infectious diseases. Although it would not take the lead on this effort, the directive did make clear that:

> The mission of DoD will be expanded to include support of global surveillance, training, research and response to emerging infectious disease threats. DoD will strengthen its global disease reduction efforts through: centralized coordination, improved preventive health programs and epidemiological capabilities, and enhanced involvement with military treatment facilities and United States and overseas laboratories. DoD will ensure the availability of diagnostic capabilities at its three domestic and six overseas laboratories, using existing DoD resources. DoD will make available its overseas laboratory facilities, as appropriate, to serve as focal points for the training of foreign technicians and epidemiologists. (PDD 1996)

Even the Department of Defense, in other words, would have to reach out to a broad range of medical professionals around the world. A decade later, the Department of Homeland Security also maintains an Office of Health Affairs focusing on biodefence, emergency medical response and international health security initiatives. At the time of writing, that office too was under the leadership of an official trained in medicine and who has been a practising doctor for many years.

The United Nations Security Council too has called upon medical professionals to become more closely involved in international security affairs. That is evident in the way that it has invited such professionals to attend some of its meetings. For example, the Security Council asked the former Executive Director of UNAIDS, Peter Piot, to address the Council during the landmark meetings of the Security Council on HIV/AIDS. Piot is another prominent international health official who initially studied medicine and graduated from medical school, but who has also been involved in high-level meetings of prominent security institutions. Security Council Resolution

1308 also called upon UNAIDS – an organization devoted to health
– to develop best-practice guidelines in relation to HIV/AIDS prevention, education, testing, counselling and treatment as a way of
helping to maintain international peace and security. This too marks
a site where different kinds of medical professionals are becoming
more closely involved in the formulation and execution of security
policy.

In addition to involving an array of medical experts more closely
in security policy, health security debates have also increased the
societal influence of many different medical professionals working
for governmental and international health organizations. The quest
for health security has, for instance, prompted the creation of entire
new organizations and emergency response initiatives dealing with
the threat of infectious diseases. In 2004 the European Union realized that the threat posed to the region by emerging infectious
diseases would require much greater cooperation and coordination
amongst member states. Realizing that Europe was not well prepared
to respond to such a regional threat, the European Union decided
to create the European Centre for Disease Prevention and Control
(ECDC) in 2005.

This Stockholm-based agency of the European Union conducts
disease surveillance on behalf of the member states of the European
Union. According to Article 3 of its founding Regulation, the mission
of the ECDC is 'to identify, assess and communicate current and
emerging threats to human health from communicable diseases'
(ECDC 2004: 3). The ECDC thus focuses heavily (though not exclusively) on infectious diseases, with a brief to identify, assess and communicate existing, as well as emerging, threats to human health. That
also makes the ECDC an important example of a new regional health
organization created partially in response to the growing concern
about the threat posed by infectious diseases.

Another new international initiative created in order to meet
the threat of infectious diseases is the Global Outbreak Alert and
Response Network (GOARN). GOARN was formalized in 2000
under the auspices of the World Health Organization. Although not
a formal international organization, it has emerged as an important
network of member states who have agreed to pool some of their

resources at the international level, to be able to mount a rapid and effective response to the outbreak of a new infectious disease irrespective of where it first emerges. The GOARN team meets regularly to sift through reports of outbreaks from official and unofficial sources. If it deems an outbreak to be of significance within the context of the International Health Regulations it then contacts one of the regional offices of the World Health Organization to investigate further, and to see whether these regional offices can make contact with people 'on the ground' to confirm the outbreak.

GOARN helps to respond to more than fifty outbreaks of disease annually (such as cholera, meningitis, yellow fever, plague, Ebola, etc.) and serves to minimize the international spread of dangerous microbes. The network not only helped to detect the SARS outbreak, but also showed that this disease was spreading beyond Asia, and linked scientists and laboratories around the world as they sought to detect the causative agents and transmission patterns of SARS (Heymann in Fidler 2004: xiii). On the back of the elevated threat perceptions about infectious disease, there have even been recent calls to divert defence funds toward some health security initiatives. For example, the Health Protection Agency in the United Kingdom has suggested that, in light of the growing centrality of health issues, it could now be legitimate to request money from government and security budgets to fund the GOARN initiative – a call echoed at the time by some officials at the World Health Organization (Aldis 2008: 371). These initiatives too enhance the societal influence of many different medical professionals by providing them with new and additional platforms from which to respond to the threat posed by infectious diseases.

Finally, health security debates have also coincided with a growing range of legal powers being made available to existing government and international agencies tasked with preventing the spread of infectious diseases. In the United States, for instance, the Secretary of the Department for Health and Human Services has the power to quarantine citizens infected with a new infectious disease. The list of quarantinable diseases in the United States is established by Executive Order of the President upon recommendation of the Secretary of the Department of Health and Human Services. The list of such quarantinable diseases today includes cholera, diphtheria, infectious tuberculosis, plague, smallpox, yellow fever and viral haemorrhagic fevers (such as Marburg, Ebola and Congo-Crimean disease).

Such powers to quarantine people are certainly not new and have a long history. But in recent years the increased anxieties about infectious diseases have led these to be expanded on at least two occasions. First, in 2003, SARS was added to the US list of quarantinable diseases. Second, in 2005, influenza brought about by novel or re-emergent influenza viruses that are causing, or have the potential to cause, a pandemic was similarly added to the list. The powers associated with this list entail that if any passenger infected with a novel influenza strain were to arrive in the United States on-board a boat, an aircraft and so forth, then the Department of Health and Human Services has the legal authority to isolate that passenger to prevent the passenger from infecting others. That is not to deny that such measures may be prudent in the event of a new infectious disease outbreak. Yet it also shows how the perception of infectious disease as a serious threat culminates in health professionals acquiring a considerable amount of control over the movements and actions of citizens who are carrying, or believed to be carrying, an infectious disease. Such quarantine powers have also been introduced in other countries.

Even more significant than these quarantine powers are the new legal powers that the World Health Organization has also acquired through the revision of the International Health Regulations (IHR). Attempts by states to deal with the international spread of infectious disease through the construction of legal norms can be traced back historically to a series of international sanitary conferences held in the second half of the nineteenth century. In 1951, the member states of the newly formed World Health Organization adopted the International Sanitary Regulations, which were renamed the International Health Regulations in 1969. However, prior to their recent revision, the International Health Regulations only made modest demands of states and applied to just six diseases – cholera, plague, relapsing fever, smallpox, typhus and yellow fever (Dry 2008: 9).

By contrast the new International Health Regulations agreed in 2005 (revised in light of experiences such as HIV/AIDS, SARS and H5N1 influenza) are much more comprehensive and have an expanded remit by applying to public health emergencies more generally. A public health emergency is defined, for the purposes of the International Health Regulations, as any extraordinary public health event that constitutes a public health risk to other states through the international spread of disease, and which potentially requires a coordinated international response. As a way of creating less uncertainty about which events must be reported, the International Health Regulations also include a decision-instrument to guide policy-makers in terms of the considerations that must be taken into account when deciding about whether or not an event is notifiable. Such public health emergencies cover diseases of which even a single case must be reported to the World Health Organization immediately – including smallpox, poliomyelitis caused by a wild-type poliovirus, any new subtype of human influenza, and SARS. Here the legal powers of the World Health Organization have been expanded in that it has acquired jurisdiction over a much wider range of diseases than just the six originally stipulated in the earlier International Health Regulations.

Beyond that expanded remit, the revised International Health Regulations also require member states to undertake new obligations in relation to the management of infectious disease. These include the establishment of national focus points for communicating information relevant to these regulations to the World Health Organization on a 7-days-a-week, 24-hours-a-day basis. The regulations also set out the minimum public health capabilities that states must ensure in terms of reporting and responding to international public health risks. The World Health Organization, in turn, has received additional powers to make temporary recommendations to mitigate any such threat. Questions still remain, of course, about how thoroughly these new measures will be implemented and enforced by member states. In the end, there is no enforcement mechanism to ensure compliance, and resources in many countries may be insufficient to make these required changes.

Due in part to these uncertainties, the International Health Regulations also formalized another important power for the World Health Organization. The latter is now permitted to draw upon information stemming from non-official sources, rather than just relying on official notifications by the states concerned. Although it had access to other informal sources of information prior to the 2005 IHR revisions and could follow up reports informally, previously the World Health Organization could only act officially on information that states volunteered. In the case of SARS, as in many other cases, that had proved a problem when China was initially not very forthcoming with information. Being able to use non-official sources expedites this process and also serves as a warning to states that, if they choose not to share information, that is unlikely to prevent the World Health Organization from becoming aware of the situation and acting upon it.

For example, the World Health Organization can now draw upon information shared through the Global Public Health Intelligence Network (GPHIN) which was developed by Health Canada in 1998. GPHIN is a fee-based system that routinely monitors internet sites, wire services, local online newspapers and so forth for reports of new disease outbreaks. It scans these sources in seven languages (Arabic, English, French, Russian, Simplified and Traditional Chinese, and Spanish) on a 24-hours-a-day basis. The results are then analysed and filtered by GPHIN officials, as well as members of the Public Health Agency of Canada. The service posts around seven to ten alerts each day. A similar internet-based alerting system is run by the International Society for Infectious Diseases in the form of ProMED-mail (the Program for Monitoring Emerging Disease), which was developed in 1994 by the Federation of American Scientists. This focuses more on new developments, i.e. either newly emerging diseases, or existing diseases emerging in new populations.

Obtaining the power to draw upon information supplied through such unofficial channels, rather than just on official information shared by member states, marks another important example of how the articulation of infectious diseases as national security threats has begun gradually to augment the social and political influence of a wide range of medical professionals – from medical experts becoming more involved in security deliberations through to officials working in international health institutions enjoying new or expanded powers. Such expansions in the societal jurisdiction of medical professionals are, as we have seen, another important hallmark of medicalization.

Magic Bullets: The Quest for Medical Countermeasures

The medicalization of security is even evident in the way that national security debates about the threat posed by infectious diseases encourage recourse to medical interventions as one of the principal ways of managing those new security threats. Rudolf Virchow, who is widely considered to be the founding father of social medicine, once famously claimed that politics is nothing but medicine on a large scale. Certainly, within the context of national security discussions about how best to manage infectious disease threats, security too has become (at least in part) practised through the means of medicine. The pandemic preparedness plans drawn up by governments are multi-faceted and often contain a range of wider public health measures in the event of a new pandemic. Yet for most governments the holy grail of securing their populations against the threat of infectious diseases remains the stockpiling of medical interventions like vaccines and treatments.

The international response to the security threat posed by HIV/AIDS already foreshadowed this move, with anti-retroviral programmes being initiated in the armed forces, and later rolled out more generally to civilian populations in Africa through unprecedented initiatives such as the US President's Emergency Plan for AIDS Relief (PEPFAR). That medical response model was subsequently also adopted in the development of domestic pandemic preparedness in many Western countries. In the United States, President George W. Bush launched the National Strategy for Pandemic Influenza on 1 November 2005. Amongst its provisions was the creation of 'surge capacity' for medical responders, as well as the drawing up of plans for rapidly distributing medical countermeasures from a strategic national stockpile to local and state agencies.

This focus on developing pharmacological countermeasures would become even more important when, in December 2006, Congress adopted the Pandemic and All-Hazards Preparedness Act. That Act established the Biomedical Advanced Research and Development Agency and tasked it with developing and acquiring new medical 'countermeasures' to protect the population against pandemic threats (as well as bioterror threats). In October 2007, the White House then issued Homeland Security Presidential Directive 21, which established the 'National Strategy for Public Health and Medical Preparedness'. One of its four elements was again the stockpiling and distributing of medical countermeasures (in addition to developing a biosurveillance capability for early warning, developing a mass-casualty care system that is sufficiently swift and flexible to deal with a catastrophic health event, and increasing community resilience by educating them about these threats and how to respond to them). Securing populations against pandemic threats has thus entailed the government acquiring and stockpiling a wide range of medicines and vaccines. Such recourse to pharmacological products is another important hallmark of medicalization processes frequently noted by scholars in other disciplines.

Emphasis on medical interventions has also been evident in the ways in which governments have been responding to the specific threat of H5N1. Governments with the requisite resources have been encouraging companies rapidly to develop new vaccines and anti-virals to reduce the spread and impact of a potential human H5N1 (or other highly pathogenic) pandemic. Since concern about H5N1 first emerged, manufacturers have effectively been in a race to develop a new H5N1 vaccine. The first products have already received approval for human use from regulatory authorities. Recognizing the more widespread desire for vaccines amongst many governments around the world, the World Health Organization in turn issued its Global Pandemic Influenza Action Plan to Increase Vaccine Supply in October 2006, and has been working with vaccine manufacturers to create a global stockpile of vaccine for the H5N1 influenza virus since 2007. So far, several pharmaceutical companies have pledged to contribute to such a stockpile, whilst the United States government too has announced its willingness to donate 20 million doses.

Yet there are several technicalities that need to be worked out, and the stockpile still does not exist at the time of writing. So far, the

World Health Organization only has pledges for around 100 million doses of vaccine (which would cover 50 million people, who need 2 doses each). In the event of an H5N1 pandemic, the World Health Organization will thus have to make difficult choices as to whether this stockpile should be used to target heavily a localized outbreak at an early stage in the hope of containing the emergence of a wider pandemic. Alternatively, the World Health Organization could try to reserve these stockpiles for low-income countries, to provide these countries with at least some measure of protection in the case of the pandemic (World Bank 2008: 57).

In either case, that push for a stockpile by the World Health Organization again shows just how widespread and pervasive the desire for having access to such medical interventions has become amongst many governments – even beyond the borders of wealthy Western states and where the requisite resources for such stockpiles often do not exist. Some of those governments without access to H5N1 vaccines have therefore also decided to invest in other pharmacological treatments which are more readily available, such as anti-viral medications like Tamiflu or Relenza. Although data about their efficacy are contested, and concerns are increasing about influenza viruses emerging that are resistant to these medicines, those moves too ultimately show how national security is becoming regarded as unattainable today without access to a range of medical interventions.

Conclusion

In the end, it does not really matter whether the threat of H5N1 was overhyped – as many have charged. In the spring of 2009, concern with H5N1 was rapidly overtaken by the need to respond to the unexpected emergence of new human infections with the pandemic H1N1 2009 influenza virus. Officials did not realize it at the time, but pandemic preparedness efforts undertaken over the past decade had been both right and wrong. They were right in pointing out that another human pandemic was due. They were wrong in focusing mostly on birds rather than on pigs as the most likely animal hosts for such a new pandemic. None of that, however, changes the underlying fact that – for at least a decade prior to the more recent outbreak of swine flu – the medicalization of security was already well under way in national security debates concerned about the threat posed by infectious diseases in the age of rapid and extensive air travel.

Those national security debates have begun subtly to redefine insecurity as a problem that is brought about not just by the military capabilities and hostile political intentions of other states, but also by the emergence of diseases within the human population. This process of medical redefinition of insecurity has in turn encouraged the growing involvement of a wide range of medical professionals in the analysis and formulation of national security policy, thereby further extending the social influence of medical professionals into this important area of politics. The medicalization of security has even compelled governments to draw up extensive pandemic preparedness plans in order to be able to respond rapidly to the emergence of a novel infectious disease – plans that have often taken the shape of acquiring extensive stockpiles of medical countermeasures. Increasingly, the provision of security thus requires the input of many different types of medical professionals and the development of new medical interventions. That renders national security discussions about pandemic threats one of the most paradigmatic manifestations of the medicalization of security which is unfolding in international relations today.

3

Poisoning Populations: Biosecurity and the Weaponization of Disease

The medicalization of security acquires an even greater scope through attempts to protect civilian populations against the threat of a biological weapon attack. Biosecurity discussions thus highlight a second set of security threats that stem from the possibility of an infectious disease being intentionally released for hostile political purposes. This focus on deliberate (rather than on naturally occurring) outbreaks also marks the main distinction between biosecurity and national security concerns. Yet, this crucial difference notwithstanding, biosecurity deliberations essentially have the same medicalizing effect in relation to our underlying understanding of insecurity. Because biosecurity discussions similarly perceive infectious diseases as security threats, they too animate the redefinition of insecurity in world politics as constituting – at least in part – a medical problem caused by the onset and spread of disease within the population.

Meeting that threat of a deliberate biological attack will again also require much closer involvement of a plethora of medical professionals in the analysis and formulation of security policy. They are needed not just for identifying the key biological agents that could be used to mount such attacks, but also for developing detailed policies about how health care providers will deal with the consequences of attack. Likewise, attempts to enhance the security of populations against the threat of such biological attacks will, once more, have to take recourse to a range of different medical interventions. That can be seen in the increased funding being directed toward researchers and institutions for the purposes of developing new medical countermeasures against biological agents. The opening up of that medical front in the War on Terror thus represents another crucial site where the medicalization of security is unfolding and expanding today.

Bio-Warfare: A Twentieth-Century Precursor to Biosecurity

According to most conventional definitions, biological warfare is defined as warfare conducted with the use of biological weapons. Biological weapons refer to any 'munitions, equipment or means of delivery including bombs, aircraft spray tanks and other devices, intended for use in the dissemination of biological agents and toxins for hostile purposes' (Guillemin 2005: 2). The development of a biological weapon commonly consists of turning a biological agent into aerosol form. That renders particles small enough not to fall to the ground immediately. Instead they travel with prevailing air currents, thus allowing them to infect humans when people inhale the air filled with those particles (Guillemin 2005: 2).

Once successfully turned into aerosol form, biological weapons usually also include a delivery component (such as a missile) that enables the aerosol to be delivered to the theatre of battle. Alternatively, a biological agent could enter the body by means of ingestion if, for example, food or water supplies were deliberately contaminated. Once deployed, biological weapons are very difficult to control. Because of their indiscriminate nature, they would almost always involve extensive civilian and non-combatant casualties. Biological weapons thus sit squarely between the worlds of health and security: the former because they consist of diseases and the latter because they are weapons used for hostile purposes.

That quality also endows biological weapons with several unique characteristics that are worth singling out – even though for analytical purposes they are usually classified in the literature as weapons of mass destruction and grouped together with chemical and nuclear weapons. Unlike nuclear weapons, for instance, biological weapons target people's biological organism rather than bringing about the massive destruction of physical infrastructure. That is a characteristic which biological weapons share with chemical weapons. Yet biological agents are also distinct from chemical weapons because of their infectious quality and their resultant ability to spread more widely. In using a chemical component at their core, chemical weapons are strictly speaking not 'infectious' at all. Biological weapons, by contrast, usually contain a 'live' bacterium or virus such as cholera, Ebola, plague, smallpox and so forth. That ability to amplify their effect by subsequently spreading to further members of the human population makes many biological weapons very dangerous, even in minuscule quantities. In those respects, it is worth singling out biological weapons from other weapons of mass destruction like nuclear and chemical weapons. All three can cause death, but it is only in the case of biological weapons that a disease is the principal weapon.

When did insecurity first become understood as something that could be caused by the deliberate release of an infectious disease within a population? Although the threat posed by bioterrorism has been vigorously debated since the late 1990s, and especially in the aftermath of the attacks of 11 September 2001, this dimension to the medicalization of security evidently has a much longer history. Historians record that the ancient Greeks and Romans already attempted to weaken their enemies by placing dead animals into their reservoirs of drinking water. Assyrians also poisoned enemy wells with a fungus (rye ergot) in the sixth century BC (Ryan and Glarum 2008: 7–8).

In medieval times infected bodies were catapulted over town walls to spread diseases, as happened in the 1346 siege of Caffa (Guillemin 2005: 3). Over a century later, the Spanish used the blood of lepers to contaminate French wine in 1495 (Ryan and Glarum 2008: 7–8). In the eighteenth century, the British Commander-in-Chief Sir Jeffrey Amherst also ordered the distribution of blankets contaminated with smallpox to Native Americans surrounding Fort Pitt in Pennsylvania (Crawford 2000: 39).

Although these are all historical examples in which diseases are alleged to have been deliberately turned into weapons, it is difficult to consider them as proper manifestations of the medicalization of security. The reason for this is that these examples predate the scientific discoveries of Robert Koch and Louis Pasteur, and therefore also the germ theory of disease (which holds that diseases are caused by micro-organisms). Even in the absence of that deeper understanding of the causes and transmission patterns of infectious diseases, it was clearly possible to use diseases deliberately for hostile purposes. Yet without the underlying scientific, micro-biological underpinnings, it was not yet possible to mass-produce, cultivate deliberately, and indeed manipulate micro-organisms in such a way as to maximize their destructive impact on a population. That marriage of the science of biology with the art of warfare would only begin to unfold in a much more dramatic fashion in the course of the twentieth century. It is also at this point that insecurity came to be understood much more widely as, among other things, something emanating from the deliberate release of an infectious disease within a population.

The Germans are thought to have been amongst the first to harness their knowledge of disease for the conduct of war when they used biological weapons against packhorses and mules (though not people) during the First World War, in an attempt to slow down and weaken the supply chains of their enemies. Historians, of course, still remember the First World War largely for its use of chemical rather than biological weapons – as epitomized by the use of chlorine gas by the German troops at Ypres, Belgium, in 1915 (Guillemin 2005: 3). Things would soon begin to change after the First World War, however. The increased use and role of airpower in warfare opened up a particularly devastating combination of scientific knowledge and a new military delivery system, which France would be amongst the first to exploit during the 1920s (Guillemin 2005: 11–13; Fidler and Gostin 2008: 46).

Evidence of how seriously states began to take the deliberate spread of infectious disease as a new source of insecurity can be found in their decision to sign the Geneva Protocol on 17 June 1925, which sought to ban the use of biological weapons in war. Strictly speaking, the protocol, which entered into force on 8 February 1928 and today has 133 state parties, only amounts to a treaty against the first use of such weapons during times of warfare – not against their development for defensive purposes, or even possessing and stock-piling them (Guillemin 2005: 5). Technically, the protocol also does not apply to internal conflicts, or to situations in which the combat-ants do not officially consider themselves to be at war (Al-Rodhan et al. 2008: 83). In retrospect the treaty nevertheless marks an early attempt to stem the new source of insecurity that was seen to emanate from the prospect of infectious diseases being deliberately released in the conduct of war.

That attempt would prove only moderately successful. Perhaps the most crucial aspect of the treaty was the fact that Japan only signed, but did not subsequently ratify, the Geneva Protocol. That left the door open for Japan to use such weapons on eleven cities during the Second World War (Al-Rodhan et al. 2008: 83), and also to use biological weapons offensively against China in the 1930s and 1940s (Fidler and Gostin 2008: 26). Japan also formed its notorious Unit 731 which experimented with cholera and hemorrhagic fevers on prisoners, in gruesome experiments. Interested in the results of their experiments, the United States government later granted these scientists immunity from war crimes prosecution in return for being supplied with the results of these and other experiments (Fidler and Gostin 2008: 46).

The Soviet Union too allegedly used biological weapons in the Second World War. Questions have been raised specifically about the large number of German deaths which occurred shortly before the battle of Stalingrad in 1942, where a large outbreak of tularaemia also occurred. The large number of deaths from inhalation tularaemia is unusual, given how rare the disease is. A prominent Soviet defector, Ken Alibek, later revealed that the Soviets had developed a tularaemia-based weapon only the year before (Ryan and Glarum 2008: 9).

Several Western countries also moved toward developing biological weapons around the time of the Second World War. Britain began its own programme during the war, focusing mostly on anthrax, and testing anthrax weapons on Gruinard Island off the Scottish coast. Fearful of a potential biological weapons attack from Germany, Britain also urged the United States to develop a similar programme. Senior officials met in the United States in December 1942 and initiated such a project at Camp Detrick in Maryland. Unlike the British programme, the American one was not restricted to anthrax: it included botulism, plague, tularaemia, Q fever, Venezuelan equine encephalitis and brucellosis as well (Ryan and Glarum 2008: 9–10). By this time, it was clear that the disease–security nexus was there to stay, and that prudence would require security analysts to factor in the possibility of a deliberate release of a disease within a population during times of war.

The three decades after the Second World War thus witnessed

the development of a wide range of secret biological weapons programmes for both offensive and defensive purposes. By this time, the
weaponization of disease was in full swing, reaching unprecedented
heights and attesting to the darker side of the health–security nexus.
By 1977 the US army alone had conducted more than 239 intentional
releases of non-infectious bacteria in order to test their dispersal qual-
ities. Those experiments included releases at the Pentagon buildings
in 1949, as well as a US navy ship sailing past the Golden Gate Bridge
in San Francisco in 1950. Further releases occurred in the cities of St.
Louis and Minneapolis in 1953, as well as in New York City's subway
system in 1966 (Ryan and Glarum 2008: 11–13). Yet with the exception of the activities of the Japanese imperial army in China, and the
possible Soviet use during the Second World War, the biological
weapons developed through those programmes are thought never to
have been deployed in battlefield conditions against human beings.
These programmes nevertheless showed just how seriously the threat
of deliberate releases of infectious diseases was being taken.

Attempts to break that chain of scientifically induced insecurity
would only regain the upper hand again in 1969, when President
Nixon made a unilateral declaration that biological weapons had no
place in US military doctrine, not least because of their poor tactical
utility (Fidler and Gostin 2008: 47). That decision also paved the way
for a new international Biological Weapons Convention (BWC) in
1972, which bound signatories to:

> never in any circumstances . . . develop, produce, stockpile or
> otherwise acquire or retain: (1) microbial or other biological
> agents or toxins whatever their origin or method of production,
> of types and quantities that have no justification for prophylactic,
> protective or other peaceful purposes; [and] (2) weapons,
> equipment or means of delivery designed to use such agents or
> toxins for hostile purposes in armed conflict. (BWC 1972)

On paper, these provisions appeared to extend significantly beyond
the earlier restraints imposed by the Geneva Protocol by further
banning the development, production and possession of biological
weapons for offensive purposes. Unlike the Geneva Protocol, this
seemed to prohibit not merely the use of biological weapons, but,
more importantly, their very development and possession.

Of course, one reason countries such as France, the United Kingdom and the United States could afford to abandon the use of disease as a weapon of war was that, in the meantime, they had all developed much more powerful nuclear weapons. In that situation, it was not actually such a substantial strategic sacrifice for those governments to undertake. Another reason for signing that applied to all non-nuclear states lay in the fact that the same ambiguity that plagued the earlier Geneva Protocol also resided at the heart of the new Biological Weapons Convention. Within the parameters of the Convention, states could still find ways for justifying the possession of such agents on defensive grounds. They could, for instance, claim that they were developing new strains of lethal, infectious microbes as a way of creating better medical responses in the event that their armed forces should be attacked in future (Fidler and Gostin 2008: 33).

Thus the Biological Weapons Convention was signed in 1972, and more than 150 states remain party to it today. As a result of that Convention, biological weapons gradually became seen as less of an overtly pressing concern, and in any case they were overshadowed by the potentially even more destructive nuclear arms race between the United States and the Soviet Union during the Cold War. Those twentieth-century biological weapons must nonetheless be considered important precursors of the contemporary medicalization of security; they already foreshadowed some of the ways in which the threat of biological weapons has moved back to the forefront of the security agenda since the 1990s. In light of that twentieth-century history of biological weapons programmes it would, in fact, be more accurate to understand the recent concern about biological attacks voiced in the context of biosecurity debates as the re-medicalization of security.

Biosecurity and the Re-Medicalization of Security

That re-medicalization of security is driven by three intersecting concerns. First, it has become clear that the Biological Weapons Convention was not actually as successful in halting biological weapons programmes as had initially been hoped. Some bioweapons programmes were indeed terminated, but others simply became shrouded in even greater secrecy (Guillemin 2005: vii). For example, it emerged toward the end of the Cold War that, despite also possessing nuclear weapons, the Soviet Union had in fact held on to the biological weapons programme until its dying days. The Central Intelligence Agency (CIA), too, retained small quantities of anthrax and shellfish toxins and cultures for tularaemia, brucellosis, Venezuelan equine encephalitis and smallpox (Guillemin 2005: 130).

During the First Gulf War in 1991, it was also revealed that Iraq had engaged in an extensive biological weapons programme. According to information made available to the United Nations inspectors, Iraq had produced 100 bombs filled with botulinum toxin. Iraq was reportedly also in possession of 50 bombs filled with anthrax, as well as a further 16 filled with aflatoxin – another naturally occurring toxin (Zubay et al. 2005: 134). Such clandestine programmes, operating in multiple countries, all exposed deeper problems associated with the Biological Weapons Convention. Most significantly of all, it highlighted the fact that there was no effective procedure for verification. States could never been entirely sure if the insecurity stemming from the possibility of the deliberate release of a biological agent had been genuinely contained by the Convention.

Further revelations emerged a decade later. In 2001, three investigative journalists revealed, in their book *Germs: Biological Weapons and America's Secret War*, that the United States too had been involved in several biological weapons projects which blurred the line between offensive and defensive use (Miller et al. 2001). The first project consisted of testing a Soviet-style anthrax bomb. CIA officials decided at the time that this test was within the permitted domain of research for defensive purposes. They decided similarly in the case of the second project, which consisted of building a small facility for making biological weapons exclusively from materials procured on the open market.

The third project sought to work on a strain of anthrax that was resistant to vaccines. Apparently not even the National Security Council under President Clinton knew about these programmes. The Clinton administration only admitted to knowledge of the last of the three, and then put it on hold. However the incoming Bush administration would soon give the green light for it to restart (Guillemin 2005: 169). Thus the deliberate use of infectious diseases as a way of posing a threat to other states defied campaigners' best-intentioned efforts to contain it.

Some still hoped that, on the back of these revelations, the Biological Weapons Convention could finally be strengthened, perhaps through agreeing an additional protocol to ensure greater compliance. In the end, any such efforts were hampered by the high number of civilian facilities involved, the technical complexity of the issues, and the fact that the Convention was now seen as insufficiently rigorous for addressing the more pressing concerns about bioterrorism (Fidler and Gostin 2008: 26). In July 2001 the Bush administration thus withdrew from the negotiations over a legally binding compliance regime and verification protocol for the Biological Weapons Convention. The reasons cited by the United States government for this decision at the time were the imperatives of military secrecy and the sensitive commercial interests of the pharmaceutical companies involved (Guillemin 2005: 168). Irrespective of whether these are deemed legitimate reasons, the difficulties surrounding the biological weapons regime show just how hard it is to keep the biological weapons genie in the box. The growing recognition that biological weapons are here to stay thus marks the first impetus behind the current re-medicalization of security that is unfolding in the context of biosecurity debates.

That re-medicalization of security is also occurring because of a second realization: recent advances in the medical field and biosciences herald the prospect not only of new medical treatments, but also of deliberately creating new types of disease. In the past, biological weapons programmes often focused on naturally occurring pathogens, and used modern science primarily for culturing them in greater numbers and weaponizing them. However, new recombinant DNA technologies could in future allow for much greater manipulation of these pathogens in terms of their genetic make-up. That, in turn, could change the characteristics of the pathogens in terms of their lethality, how stable they are in aerosol form, their resistance to conventional antibiotic treatment, and even their ability to resist modern detection and diagnosis systems (Petro et al. 2003: 162).

Microbiologists and biomedical experts with detailed knowledge about the technical issues involved warn that it is not inconceivable that new technologies could even herald a new era of bioweapons that 'target specific human biological systems at the molecular level' (Petro et al. 2003: 162). In civilian research, scientists are already capable of introducing foreign genes into the DNA of plants and animals so as to produce new proteins. They can, for instance, now breed goats producing insulin in their milk. Such 'transgenic' technology could also be used to produce large quantities of toxins, and even 'transgenic insects, such as bees, wasps, or mosquitoes, could be developed to produce and deliver protein-based biological warfare agents' (Petro et al. 2003: 163). Advances in nano-technologies could also yield more efficient ways of weaponizing biological agents (Petro et al. 2003: 164).

The harrowing possibilities for such new bioweapons thus include their being engineering to be much more predictable and targeted in their effects, as well as new agents being produced that will not be recognized by expert communities and that could even evade existing medical countermeasures. These possibilities further include making existing pathogens produce new or quite different symptoms, which would again make detection of an attack much harder initially (Petro et al. 2003: 164). The mere prospect of such scientific developments poses deep challenges to existing biological weapons control regimes and counter-proliferation policies, rendering international regimes to counter and constrain these developments perhaps much more relevant than at any previous time in human history. So far, however, the race to weaponize infectious diseases has not only resisted the best of these diplomatic containment efforts, it has now also entered a dangerous new phase fuelled by recent scientific advances. That is a second important factor prompting the current re-medicalization of security.

Bioterrorism: Disease as Terror

The third and most important driver of the present re-medicalization of security is the possibility of such bioweapons also proliferating

to non-state actors, especially terrorist groups. Not only are terrorist groups more difficult to deter because of their smaller size and
increased mobility (compared to nation states), but the tactic of ter-
rorizing the population also means that such an attack may not be
contained to times of war. Conceivably, it could occur at any time,
thus requiring states to prepare continuously for an 'invisible' threat
that could manifest itself at any time. Here the sense of insecurity is
exacerbated not necessarily by the creation of more 'sophisticated' or
dangerous diseases, but by the inability to contain that source of insecurity temporally. What is more, the deliberate use of such weapons
by terrorist groups also raises the very real possibility that terrorists
might even have sufficient time to leave the scene of the release before
it is detected. Metaphorically speaking, such groups could thus
'reload', i.e. retreat, produce more such agents and carry out repeated
attacks in a way that would inflict even more damage and would
complicate a response.

If definitions of terrorism are notoriously difficult to agree, the
same is true regarding the more specific activity of bioterrorism. In
the United States, the Federal Bureau of Investigation (FBI) defines it
as the 'unlawful use of viruses, bacteria, fungi, toxins or other pathogenic material against a government, the civilian population, livestock, crops or any segment thereof, in furtherance of political, social
and/or economic objectives' (Al-Rodhan et al. 2008: 41). Interpol
(2007: 7) has proposed a similar definition: 'the intentional release
of biological agents or toxins for the purpose of harming or killing
humans, animals or plants with the intent to intimidate or coerce a
government or civilian population to further political or social objectives'. These definitions hinge on what uses of such materials are
deemed 'lawful', and what political, social and economic objectives
are in turn deemed to be illegitimate.

Of course such 'academic' issues are unlikely to preoccupy terrorist groups. From their perspective, many characteristics of a
biological agent may, in fact, be deemed tactically beneficial. Several
biological agents are naturally occurring and can, in principle, be
readily acquired. Furthermore, terrorist groups would only require
small quantities to have substantial effects on human populations.
Biological agents are also imperceptible to the human eye. Once

released in public, they would initially evade the human senses of smell or taste. Although that makes biological weapons visually less striking than a conventional explosive device in terms of staging a dramatic attack, it also gives a potential terrorist crucial time to escape the site of the release undetected. Finally, the very same quality that has long made biological weapons of dubious military usefulness – their inability to differentiate between civilians and combatants – are unlikely to deter would-be terrorists.

However, those perceived 'advantages' of biological weapons also need to be balanced with some of the tactical disadvantages associated with their use. Several such drawbacks exist. First, there is the risk that during the release the terrorist might become infected with the agent as well, although in the era of suicide bombings that is unlikely to be a huge deterrent. Second, there is still a considerable degree of technical difficulty involved in successfully cultivating, stabilizing and weaponizing biological agents. Finally, the fact that biological weapons attacks are heavily susceptible to unpredictable weather conditions, such as wind and levels of cloud cover, means that any such plot could easily fail (Ryan and Glarum 2008: 35). For these reasons, expert opinion still remains divided as to how probable such an attack is today. Yet it is a scenario that even ardent sceptics cannot rule out altogether.

Two events in the past decade have certainly increased the concern about such a scenario becoming reality. First, the attacks of 11 September 2001 on New York City and Washington, DC, demonstrated that terrorists – if capable – might not shy away from orchestrating mass-casualty attacks on civilian populations. Second, and at a time when the United States was still reeling from the attacks on the World Trade Center and the Pentagon, two batches of anthrax letters were then also posted in the United States from mail-boxes in Princeton, New Jersey. The first batch, thought to have consisted of approximately five letters, was sent to media offices on around 18 September 2001. These included American Media Incorporated, a number of broadcasters and editors based in New York City, and a tabloid publisher in Boca Raton, Florida. These initial letters were mostly dismissed as hate mail and/or were left unopened at the time.

A second batch of letters was mailed on 8 October 2001, two of which went to Democrat senators in Washington, DC. The first was opened on the morning of 15 October in the Hart office building of the Senate majority leader, Tom Daschle. It would take a week before it was established that these infections had actually come from letters, by which time many more persons had become exposed to the anthrax. It was also discovered later that the letters contained the Ames strain of anthrax, which had been used for several years in the US biological weapons programme. This would point to a domestic rather than foreign source for the release (Guillemin 2005: 173–6).

Although the attacks of 11 September 2001 and the anthrax letters were crucial catalysts in terms of placing the threat of bioterror at the heart of the international security agenda, anxieties about such biological attacks also predate the events of 2001 by at least half a decade. In 1995 the Aum Shinrikyo cult in Japan had already received widespread media attention when it released sarin nerve gas into the Tokyo subway system. The attack was carried out with a chemical rather than a biological substance. Nor was it a very sophisticated operation, effectively relying on the use of an umbrella to poke holes into plastic bags. The release killed 12 people nonetheless, and hospitalized around 1,000, with thousands more needing to seek medical care. In fact, the 1995 operation was not the first time the cult had struck. A similar attack had occurred in the town of Matsumoto eight months earlier killing 7 people (Guillemin 2005: 158).

The Aum Shinrikyo cult was first established in 1984 by Shoko Asahara as a countermovement to the perceived decadence of modern societies. The cult ultimately hoped to create a new type of society, and eventually grew in size to between 10,000 and 60,000 members (Rosenau 2001: 291). The cult was operating internationally, with various contacts in post-Soviet Russia, Australia, Germany, Taiwan and the former Yugoslavia. It even had an office in New York City. It was also well financed, with funding in the range of an estimated US$20 million (Guillemin 2005: 159). The cult intended to use biological weapons such as anthrax, Q fever, Ebola and botulinum toxin on ten separate occasions (Ryan and Glarum 2008: 16). After being arrested, the head of their germ development, Seiichi Endo, later revealed that, from 1990 to 1993, the cult had released aerosolized anthrax and botulinum toxin on several occasions at Japan's legislature (the Diet) and the Imperial Palace, as well as several other places in Tokyo and even at the US military base of Yokusaka (Zubay et al. 2005: 134–5). Fortunately for those involved, nobody became infected, most probably because the strain used was similar to that used in animal vaccination, which is of little danger to humans and has low virulence (Zubay et al. 2005: 135).

The precedents set by Aum Shinrikyo prompted a growing climate of fear in which it was felt that more concerted efforts needed to be undertaken to protect populations in the event of such an attack. Long before the tumultuous events of the autumn of 2001, these incidents showed that a bioterrorist attack is more than just a hypothetical possibility – even if the attempt to place a more precise probability on such an attack occurring is fraught with difficulties. In practice, developing and procuring biological weapons remains a complicated process, which requires selection of the desired biological agent, obtaining this agent, then working upon it in such a manner that it can become weaponized, before also creating a method for disseminating it (Fidler and Gostin 2008: 35). A report issued by the US General Accounting Office thus found that:

> In most cases terrorists would have to overcome significant technical and operational challenges to successfully make and release chemical or biological agents of sufficient quality and quantity to kill or injure large numbers of people without substantial assistance from a state sponsor... [S]pecialized knowledge is required in the manufacturing process and in improvising an effective delivery device for most chemical and nearly all biological agents that could be used in terrorist attacks. Moreover, some of the required components of chemical agents and highly infective strains of biological agents are difficult to obtain. (GAO 1999: 1–2)

That more sceptical assessment predated the attacks of 11 September 2001 and the anthrax letters of October 2001.

Others have also taken heart from the fact that the Aum Shinrikyo group ultimately failed to procure biological weapons – despite its clear intentions of doing so. In many ways the group fulfilled most of the ideal conditions that ought to have led to success in terms of producing such weapons, including having a network of front companies, possessing key staff, funding, sufficient time and so forth. Although it is difficult to come to firm conclusions given the classified nature of much of the information surrounding the cult's activities, Rosenau argues that the group encountered at least three significant difficulties: (1) acquiring sufficiently lethal strands of key biological agents such as anthrax bacilli; (2) challenges in terms of finding efficient ways of delivering and dispersing the agent; and (3) internal organizational difficulties (Rosenau 2001: 293). Even a well-funded non-state group like Aum Shinrikyo thus encountered considerable obstacles in developing viable biological weapons.

Diverging assessments of the likelihood of a biological attack by terrorists also extend all the way to the highest levels of government. Even in the United States some senior policy-makers have expressed unease with the strong emphasis placed on bioterrorism. Charles Allen, the Chief Intelligence Officer of the Department of Homeland Security (DHS), testified before Congress that 'in general, terrorist capabilities in the area of bioterrorism are crude and relatively unsophisticated, and we do not see any indication of a rapid evolution of capability' (cited in Klotz 2008: 109). Although not denying the threat, Admiral William J. Crowe, Jr, who is a former Chairman of the Joint Chiefs of Staff, has also insisted that 'these terrorists cannot destroy us . . . We are a country of nearly three hundred million people with infrastructure spread across a nation that has the fourth-largest landmass in the world. This is not thermonuclear war we are facing . . . The real danger lies not with what the terrorists can do to us but what we can do to ourselves when we are spooked' (cited in Klotz 2008: 109).

The Commission on the Prevention of WMD Proliferation and Terrorism, by contrast, came to a very different view in its more recent report of December 2008. The commission concluded that 'it it is more likely than not that a weapon of mass destruction will be used in a terrorist attack somewhere in the world by the end of 2013'. Crucially, it also found that 'terrorists are more likely to be able to obtain and use a biological weapon than a nuclear weapon' (Commission on the Prevention of WMD Proliferation and Terrorism 2008: xv). Although the commission accepted the advice of the intelligence community that the capabilities of non-state actors to produce biological weapons are rudimentary, the commission did note that such organizations had the intent of upgrading those capabilities (Commission on the Prevention of WMD Proliferation and Terrorism 2008: 11). Time will eventually tell who is right, but already there is sufficient concern about the possibility of biological attacks for this to emerge as another area of contemporary world politics where insecurity is being redefined, in part, as being a medical problem caused by the onset and spread of disease.

The administration of George W. Bush, for one, was not going to be seen sitting idly by. After turning its attention away from the negotiations on the Biological Weapons Convention, it began to focus much more closely on a number of smaller states and non-state groups (including terrorists) who might be interested in acquiring, developing and using biological weapons against the United States and its allies. One way the Bush administration sought to meet that challenge was by turning to the United Nations Security Council, which adopted Resolution 1540 on 24 April 2004 under Chapter VII of the United Nations Charter. The resolution, pushed for very strongly by the United States, dealt with weapons of mass destruction in general, thus also covering biological weapons.

The overall intent of Resolution 1540 was to strengthen the international regime on the proliferation of weapons of mass destruction. At the time, that regime essentially consisted of three treaties: the Treaty on the Non-Proliferation of Nuclear Weapons (1968); the Convention on the Prohibition of the Development, Production and Stockpiling of Bacteriological (Biological) and Toxin Weapons and on Their Destruction (1972); and the Convention on the Prohibition of Development, Production, Stockpiling and Use of Chemical Weapons and on Their Destruction (1993). The United States had identified several problems with that regime (Parker and Pate 2005: 167). Membership of these treaties was not universal. Of the world's 194 countries, 189 were party to the nuclear weapons regime, 167 to the chemical weapons regime, and 153 states to the biological weapons regime. Therefore the regime possessed a 'horizontal' gap in terms of membership in that not all states had signed up. Moreover, those treaties only covered states and did not apply to non-state actors such as terrorist groups – giving rise to a 'vertical' gap as well.

In terms of biological weapons in particular, there was at the time no international organization responsible for enforcing or monitoring the controls on biological weapons (Parker and Pate 2005: 167).

Resolution 1540 hoped to close some of these gaps by legally requiring states to 'refrain from providing any form of support to non-State actors that attempt to develop, acquire, manufacture, possess, transport, transfer or use nuclear, chemical or biological weapons and their means of delivery'. The resolution also called for states to introduce laws and effective control measures prohibiting non-state actors from working with such materials either directly or indirectly by transporting them or financing such activities. Such control measures include actual physical controls on the availability of such materials, as well as border control measures, law enforcement measures and so forth.

These provisions would close the horizontal gap in that (unlike treaties) Security Council resolutions are legally binding on all states, and individual states cannot opt out or refuse to ratify them. At least in principle, the resolution thus has universal coverage. The resolution also addressed the vertical gap by explicitly dealing with the issue of non-state actors (Parker and Pate 2005: 167). It was thus an important legal mechanism for addressing the threat of biological weapons. Yet, mindful of the weaknesses exposed in earlier attempts to curb biological weapons through international law, the US administration also decided not to put all of its eggs in one basket. The task of enhancing the security of populations against biological attacks would also have to take other forms in case these new legal instruments proved insufficient in halting the threat of biological attacks.

We Need a Medic: Medical Professionals in Defence of the Nation

Responding to the threat of bioterrorism also required opening up a domestic, medical front in the War on Terror. That medical front is made up, on the one hand, of terrorists potentially weaponizing a range of infectious diseases. On the other hand, it consists of sustained efforts by a range of biomedical researchers and institutions to develop rapidly new medical countermeasures to protect their populations against such possible attacks. The latter task inevitably also requires the greater involvement of a swath of different medical professionals. Biomedical experts and researchers, for instance, are needed for drawing up a list of the most likely and dangerous pathogens that could be used for the purposes of a terrorist attack, and for developing new medical countermeasures against such biological agents. Health care providers, moreover, will need to become involved, in terms of mapping out how doctors and hospitals will respond in the event of an attack, and how to liaise with the relevant government authorities. Public health experts, in turn, will also be required for designing and running surveillance systems that would detect the release of those agents within the proximity of human populations. Biosecurity concerns about biological weapons too, therefore, encourage a further augmentation in the societal jurisdiction of a broad array of medical professionals by involving them much more closely in biodefence and biosecurity policy.

In the United States, as elsewhere, the first step in creating a security policy to meet those threats has been to identify the likely pathogens that may be used in such an attack. With this objective, the United States government convened an expert panel of the Working Group on Civilian Biodefense in 1999. The panel's task was to identify a range of factors that could be used in assessing the risk of particular pathogens. The most relevant factors identified by the group included the potential to cause high morbidity and mortality through human-to-human transmission, the possibility of being produced in stable aerosol form and in large quantities, and little or no vaccine immunity in the population, perhaps with prior use in biological weapons programmes (UPMC 2009).

Later the American government also turned to other professionals at the Centers for Disease Control and Prevention (CDC) and instructed them too to draw up another list of such 'unlawful' agents that could be used for mounting a terrorist attack. The CDC, which is the agency tasked with protecting American citizens from the spread of infectious disease and run by the US Department of Health and Human Services (HHS), developed a simple rating system that takes into account several factors, including the biological characteristics of the agents, as well as the likelihood of them being successfully weaponized for bioterrorist purposes.

At the top of their list are what they have called 'Category A' agents. These are the agents seen to pose the greatest threat to the US population. They are highly infectious, can be easily disseminated, induce high mortality rates and are difficult to treat. An attack using those agents would have highly disruptive effects upon a civilian population. They include anthrax, botulism, plague, smallpox, tularaemia, viral hemorrhagic fevers (e.g. Ebola, Marburg) and arena viruses (e.g. Lassa, Machupo). In comparison, Category B agents have lower mortality rates. They tend to induce only 'moderate' morbidity and can be treated more readily. The list of such agents is more extensive and includes brucellosis, various food safety threats (such as Salmonella species and Escherichia coli), glanders, Q fever, ricin, typhus fever, viral encephalitis and so forth. The final Category C covers those emerging pathogens with potential for weaponization, such as Nipah virus and hantavirus.

Of course, pursing a strategy of asking experts to identify particular pathogens has one rather significant drawback. That approach is not exhaustive and is not helpful in the case of a terrorist attack with a newly created biological weapon. For this reason, the Secretary of the DHS, in consultation with the Secretary of the HHS, has periodically to review that list. If these assessments determine that an agent poses a serious threat to the United States, the DHS then issues a Material Threat Determination (MTD), which triggers a process to begin acquiring medical countermeasures (UPMC 2009). This elaborate method of identifying the pathogens that could be plausibly weaponized for terrorist groups is one way in which bioterrorist concerns are encouraging the closer involvement of medical researchers and professionals in security policy.

Professionals working at public health organizations have also become more intimately involved in the task of securing populations against such threats by helping in the design and running of new surveillance systems for detecting the release of such pathogens within civilian populations. Detecting a biological weapons attack is far from straightforward, given that biological weapons evade the human senses of taste, smell and sight. An outbreak would not necessarily be immediately evident until symptoms began to emerge. In the United States, Project BioWatch was thus launched in 2003 with a view to developing a national early warning system aimed primarily at detecting a biological attack using an aerosolized agent.

The BioWatch system was intended to fulfil three functions crucial for containing any release of a biological agent. First, it was supposed to provide early warning of the release of such an agent, thus facilitating a rapid containment response before the agent had spread too widely. Second, the system was intended to help gather forensic evidence for the purposes of establishing who was responsible for the release. The samples collected by the filters used in the BioWatch system could subsequently be used in the forensic search for the likely origin of the agent, perhaps giving clues to the likely perpetrators of the release. Finally, the network of multiple sensors spread across a city was also supposed to help to determine the geographic extent of the release. In the event of an attack taking place, this would help authorities responding to the release to determine the size and location of the population affected by it.

In practice, this mechanism for improving the security of the United States against the effects of a bioterrorist attack could not function without the input of a range of scientists and qualified biomedical professionals. For instance, the project involved erecting an elaborate network of environmental sensors (or stations) in at least thirty-one cities, which continuously analyse particles in the air through a filter system. The exact number of cities has not been disclosed, nor the particular cities that make up the network – although filters are reportedly located in Philadelphia, New York City, Washington DC, San Diego, Boston, Chicago, San Francisco, St. Louis, Houston and Los Angeles (Shea and Lister 2003). These filters are collected daily and analysed at the CDC for traces of anthrax, brucellosis, glanders, meliodosis, plague, smallpox, and tularaemia. The entire process has a turnaround time of at least thirty-six hours (Ryan and Glarum 2008: 262).

Running and maintaining this network of filters is a complicated operation, requiring the collaboration of several government agencies, including public health institutions. Although the Science and Technology Directorate at the DHS has overall oversight of the programme, the Environmental Protection Agency is responsible for maintaining the actual sensor units and collecting the filters, whilst the CDC has responsibility for coordinating the laboratory analysis, which is carried out in state and local public health laboratories. Running the network properly is thus an inter-agency operation requiring the contribution of public health experts as well.

Its sound intentions notwithstanding, the implementation of Project BioWatch has proved controversial in practice. Beyond the broader question of how likely a large-scale bioterrorist attack actually is, a range of technical issues have cropped up around whether this technology would detect underground or indoor releases, as well as a range of other technical issues regarding the appropriate location of the sensors (Shea and Lister 2003). BioWatch also cannot detect the outbreak of a biological weapons attack immediately, because the filters are retrieved every 24 hrs and then still require time to be examined. Additional problems with the programme include both its cost and the lack of follow-through (Ryan and Glarum 2008: 264).

In January 2007 the Office of the Inspector General at the DHS issued a report highlighting several shortcomings in the management of the project. These shortcomings involved the identification of several non-compliance issues relating to the field collection of samples, the transport of filters, and laboratory operations that could allow samples to become cross-contaminated (DHS 2007). This has led to changes to BioWatch being proposed, including transferring overall responsibility for the programme to a new Office of Health Affairs at the DHS. There are now also plans to use new types of sensor technologies that would reduce the detection time to four to six hours.

Project BioWatch has been complemented by the launch of Project BioSense – a web-based software program that collects public health data from across the United States on a daily basis and that similarly requires the input of medical professionals. It too is run by the CDC. The purpose of the BioSense program is to detect statistical anomalies that could indicate the occurrence of a biological attack but that may otherwise go unnoticed. Here it is not the pathogen itself that would be directly picked up by a sensor, but the clusters of unusual but similar symptoms that the pathogens would induce amongst human beings who then report to their local doctors or hospitals. Yet probing questions have been raised about the value of BioSense as well, especially in terms of the utility of the data it collects and the limited scope of its coverage (thirty cities in less than twenty states) (Ryan and Glarum 2008: 265). It too was subject to a review by the Government Accountability Office (GAO 2008), which found that the cost-benefit considerations in relation to BioSense remain unclear, and that stakeholders from local through to federal levels expressed mixed views about the utility of the data gathered.

Public health experts have, finally, also been called upon to help to secure the nation by mapping out the protocols for how health care providers are to respond to a biological weapons attack. Given that a biological weapon works through the deliberate release of a disease, health care providers become one of the first lines of defence against such an attack. That process has not only required the development of bioterrorism response plans for various domestic health agencies and providers within the United States. It has also entailed such professionals linking up internationally with their counterparts in other countries. The World Health Organization, for example, has led several international activities in response for calls for it too to be involved in the event of biological attack. In 2006 the United Nations adopted its Global Counter-Terrorism Strategy, which called upon the World Health Organization to provide technical assistance to states in terms of improving their health care systems to prepare for potential bioterrorism attacks (Al-Rodhan et al. 2008: 94). In fact the World Health Organization has been developing a strategy to deal with the health impacts of such biological incidents since 2002, and now runs technical and training programmes on national preparedness. It has also established a Chemical and Biological Weapons Scientific Advisory Group, which provides expert advice to the Secretariat on health-related issues associated with chemical and biological weapons (Al-Rodhan et al. 2008: 95–6).

Opening up the medical front in the War on Terror has therefore done more than just redefine insecurity as something caused by the onset and spread of disease. It has also augmented the societal influence of a broad range of medical professionals – ranging from biomedical researchers working away in laboratories all the way through to health care providers and prominent national and intergovernmental health institutions such as the World Health Organization. It has done so by inviting those different medical experts and officials to play an increased role in the formulation and execution of various security policies relating to biodefence and bioterrorism. As we have seen, such augmentations in the societal jurisdiction of medical professionals are also another crucial hallmark of medicalization.

BioShield: Developing New Medical 'Countermeasures'

It is a truism that the so-called 'War on Terror' has taken many forms, including recourse to military force – as attested to by the continuing campaigns in Afghanistan and Iraq. Closer to home, however, the War on Terror is being fought not through guns and bombs, but also through the development of new vaccines and pharmacological treatments to counter the effects of a biological attack. As early as 1999 the United States Congress instructed the HHS and the CDC to create a national stockpile system capable of storing medicines and medical equipment that could be quickly made available in response to a bioterrorist attack (Al-Rodhan et al. 2008: 102).

Three years later the US government passed the Public Health Security and Bioterrorism Preparedness and Response Act of 2002. That Act too focused on technological measures to improve health security in the United States. It provided for stockpiling emergency supplies of medicines and vaccines. It also put the Secretary of Health in charge of accelerating research into countermeasures against pathogens that could be used as biological weapons (Guillemin 2005: 183). Medical countermeasures, ranging from antibiotics and vaccines through to anti-toxins and anti-virals, have thus become a key pillar of biosecurity policy in the United States.

In December of that same year President George W. Bush took a much more proactive and pre-emptive stance when he announced a controversial national smallpox vaccination programme that would target 500,000 key civilian, as well as 500,000 military, personnel. Take-up of the vaccinations went well in the military populations, but far less well in the civilian groups (Fidler and Gostin 2008: 100–1). Even when a smaller vaccination programme was implemented, it resulted in 145 adverse events and 3 deaths. Several servicemen refused a similar attempt to vaccinate all US service members against anthrax. Those who refused were reportedly demoted, dismissed or court-martialed. That, in turn, led to a class-action lawsuit which placed an injunction on the vaccination procedure and eventually forced the policy toward voluntary vaccination (GHW 2008: 117). The vaccination episode laid bare some of the complex medical, logistical and legal difficulties involved in seeking to combat the threat of bioterrorism through the use of such medical products. Yet it also marked the clearest example yet of how the War on Terror would be fought through medical interventions as well.

It was surpassed, in that respect, only by Project BioShield, proposed by President George W. Bush in his 2003 State of the Union address. BioShield is the most prominent project in the United States focusing on the development of medical countermeasures. The core mission of this programme was to increase the medical defences of the United States through new vaccines and treatments for a range of possible pathogens that could be used to attack the United States. It was signed into law by President Bush on 21 July 2004 as the Project Bioshield Act, and was initially allocated around US$5.6 billion – mostly for the procurement of medical countermeasures over a ten-year period. The majority of that money was directed at the HHS. From there, much of the funding went to the National Institute of Allergy and Infectious Diseases (NIAID) in order for research to be conducted into designing countermeasures for the most likely biological weapons agents, including smallpox, anthrax, tularaemia, plague, botulinum toxin and hemorrhagic fever viruses (Guillemin 2005: 183–4).

Project BioShield is run jointly through the DHS and the HHS. It has three core objectives. First, it makes funding available to purchase significant stockpiles of medicines and vaccines that could be used to counter specific agents that may be used in biological attacks. Second, it creates additional funding streams for research into new pharmaceutical products that could be used to respond to any attack with biological agents. Third, Project BioShield has made significant changes to the authorization process for the deployment of new medicines, allowing the Food and Drug Administration to move toward a more rapid dispersal system for new medications.

Overall, the intention of Project BioShield was thus to create powerful incentives and rewards for commercial companies to develop new medicines and vaccines for disease caused by biological agents. This was deemed necessary at the time given that there is no regular commercial market for these products, and artificial incentives thus needed to be created. The project did not, however, amount to a blank cheque for large pharmaceutical companies. Confirmation of final purchase by the government was still dependent on clinical trials showing that the drugs were safe and effective. In practice this meant that companies still carried considerable commercial risks, especially if their products failed such tests.

As with its related projects, BioWatch and BioSense, the implementation of BioShield has run into practical difficulties. First, there have been problems associated with the delivery of some of the medical components, most notably the anthrax vaccine. On 4 November 2004, the HHS had awarded a US$877.5 million contract to VaxGen in order to procure some 75 million doses of a new anthrax vaccine that could be used in the Strategic National Stockpile (SNS). These doses were meant to be procured over a three-year period, with 25 million of them to be available within two years. Yet after two years, on 19 December 2006, VaxGen announced that the contract had been 'terminated for default' by the HHS. That meant the government would now effectively have to start again from scratch (Franco and Mair 2007: 290).

A subsequent report by the Government Accountability Office (GAO 2007) found three contributing factors for this significant failure. First, the contract was given to a small firm which was in the initial stages of developing its product. In light of its small size, the company had not properly assessed the issues surrounding mass manufacturing and stockpiling. Second, the management of VaxGen had taken unacceptable risks in agreeing the contract, given its lack of expertise in mass-producing vaccines and the tight production timeline. That gave rise to serious questions as to whether they should even have been contemplating applying under the BioShield programme. Finally, the report also found that there was uncertainty about the 'acceptance' criteria that would be applied to the vaccine by the government.

Beyond these procurement issues, a second problem with Project BioShield is that many large pharmaceutical companies with the capacity to mass-manufacture such products have tended to shy away from it. The incentives, in other words, have not proved sufficient to lure those companies in. Representatives of those companies argue that a significant incentive problem remains for their organizations, as the government will only purchase products that are proven to be effective after thorough evaluation and that have no significant commercial market. That caveat was introduced in order to prevent large drug companies from getting money for products that were commercially viable, and to prevent them using Bioshield money to develop new drugs, only to then sell them on at great profit to the public at large (Klotz 2008).

Yet precisely because there is no commercial market for these types of treatments, and the US government remains the only realistic purchaser, this makes the development of such products a very 'high-risk' strategy for pharmaceutical companies. If the product is successful, they stand a good chance of reaping financial rewards, but if the products fail the evaluation, they carry the commercial risk for this failure. Such a high-risk strategy is difficult for commercially operating companies to adopt, especially for small to medium-sized bio-tech companies which could potentially go under on the back of such a failure. Moreover, even if a product does pass the initial evaluation and is accepted for procurement by the government, companies have voiced additional concerns about potential legal liabilities in terms of the safety or efficacy of the new products.

Due in part to these difficulties, only six products have so far been developed in response to eleven requests for proposals issued by the HHS for biodefence countermeasures, and none of those were developed by a major pharmaceutical company (Matheny et al. 2007: 228). Acknowledging these concerns, the Bush administration then made an additional US$1 billion available for setting up the Biomedical Advanced Research and Development Authority (BARDA), which helps not only with the cost of creating new manufacturing facilities, but also with reducing the liability of companies if drugs not licensed by the Food and Drug Administration are used in the event of a bio-terrorist attack (Ryan and Glarum 2008: 257). Notwithstanding these difficulties, the United States continues to maintain a stockpile of medical countermeasures against a range of biological agents, includ-ing 182.5 million doses of second-generation smallpox vaccine (Mair 2006: 334).

Beyond these technical and commercial issues, moreover, there is an even bigger question mark that looms over Project BioShield: is the development of medical countermeasures, especially vaccines, really the correct approach to adopt in relation to the threat of bio-terrorism? Based in part on his extensive and first-hand experience with the Soviet biological weapons programme, Ken Alibek argues that, while it would take around three to four years to produce a drug-resistant or more virulent pathogen, it would currently take around ten to fifteen years to develop and get approval for a vaccine (Alibek and Bailey 2004: 132). Even if that process could be shortened significantly through funding and an altered regulatory environment, vaccines may not be a realistic prophylaxis in civilian populations because of the immense expense that would be involved in vaccinat-ing the entire civilian population of a country like the United States – not to mention the possible medical side-effects produced by such mass vaccinations.

Authorities also do not know which agent, or combination of agents, will be used. That means they do not even know, prior to an attack, which vaccinations to carry out. Furthermore, vaccines are not actually available for all types of biological agents that might be released, and it is also possible that a biological agent may be engi-neered to evade current vaccines (Alibek and Bailey 2004: 132). More importantly, administering vaccines also makes little sense after an attack has emerged, given that they need to be taken several days and even weeks before exposure. This also represents one of the key dif-ferences between civilian and military populations, in that (provided there is sufficient lead time) one can usually vaccinate soldiers prior to their deployment (Alibek and Bailey 2004: 133). Arguably, it would therefore be better for civilian funds to be directed toward research into emergency prophylaxes and therapies to be used at the time of, or in the immediate aftermath of, an outbreak. More than five years after it was announced, such larger and quite fundamental questions continue to loom over Project BioShield.

Nonetheless Project BioShield too shows how – on the home front – the War on Terror continues to be waged through recourse to medical treatments and interventions. These medical counter-measure programmes not only have commanded the closer involvement of a range of medical professionals in security policy, but have also made available considerable amounts of funding for bio-medical researchers in this area. For fiscal year 2009 (FY 2009) alone, President George W. Bush proposed approximately $8.01 billion in federal funding for civilian biodefence programmes. At the time, that figure amounted to approximately 0.26 per cent of the total FY 2009 US federal budget of $3.107 trillion (Franco 2008: 131). As was the case with earlier budgets, the majority of that funding will flow toward the HHS, which is set to receive $4.17 billion (52 per cent) of the $8.01 billion total for FY 2009 (Franco 2008: 131).

Some of these HHS funds are subsequently allocated to the CDC and the National Institutes of Health. The National Institutes of Health were the top recipients of funds for FY 2009 with a budget of $1.64 billion, which it, in turn, directs toward the National Institute of Allergy and Infectious Diseases (NIAID) for biodefence research initiatives (Franco 2008: 138). That research revolves around the clinical evaluation of vaccines and other medical treatments for use against pathogens.

The CDC, by contrast, saw an increase of $46 million for various biosurveillance activities (BioSense, quarantine stations at ports and laboratory reporting). The biodefence budget also included a further $18 million for the Strategic National Stockpile, as well as $42 million for food defence initiatives run by the Food and Drug Administration (Franco 2008: 135). Finally, the proposed budget for FY 2009 also includes $111.6 million (a $34.5 million increase) for the Office of Health Affairs at the DHS, which manages Project BioWatch. The purpose of the increase is to fund next-generation detection systems (Franco 2008: 140). Looking at US government funding for civilian biodefence research for the period of FY 2001 – FY 2009, the HHS has thus received $31.7 billion of the roughly $50 billion (Franco

2008: 132). Many different medical professionals and researchers are not only becoming more closely involved in security policy, they are also receiving substantial funding for those activities.

Unsurprisingly, thse levels of funding have proved controversial in many quarters. An open letter published in *Science*, with more than 700 signatories, complained about the effect that the prioritization of biodefence was having on research carried out at the National Institutes of Health. The letter pointed to a 'massive influx of funding, institutions, and investigators into work on prioritized bioweapons agents' and a 1,500 per cent increase in the number of grants awarded by NIAID referencing those agents (from 33 in 1996–2000 to 497 in 2001 – January 2005 (Altman et al. 2005: 1409). The letter went on to criticize how funding was being diverted from research projects of high public health importance to biodefence ones with a low public health importance (Altman et al. 2005: 1409).

The picture may not be quite so clear-cut, however. Gerald Epstein (2007: 354) counters that 'the drafters of this letter approached intellectual dishonesty' because it did not acknowledge that the net increase in the National Institutes of Health budget did not come at the expense of other internal National Institutes of Health funding, and non-biodefence funding actually continued to grow throughout that period. He points out that 'the new NIH funds were security dollars and not science dollars, although science certainly benefited from the decision to allocate them to NIH'. From the point of view of those interested in civilian projects, this money may be considered wasted, but Epstein notes that it did not come at the expense of existing funding. More importantly, it means that substantial amounts of 'security' funds seem to be flowing to medical professionals.

These tensions regarding the levels of biodefence funding for medical institutions and researchers have prompted attempts to carve out a middle ground between these positions. This can be done by arguing that security concerns about bioweapons and public health concerns about the spread of infectious diseases are not mutually exclusive. According to such arguments, anything that benefits the one can also benefit the other. That would effectively render as 'dual use' much of the current funding directed toward bioterrorism.

Surveillance systems designed and deployed for tracking a possible terrorist attack may, for example, also be of use in terms of tracking a newly emerging infectious disease. Fidler and Gostin, who use the notion of 'biosecurity' precisely in order to combine the concerns about bioterrorism with those about naturally emerging infectious diseases, argue:

> Expanding the concept of biosecurity to include infectious disease threats requires substantial improvements in public health infrastructure. Investments in national and international biosecurity make little sense without upgrading public health systems. Investments in laboratories, surveillance, data systems, and public health workforce capabilities frequently aim to create 'dual use' capacities for defense against biological weapons and against disease epidemics. Biosecurity means having both security and public health firmly planted in the realm of the 'high politics' of foreign policy and international relations. (Fidler and Gostin 2008: 10–11)

Other analysts, by contrast, have charged that it is 'an indictment of scientific and political leaders that they only appear willing to develop a sense of common purpose in the aftermath of adversity' (Durodie 2004: 264).

It remains unclear exactly how easily systems and staff training for detecting specific agents of bioterrorism can be redirected toward wider public health tasks. Tangible problems can emerge once this kind of 'dual-use' argument is translated into practice. For instance, Project Bioshield contains a 'no significant commercial market' clause which means that its funding will only cover the development of new medical products that do not have wider commercial applicability. This has encouraged institutions such as the National Institutes of Health to develop a 'one bug / one drug' strategy, whereby researchers try to develop countermeasures for specific pathogens, rather than concentrating on measures with a potentially wider range of applicability. These kinds of measures, although they may provide better security, are deemed by commercial companies to be too risky to pursue because they may end up also having a significant commercial market, and may therefore be declined for procurement by the government. Klotz argues in this regard that 'the one bug / one drug strategy is not really a two-way street. Countermeasures developed to combat endemic infectious disease would have direct benefit to biodefense, but benefits to endemic infectious disease from developments focused on biodefense are less likely' (Klotz 2008).

Another point often ignored by advocates of the 'dual-use' approach to bioterrorism and infectious disease measures is that, by increasing the amount of people and laboratories working with such agents for the purposes of biodefence, the possible theft of biological materials also becomes more likely. Simply put, these efforts are putting ever more people in contact with such materials. According to recent estimates, there are now more than 400 laboratories giving access to such biological agents to around 15,000 individuals – a very high number for the security institutions to run checks and controls on (Pelletier 2008: 114). The chances of biological agents falling into the hands of radical groups has thus increased as a result of these measures, and that needs to be balanced against any 'dual-use' gains that accrued for public health. The anthrax letter sent within the United States in October 2001 may in the end prove to have been such a case in point – although the investigation into those events is still ongoing.

Finally, all of this increased attention on bioweapons also increases the risk of accidents. Accidents involving biological materials have already been chronicled (Fidler and Gostin 2008: 181). Live anthrax was mistakenly sent from a laboratory in Maryland to a hospital in California by a biodefence contractor, Southern Research Institute. At the Public Health Research Institute in New Jersey, mice infected with bubonic plague reportedly went missing. Samples containing a dangerous and humanly transmissible strand of the pandemic influenza virus (H2N2) were accidentally distributed by the College of American Pathologists to 3,747 laboratories in eighteen countries (Fidler and Gostin 2008: 182). There were also laboratory-contracted cases of tularaemia at Boston University. These were not even reported to public health authorities in a timely manner, and yet the university has since been awarded a contract to build a Biosafety Level 4 laboratory (the highest level). Nor were bacterial infections contracted at the Texas A&M University reported until the following year (Fidler and Gostin 2008: 181). Trying to wage the War on Terror through an elaborate medical countermeasures programme is thus also accompanied by the constant risk of accidents occurring. That too must be balanced against any 'dual-use' gains for public health associated with biodefence. However, there can be no doubt that, in trying to neutralize the threat of a biological attack, biosecurity policies in the United States have taken extensive recourse to medical interventions and have made substantial funding available for both developing and stockpiling a range of new medical countermeasures.

Conclusion

The continued wrangling about the validity of dual-use arguments, and about the appropriate level of biodefence resources, shows that the medicalization of security cannot be reduced to the selfish interests of medical professionals alone. Biodefence marks the one domain of health security which has encountered by far the biggest resistance from within the international public health community. Yet that should not detract from the more fundamental point that these biosecurity concerns similarly encourage the medicalization of security. Like national security concerns about pandemic threats, such biosecurity discussions too construe and redefine insecurity as a medical problem caused by the rapid and unexpected onset of a lethal disease within the population.

In fact biosecurity policies further extend the scope of that medical redefinition of insecurity in international relations. They do so by concerning themselves with an additional set of diseases that could be deliberately released for hostile purposes – rather than just focusing on ones that might break out naturally. Apprehension about the threat of bioterrorism also removes any residual temporal constraints surrounding the threat posed by a disease outbreak. With the War on Terror, the threat of biological weapons use is no longer limited to periods of interstate war; it can hypothetically manifest itself at any time. Like pandemic preparedness, biosecurity too thus requires constant vigilance.

Managing that source of insecurity in the twenty-first century is again only feasible with the much more intimate involvement of a wide range of medical experts in the formulation and implementation of security policy. Notwithstanding its controversial nature, the endeavour to achieve greater biosecurity by developing new medical countermeasures has, in the end, found many willing helpers amongst a wide group of medical professionals. Here too the range of activities carried out by the medical professions in society is thus extended into the realm of security policy. Once more, the task of enhancing the security of populations against that threat of biological attack has also taken extensive recourse to the development and stockpiling of medical interventions. Viewed collectively, these factors render the medical front of the War on Terror a second crucial site where the medicalization of security is unfolding in contemporary international relations. It is not the last.

4

A Global Pharmacy for the Poor? Endemics and Other Human Insecurities

Human security activities aimed at improving global health advance the medicalization of security in world politics farther still. In the context of the human security agenda, insecurity similarly becomes understood as a problem or predicament brought about by the onset of disease. Yet the specific diseases generating that human insecurity are different, more numerous and also much more wide-ranging. Because the human security agenda posits the individual human being (rather than the state or the population) as the privileged referent object of security, virtually any lethal disease – whether communicable or not – can become considered as a source of insecurity. That renders the human security framework a much more sweeping attempt to medicalize security in the twenty-first century. Thus the human security list of health-related threats is also much longer than in the previous two cases. It even includes many diseases endemic in developing countries – like HIV/AIDS, tuberculosis and malaria.

Managing the threat posed by these endemics will again require concerted and intensified efforts by a range of medical professionals. In fact, the goal of minimizing these sources of human insecurity has already spawned an extensive and increasingly well-funded international health movement since the turn of the century – a movement which involves a large number of medical researchers and practitioners whose aim it is to procure and roll out a range of medicines and vaccines in the global South. Through a variety of different international actors and initiatives, these efforts push the medicalization of security far beyond the borders of the West, broadening its geographic scope to reach most other parts of the world as well.

The Endemic Killers: HIV/AIDS, Tuberculosis and Malaria

How does insecurity become redefined as a medical problem caused by the onset of disease within the context of human security debates? Here the medical redefinition of insecurity is made possible because the human security framework changes the primary referent object of security. Initially the concept of 'human security' was advanced by the United Nations Development Program (UNDP) after the end of the Cold War. It put forward an alternative 'people-centric' account of security that would privilege the needs and welfare of individuals as they go about their daily lives.

Human security advocates charged that the excessive focus on the military capabilities of states in national security approaches obscured the extent to which people in many parts of the world are threatened every day by a growing range of non-military issues. 'The concept of security', the influential 1994 *Human Development Report* lamented in this regard, 'has for too long been interpreted narrowly: ... It has been related more to nation-states than to people. . . . Forgotten were the legitimate concerns of ordinary people who sought security in their daily lives' (UNDP 1994: 22). In the twenty-first century security thinking should therefore focus much more closely on the needs of ordinary individuals.

Placing the individual at the centre of security thinking considerably widens the concept of security beyond its traditional focus on the deployment of armed force. The aim of the human security framework is thus to achieve a much wider 'safety from constant threats of hunger, disease, crime and repression . . . [and] from sudden and hurtful disruptions in the patterns of our daily lives – whether in our homes, our jobs, in our communities or in our environments' (UNDP 1994: 3). A whole host of wider social ills that threaten the survival and well-being of human beings on a daily basis now become considered legitimate security concerns as well. Much in this vein the 1994 *Human Development Report* identified no less than seven different areas that needed to be addressed in terms of achieving human security: economic security, food security, environmental security, health security, personal security, community security and political security (UNDP 1994: 24–5).

The reference to health security in the report indicates that the threat of disease is one of those crucial, wider concerns that acquire a renewed salience for the human security framework. Yet why exactly should disease be considered a source of insecurity with the human security framework? The precise relationship between health and human security was not actually spelt out in the 1994 report. The latter did not even define the notion of 'health security' in any meaningful detail.

The follow-up report by the Commission on Human Security, entitled *Human Security Now*, published nearly a decade later in 2003, rectified that oversight by devoting an entire chapter to the theme of 'health security' as one of the most important components of human security. Health is essential to human security, it argued, because 'the very heart of security is protecting human lives. Health security is at the vital core of human security – and illness, disability and avoidable death are "critical pervasive threats" to human security' (Commission on Human Security 2003: 96). Human security advocates thus consider diseases to constitute security threats by virtue of the simple and uncontestable fact that they cause premature death.

The deliberate inclusion of health threats in the 'vital core' of human security renders the human security framework another site in contemporary world politics where insecurity is becoming construed, at least in part, as something brought about by the onset of disease. Here too insecurity is no longer seen to be caused principally by the use of armed forces, but also by the spread of disease. Unlike earlier manifestations of the medicalization of security, however, the human security agenda does not restrict its concern to a small number of new and particularly infectious diseases; it attempts to address a whole range of diseases that cause premature death. For that reason the human security framework also remains much more attuned to the burden of diseases in the global South where a range of much less 'sensational' illnesses, such as HIV/AIDS, malaria and tuberculosis, remain endemic in many low-income countries with comparatively weak health infrastructures.

Collectively, these three diseases alone are estimated to account for around 5 million 'premature' deaths annually. In its 2007 update on the AIDS pandemic, the Geneva-based UNAIDS estimated that there had been approximately 2 million deaths due to AIDS-related illnesses in 2007, whilst a further 2.5 million people became newly infected. The World Health Organization estimates that 247 million people were also infected with malaria in 2006, with close to 1 million people dying from malaria that same year – the majority of whom were children under the age of five. Tuberculosis, which is now re-emerging in multi-drug-resistant form, is estimated to be responsible for around a further 2 million deaths annually. Most of these deaths occurred amongst persons aged between fifteen and fifty years.

HIV/AIDS

Obtaining more precise mortality figures for these three diseases is fraught with methodological difficulties, especially in countries with public health systems that do not cover the entire population. In the case of the AIDS pandemic, for example, it is impossible to determine exactly how many people are living with HIV/AIDS in the world, and how many are dying from AIDS-related illnesses. Generating such data would not only be impossible in light of considerable financial and logistical constraints, but would also necessitate testing virtually every member of the human population for HIV – raising difficult ethical questions around compulsory and routine testing. That is why the figures provided by UNAIDS are estimates, rather than precise figures (see table 4.1).

What is more, UNAIDS has a very strong advocacy mission and some epidemiologists have openly quested how accurate the figures presented by them are (Chin 2007: 170). Others have also drawn attention to the complex political and bureaucratic difficulties associated with generating such figures (Pisani 2008: 14–42). It is worth noting that UNAIDS has itself recently revised its estimates downwards for many countries, in light of new studies that have been conducted and new data that have been emerging.

Nevertheless in sub-Saharan Africa AIDS appears to have already established itself as the leading cause of adult deaths. According to the World Health Organization's *World Health Report 2004*, AIDS-related illnesses have become the world's leading cause of death

Table 4.1		
Region	Adults and children living with HIV/AIDS	Adult and child deaths due to AIDS
Sub-Saharan Africa	22 million	1.5 million
Middle East and North Africa	380,000	27,000
South and South-East Asia	4.2 million	340,000
East Asia	740,000	40,000
Oceania	74,000	1,000
Latin America	1.7 million	63,000
Caribbean	230,000	14,000
Eastern Europe and Central Asia	1.5 million	58,000
Western and Central Europe	730,000	8,000
North America	1.2 million	23,000
Total	33 million [30 mil. – 36 mil.]	2 million [1.8 mil. – 2.3 mil.]

Source: Figures from UNAIDS 2008: 214–33

and loss of life-years among 15–59-year-olds (WHO 2004a: 155). In terms of mortality, HIV/AIDS was also estimated to be the fourth-largest cause of death in the world in 2002 (after ischaemic heart disease, cerebrovascular disease, and lower respiratory infections), and, depending on how successful ongoing prevention and treatment programmes are, is projected to become the third-largest cause by 2030. In terms of disability-adjusted life-years – a measure which not only takes into account direct mortality but also accounts for when this mortality occurs in the lifespan of an individual – HIV/AIDS was estimated to be the third-largest cause of death in 2002 (after perinatal conditions and lower respiratory infections), and is expected to be the leading cause by 2030 (Mathers and Loncar 2006). Given that there is still no cure for AIDS, and that, as of 2007, only around 30 per cent of those estimated to be in clinical need of anti-retrovirals (ARVs) have access to them, HIV/AIDS represents a serious human security threat for people living with the disease (WHO 2007d: 5).

Even when people live for several years with HIV before succumbing to AIDS-related illnesses, they may not survive the stigma and violence inflicted upon them by their fellow human beings. In the worst-case scenario, that stigma can generate further threats to their survival. One particularly tragic episode in that respect, and one that caught the world's media attention, occurred in December of 1998. Gugu Dlamini died at the age of thirty-six as the result of a beating inflicted by her neighbours in the outskirts of Durban, South Africa, after she revealed her HIV-positive status – on World AIDS Day. Human Rights Watch (2003) has documented how domestic violence frequently erupts in families following HIV infection; in some cases, wives are simply strangled to death after revealing their status. In such tragic cases, HIV/AIDS infection can lead to premature loss of life even before the disease has run its full course.

Violent attacks continue to occur in many countries, especially where there is still a strong stigma attached to the illness. In 2007 a Tanzanian woman, Tumaini Mbogela, was similarly beaten by her husband after returning home from a voluntary counselling centre in Makete, where she had taken the HIV test advocated by the Tanzanian government in a nationwide drive to increase testing (BBC 2007). Such attacks effectively render an HIV infection a double source of human insecurity: both because of its clinical manifestations and because of the social stigma attached to it.

Tuberculosis

Tuberculosis is another cause of significant premature mortality that human security advocates are trying to address in the developing world. The symptoms of tuberculosis, which primarily affects a person's lungs and respiratory system, include a persistent cough, weight-loss, fatigue, shortness of breath and night sweats. The bacilli that cause the disease are contagious and are spread when an affected person sneezes, talks or spits, thereby enabling the germs to spread through the air. Once the bacilli enter the human body, however, they can lie dormant for many years. This means that not all of those who have been infected with tuberculosis bacilli are clinically ill. Indeed it is estimated that around a third of the world's population is actually infected with dormant tuberculosis germs.

In response to the rise of tuberculosis cases following years of neglect by public health institutions in the 1970s and 1980s, and the emergence of multi-drug-resistant tuberculosis, the World Health Organization declared a 'Global Tuberculosis Emergency' as early as 1993 (Koch 2008). In descending order, the ten countries with the highest estimated numbers of persons with clinically manifesting tuberculosis in 2008 (not adjusting for the overall size of the population) are India, China, Indonesia, South Africa, Nigeria, Bangladesh, Ethiopia, Pakistan, the Philippines and the Democratic Republic of Congo (WHO 2008a: 19). According to the latest available figures supplied by the World Health Organization (WHO 2008a: 3), there were some 9.2 million new cases of tuberculosis in 2006 and 14.4 million prevalent cases, including half a million cases of multi-drug-resistant tuberculosis (MDR-TB). That same year, tuberculosis killed an estimated 1.7 million people, of whom 200,000 were people also living with HIV/AIDS at the time.

Medical treatment for tuberculosis was introduced in the 1950s through multi-drug treatments. Prior to that, tuberculosis was still a leading cause of death around the world. Today such treatment is usually undertaken through the prescription of medicines (like isoniazid, rifampicin, pyrazinamide, streptomycin and ethambutol). The use of these medicines presents a range of practical problems, however, especially in low-income countries with patchy health care systems. In order to be effective, the medicines must be taken for six to eight months without interruption – even though people may begin to feel better much earlier.

If this strict medical regime is not adhered to, the bacteria will not be completely eradicated from the body and drug-resistant versions may begin to emerge. Partly due to the weaknesses in supervising the administration of these medicines, tuberculosis has already made a strong comeback in recent decades. This includes the rise of MDR-TB, i.e. tuberculosis that has become immune to the two strongest anti-TB medicines: isoniazid and rifampicin. MDR-TB is more difficult to treat because it takes longer to cure. It is also more expensive to treat, and the medicines for it tend to have more serious side-effects.

Fortunately, second-line treatments for MDR-TB have since been developed (such as Capreomycin, Kanamycin and Amikacin). Yet frequently these medications too have not been administered in accordance with the recommended guidelines, giving rise to yet a third and even more serious form of tuberculosis: extremely drug-resistant tuberculosis (XDR-TB). XDR-TB is a form of MDR-TB that is also resistant to three or more of the six classes of 'second-line' treatments that have been developed for MDR-TB. In response to the continuing problem of rising drug resistance, the World Health Organization pushed for and supported the use of Directly Observed Therapy – Short Course (DOTS) in the 1990s. The DOTS treatment method essentially requires medical staff to oversee the administration of the drugs and ensures that patients have a sufficient supply of medicines, so as to prevent them from developing resistance (Crawford 2007: 201). Nevertheless, the continuing levels of mortality caused by tuberculosis, in conjunction with the growing problem of drug resistance, mean that tuberculosis too is considered a direct threat to human security for many people living in low-income countries.

Malaria

The same is true of malaria, which has similarly become a disease of considerable concern to human security advocates. In contrast to HIV/AIDS and tuberculosis, malaria is not spread directly between persons and therefore not communicable in the strict sense of the term. Yet it too remains endemic in many low-income countries, where it continues to cause significant mortality. Historically, malaria was thought to be transmitted through foul-smelling marshes, hence the name 'mal-aria' (bad air). The germ theory of disease would lay the groundwork for the subsequent discovery that malaria is in fact caused by Plasmodium parasites spread by the female of the Anopheles genus of mosquitoes. Female mosquitoes of that genus suck human blood in order to fuel the production of their eggs, and in that process can transmit the malaria parasite (Crawford 2007: 40).

Once it enters the human bloodstream, the parasite feeds on haemoglobin – a protein that carries oxygen through the human body. The parasites also rapidly multiply in the liver and in the red blood cells, eventually causing the red blood cells to rupture. Toxins are then released into the body producing the fever characteristic of malaria. That process also enables the parasites to infect yet further new red blood cells.

The most common clinical symptoms of malaria include the onset of fever, headaches, chills and vomiting, usually around ten to fifteen days after a person becomes infected. In 'benign' forms of malaria, these symptoms usually disappear within a couple of days of treatment. In cases of 'malignant' malaria, however, further symptoms can emerge, including breathing problems, fits, liver failure and shock. Malaria can also affect the brain and central nervous system, at which point it is usually fatal. Therefore, it is important to bear in mind that not all malaria is the same. In fact there are four different types of malaria that occur in human beings: Plasmodium falciparum (malignant), Plasmodium vivax (benign), Plasmodium malariae (benign) and Plasmodium ovale (benign). The most commonly occurring forms amongst these are Plasmodium falciparum and Plasmodium vivax. The former also remains the most deadly form of malaria (WHO 2007b).

The majority of deaths attributable to malaria occur in children under the age of five. They are particularly susceptible to malaria because immunity only builds up gradually, and usually does not function properly until the age of four to five years (Crawford 2007: 36). In terms of their geographical distribution, most malaria cases and deaths today occur in sub-Saharan Africa. The disease also affects many other regions of the world – including Asia, Latin America, the Middle East and even parts of Europe. The key factors determining a region's susceptibility to malaria include patterns of rainfall, the proximity of human populations to mosquito breeding grounds, and the particular species of mosquitoes prevalent (as malaria is only spread by females of certain species of mosquitoes of the Anopheles genus) (WHO 2007b). Thus malaria is not usually transmitted at temperatures outside of the range of 16 to 30 degrees Celsius. Furthermore, the mosquitoes that spread the malaria parasites also need reservoirs of water at the larval stage (Crawford 2007: 40).

There are a number of measures that can be taken to prevent the spread of malaria amongst human populations, including the use of insecticides against mosquitoes, or the use of insecticidal nets that reduce the number of mosquito bites (because most species of mosquitoes carrying malaria bite at night). Medical treatments for malaria are also available, but mostly just shorten the duration of the illness. They also moderate symptoms and reduce possible medical complications. As in the case of tuberculosis, the emergence of strains of malaria resistant to anti-malarial drugs is also becoming a growing concern. In many parts of the world the parasite has already become resistant to traditional treatments such as chloroquine, making it almost inevitable that malaria will – along with AIDS and tuberculosis – continue to claim many lives in future. That continuing death toll marks the first reason why endemic diseases like malaria, tuberculosis and AIDS are construed as sources of insecurity within the human security framework. Yet that is not the only reason.

Endemic Disease and Other Human Insecurities

Human security advocates are also mindful of the fact that endemic diseases have a plethora of wider social, political and economic ramifications and can thus adversely affect other dimensions of human security as well. Beyond its immediate clinical manifestation, poor health 'is intimately intertwined with poverty, inequality, violence, environmental degradation, and the myriad of other human security challenges that face individuals and communities' (Takemi et al. 2008a: 1). Good health, for instance, allows sick adults to resume work thus also helping to secure the material well-being of their families. Good health also allows children to stay in school and become better educated, and so forth (Commission on Human Security 2003: 96).

From the human security perspective, health is therefore not only essential for human security; it also plays a more instrumental role. The other dimensions of human insecurity are unlikely to be successfully addressed in the long run if the burden of disease is not first minimized in populations. This marks the second reason why endemic diseases are singled out in the human security framework as constituting an important source of insecurity. The wider impact of endemic diseases on health security, economic security and food security in the global South are seen to be especially pertinent in this respect.

Health security

Because of their clinical manifestations, endemic diseases place an additional burden on health care infrastructures that are often already struggling to meet demand. A study of the impact of HIV/AIDS on the health sector in South Africa conducted in 2003 found that the AIDS epidemic was having several adverse impacts. It was causing the loss of health care workers and generating increased levels of absenteeism. Around 16 per cent of the health care workforce in the Free State, Mpumalanga, KwaZulu-Natal and North West provinces were HIV-positive. It also found that the rise in the number of HIV/AIDS patients seeking clinical care had led to an increased workload for health care staff, and that this too was lowering staff morale. With some 46.2 per cent of patients in public hospitals being HIV-positive, the study concluded that, at times, non-AIDS patients have even been 'crowded out' of the system in order to accommodate patients living with HIV/AIDS (Shisana et al. 2003).

A study from Kenya based on a sample of hospitals detected similar trends. It found an increase in AIDS-related admissions and 50 per cent of patients on medical wards to be living with HIV/AIDS. Focus-group discussions conducted in the context of the study also revealed that one of the reasons why the Kenyan health care systems had such high levels of attrition was the fear of becoming infected with HIV (in addition to high workloads, poor remuneration and poor working conditions) (Cheluget et al. 2003). A study of the impact on Swaziland in turn estimated that up to 80 per cent of bed occupancy in the medical and pediatric wards was related to HIV/AIDS (Kober and van Damme 2006).

Although the impact of HIV/AIDS on the health care sector is comparatively much better studied than the impact of tuberculosis and malaria, the World Health Organization also finds that, in countries facing a heavy malaria burden, 'the disease may account for as much as 40 per cent of public health expenditure, 30–50 per cent of inpatient admissions and up to 60 per cent of outpatient visits' (WHO 2007b). These studies highlight the more indirect effects of endemic diseases on human security as the disease burden also ripples through much wider social structures – including fragile health care systems.

Economic security

Defined as 'an assured basic income – usually from productive and remunerative work, or in the last resort from some publicly financed safety net' (UNDP 1994: 25), economic security is another important component of human security affected by endemic diseases. The World Health Organization estimates that, in countries with intensive transmission of malaria, the disease generates a loss of 1.3 per cent of annual economic growth. That is because malaria creates both direct and indirect costs. The former include expenditures made by individuals or other members of their family for preventing the disease (such as the purchase of mosquito nets). They also include those costs that arise when the disease manifests itself (such as doctors' fees, transport to health care facilities, etc.). On a macro-level, the indirect costs include expenditures made by governments at local and national levels to meet such expenses (RBM 2008). The World Health Organization estimates that, in Africa alone, malaria is already shaving US$12 billion off GDP annually – even though it could be treated for a fraction of that cost (WHO 2005). The organization argues further that those costs associated with malaria help to explain, when viewed over longer periods of time, some of the divergence in economic growth between the GDP of countries with and without malaria (WHO 2007b).

Turing to the economic impact of HIV/AIDS, the few household studies that have been carried out to date also suggest the impact to be twofold. Households affected by HIV/AIDS are likely to experience a reduced earning capacity. That is because people are unable to work, or are tied down to caring for the affected family member. A 2002 comparative study of rural and urban households in South Africa, conducted by Booysen and Bachmann (2002) showed that those households affected by HIV/AIDS only have on average 50–60 per cent of the per capita income of non-affected households. In addition, HIV/AIDS generates costs for treatment and – in the case of death – further funeral expenditures, legal costs, medical bills and so forth (Drimie 2003). Other studies carried out for the World Bank similarly suggest increased expenditure by these households on medical care and funerals, as well as a reduction in spending on non-food items (see Barnett and Whiteside 2006: 203–5).

Household studies of the impact of tuberculosis have made similar findings. A study carried out in Thailand, for instance, found that, in households below the poverty line, the average out-of-pocket expenditure for treating the disease amounted to 15 per cent of the annual household income, and incomes were also reduced by 5 per cent due to the illness (Kamolratanakul et al. 1999). A study of urban and rural families affected by tuberculosis in India found that, on average, the disease and its treatment led to the loss of eighty-three days of labour and three months' worth of wages. The study also observed that some children dropped out of school as a result and took up employment in order to support the family (Rajeswari et al. 1999). A paper analysing the economic impact of tuberculosis at the macro-level estimated an annual loss of between US$1.4 and 2.8 billion in economic growth worldwide (Grimard and Harling 2004). Another attempt at a ten-year macro-projection over the period 2006–15 estimated that 'the economic burden of deaths associated with TB (including HIV coinfection) in Sub-Saharan Africa is $519 billion (95% CI, $475–$563) when there is no DOTS coverage' (Laxminarayan et al. 2007: 16). These studies show that endemic diseases can have a further adverse impact on human security in that they undermine the ability of individuals and households to ensure their economic security.

Food security

Links have also been identified between infectious diseases and food security, especially in the case of HIV/AIDS. Food security is defined as requiring 'that all people at all times have both physical and economic access to basic food. This requires not just enough food to go round. It necessitates that people have ready access to food' (UNDP

1994: 27). The crucial point here is that the physical availability of food is only part of the equation when it comes to food insecurity. Even when such food is physically available, people may still experience hunger and starve if they do not have access or entitlement to this food. During many famines the problem is the lack of purchasing power and the poor distribution of food, rather than the absence of food itself. That distinction is crucial because HIV/AIDS can generate food insecurities by skewing the access of certain individuals and groups to food. The negative impact of HIV/AIDS on food security has prompted the famine researcher Alex de Waal to advance a 'new-variant famine' thesis which argues that AIDS weakens the ability of communities to resist famine by killing young adults and women whose labour is most needed and, indeed, especially crucial for planting and harvesting seasonal crops (de Waal 2002).

A study of 1,889 rural households in northern Namibia, southern Zambia and around Lake Victoria in Uganda, carried out by the Food and Agriculture Organization, found that households affected by HIV/AIDS are finding it increasingly difficult to ensure their food security, particularly if they are headed by women (FAO 2003). A study of fifteen villages in three districts of Malawi carried out by Shah et al. (2002) found, further, that many households affected by HIV/AIDS also experienced loss of labour (70 per cent), reported delays in agricultural work (45 per cent), leaving fields unattended (23 per cent) and changing crop composition (26 per cent). However, much of the impact depended upon when the disease arrived (i.e. pre- or post-harvest), the existence of other stress factors and the relative economic status of households. Although HIV/AIDS is therefore unlikely to create a 'supply-shock' in terms of food production in and of itself, it can nevertheless have negative implications for households by interacting in complex ways with their ability to secure access to food (de Waal 2006: 89–92; Gillespie 2006).

From the human security perspective, all these indirect effects of endemic diseases matter as well. They render endemic diseases in low-income countries a two-fold source of human insecurity. They continue to claim directly a large number of lives every year. But they also complicate the wider achievement of human security by having knock-on ramifications for other crucial dimensions of human security – such as health security, economic security and food security. Drawing attention to these manifold human insecurities caused by endemic diseases in the global South considerably expands the scope of the medicalization of security. Now it is not just a number of infectious diseases with pandemic or bioweapons potential that become construed as sources of insecurity, but also a much longer list of diseases already affecting millions of people around the world. Anything that causes the human organism to function abnormally, or to cease functioning altogether, can now be considered a source of insecurity. That immense breadth of the human security approach also renders it one of the most comprehensive attempts yet to medicalize security.

WHO is in Command? The Traditional Landscape of Global Health

Such extensive stretching of the security concept has understandably left many security analysts uncomfortable and wondering just how viable the human security framework really is in the long run. No doubt some will have echoed Roland Paris's searching question about whether the human security agenda amounts to a real paradigm shift in security thinking, or whether it is going to turn out to be 'hot air' (Paris 2001). The events of 11 September 2001 and the subsequent re-orientation of the international security agenda around the threat of international terrorism have certainly done much to steal the thunder from the rising human security agenda. Yet looking back over the past decade, the counterintuitive finding is just how extensively the broader human security concern with global health has already transformed the institutional and funding landscape for international health issues. As in the prior cases of pandemic preparedness and biosecurity, here too the medical redefinition of insecurity has facilitated a gradual augmentation of the influence of many different medical professionals.

First, human security advocates concerned about global health too have called upon those working in the field of security to reach out to the medical professions and to seek greater levels of collaboration.

The 2003 report by the Commission on Human Security had already called for the establishment of a new balance between 'individual, state and global responsibilities for health and human security' (2003: 108), and for cultivating much closer ties between the security and health communities:

> Health and security have long been distinct fields, to the detriment of both. Health has been seen as a 'medical problem', and security, as a matter of military defence. The state was responsible for the health and defence of the public, but it assigned these responsibilities to unconnected ministries. People in all countries want good health and human security. And maintaining artificial distinctions between 'health' and 'security' distorts the priorities of what the public wants in most democratic societies.(Commission on Human Security 2003: 109)

A 2007 report by the World Health Organization echoed that call, urging that 'professionals and policy-makers in the fields of public health, foreign policy and national security should maintain open dialogue on endemic diseases and practices that pose personal health threats, including HIV/AIDS, which also have the potential to threaten national and international health security' (WHO 2007a: 67). Here human security concerns about endemic diseases begin to encourage a further expansion of medical jurisdiction by again calling for a broad range of medical professionals to become more closely involved in security deliberations (and vice versa).

Second, human security discussions have also led to calls for greater international political priority to be given to the task of reducing the global burden of disease. That is to be accomplished by making health issues a much more central component of the 'high' politics of foreign policy. These calls have already been heeded in the policy-making community. In September 2006 the foreign ministers of Norway and France invited their counterparts from Brazil, Indonesia, Senegal, South Africa and Thailand to form the Global Health and Foreign Policy Initiative. The purpose of the initiative is to 'build the case for why global health should hold a strategic place on the international agenda'. It hopes to achieve this by 'exploring how foreign ministers and foreign policy could add value to health issues of international importance' and also by 'showing how a health focus could harness the benefits of globalization, strengthen diplomacy and respond to new thinking on human security' (Oslo Ministerial Declaration 2007: 1373). The following year, these foreign ministers also agreed the Oslo Declaration. The declaration committed its signatories to adopting a 'health lens in foreign policy', and carved a future agenda around an extensive range of points for collaborative action (Oslo Ministerial Declaration 2007: 1375). Here the social and political influence of the medical professions is enhanced not so much by expanding their societal jurisdiction, as by elevating the treatment and prevention of disease to a much more urgent matter of 'high' politics and foreign policy.

Finally, and most importantly, broader human security concerns about global health have also prompted an explosion in the number of new actors, initiatives and funders involved in the field of global health. Many of these are principally aimed at healing people around the world, or preventing them from becoming sick in the first place. They hope to achieve that through recourse to a range of medical interventions. Thus the human security approach has also aimed 'to strengthen the interface between protection and empowerment' (Takemi et al. 2008b: 14). In other words, rather than focusing solely on state-based initiatives, the human security approach also tries to reach neglected populations directly. It seeks to empower them from 'below' by alleviating their disease burden. This will require a range of new international initiatives aimed at rolling out medical treatments in the global South. As a result of this quest, the international influence of medical practitioners and researchers will become augmented further still. They now have at their disposal a much greater range of new and better-funded international platforms from which to launch new treatments directly to people living in developing countries.

The number of such new global health initiatives that have been created since 2000 can be mind-boggling and has already transformed the institutional landscape of global health into a complex patchwork of international, national and non-state-actor initiatives running novel – and sometimes overlapping – global health programmes. Some would say the global health landscape has become almost unrecognizable (see Kay and Williams 2009). In order to appreciate better the extent of that profound sea-change in the number and nature of global health actors, it is worth first considering what the traditional institutional landscape of international health used to look like for most of the latter half of the twentieth century.

The cornerstone of that traditional landscape was undoubtedly the World Health Organization (WHO), founded in 1948. Organizationally, the WHO consists of its headquarters in Geneva as well as six regional offices in Europe (Copenhagen), Africa (Brazzaville, Congo), the Americas (Washington, DC), South-East Asia (New Delhi), the Eastern Mediterranean (Cairo) and the Western Pacific (Manila). These regional offices enjoy a significant degree of autonomy within the organization as a whole. The organization also maintains further links with more than 140 country offices. Its core decision-making body, the World Health Assembly, consists of representatives from all of the WHO's 193 member states and meets once a year in Geneva (usually in the month of May).

The Constitution of the WHO, drafted after the Second World War, established the institution as the focal point of international health concerns and spelled out some ambitious goals in the area of global health. It argued that the enjoyment of the highest attainable standard of health is the fundamental right of every person, that the health of all peoples is fundamental for achieving lasting peace and security, that unequal development is a danger when it comes to the control of disease, and that advances in medical knowledge should be extended to all peoples (WHO 1946: 1). These goals represent a potent mix of humanitarian and interest-based motivations for addressing international health issues. They are not always achieved, however, because the World Health Organization – as an inter-governmental organization – possesses no independent enforcement powers to implement them. In that regard, it is reliant on the actions of member states.

What is more, the organization has historically also been plagued by considerable political and diplomatic wrangling between states – something encouraged by the nature of its budget. Its biannual budget (US$4.2 billion for 2008–9) is made up of two separate components. One is the core budget which consists of mandatory subscriptions paid by the member states. That part of the budget, also referred to as 'Assessed Contributions', covers the day-to-day operating costs of the organization and essential programmes of benefit to member states. These assessed contributions are worked out according to a formula that takes into account the size of a country's population and economy. The United States continues to contribute 22 per cent of these assessed contributions. In addition to the United States, the largest contributors are Japan (16.63%), Germany (8.58%), United Kingdom (6.64%), France (6.30%), Italy (5.08%), Canada (2.98%), China (2.67%), Mexico (2.26%), and the Netherlands (1.87%) (WHO 2007c).

Yet, in reality, the WHO's budgetary picture is far more complex than that, and allows the organization all too easily to become hostage to political wrangling by member states. For instance, the relative ranking of these contributors changes when additional voluntary contributions made by member states are taken into account – the second component of the budget. The United Kingdom, Canada and Norway, in particular, make substantial voluntary contributions. That is part of a larger trend whereby many donors prefer to give voluntary contributions over which they have a greater influence and which tend to be more project-specific (GHW 2008: 2006). Indeed, it is striking that the core budget of assessed contributions consists of less than US$1 billion, and so represents less than a quarter of the WHO's biannual budget. The majority of the budget is in fact made up of those voluntary contributions which tend to be earmarked for specific projects, such as developing vaccines or rolling out immunization programmes. Here the donors can exert subtle but substantial pressure over the use to which this funding is put.

These budgetary arrangements can place the secretariat of the World Health Organization in a difficult position. That can be seen, for example, in how the organization has come under considerable pressure from the US government, its largest contributor, over various issues. Members of the US government have in the past tried to pressure the World Health Organization to withdraw official reports critical of the US policy on intellectual property rights. One such episode reportedly occurred in March 2006 when the US Ambassador to the United Nations in Geneva visited the Director General of the World Health Organization, Lee Jong-wook, to express Washington's displeasure at the public commentary of a regional WHO official. The official had warned the Thai government that it should think carefully about the health consequences of entering a bi-lateral free trade agreement with the United States that would surrender Thailand's sovereign right to produce or import generic medicines. He also warned that the agreement might lead to increases in the price of many medicines used in Thailand. The next day the WHO official was recalled and assigned to a different regional office (Williams 2006).

On another occasion, the World Health Organization also came under pressure to withdraw and water down measures it was proposing in its Global Strategy on Diet, Physical Activity and Health, as they were perceived as threatening to the sugar industry (Cannon 2004). The sugar industry had written several strong letters to the Director General of the World Health Organization, Gro Harlem Brundtland, and threatened to lobby Congress to withhold US contributions to the World Health Organization (Hagmann 2003). The organization thus has to walk a fine line between serving its membership as a whole and satisfying the interests of countries making significant voluntary contributions. Notwithstanding such sensitive political issues, the World Health Organization has long been perceived to occupy centre stage in the institutional landscape of international health.

Partially in recognition of some of the limitations of a large inter-state organization like the World Health Organization, the institutional landscape of international health has traditionally also included several non-governmental organizations. Though certainly not an exhaustive list, three such organizations have played a particularly prominent role in international health: the International Committee of the Red Cross, Médecins Sans Frontières and Oxfam. Deriving its name from the Oxford Committee for Famine Relief, which was founded in Britain in 1942, Oxfam has been active in the field of health – even though its central mission is related to poverty. Oxfam is particularly concerned with enhancing access to basic health services, essential medicines, water and sanitation, as well as responding to HIV/AIDS.

Founded over a century ago, the International Committee of the Red Cross provides humanitarian assistance and protection to civilian and military victims of war and armed violence, on a basis of political neutrality. Although its headquarters are located in Geneva, the Red Cross is based in around eighty countries and employs more than 11,000 staff. As part of its efforts, the Red Cross has also been involved in health issues, as its members try to ensure that the victims of armed conflict have access to essential preventative medicine and treatment. Their work routinely includes repairing damaged health care infrastructure, conducting epidemiological surveillance and training medical staff. In cases of famine, it also assists in intensive feeding programmes. During times of war, members of the Red Cross can also perform surgery to heal injuries, and provide assistance to persons who have become disabled as a result of conflict.

Established by doctors and journalists more recently, in 1971, Médecins Sans Frontières is perhaps the best-known non-governmental organization devoted to international health issues. It focuses on the provision of medicine and emergency aid to people affected by armed conflict, epidemics, and natural or man-made disasters, or who are otherwise excluded from access to health care. The activities of Médecins Sans Frontières are thus wide-ranging, covering anything from running hospitals and clinics and performing surgery, through to carrying out vaccinations, feeding undernourished children, dispensing drinking water, providing blankets and shelter, and so on. Today the organization has sections in nineteen countries, and operates in more than sixty. In conjunction with the state-based World Health Organization, non-governmental organizations such as Médecins Sans Frontières have also long formed core elements in the institutional landscape of international health. Yet, since 2000, that traditional landscape of global health has been transformed radically.

Global Pharmacology: Creating an International Curing Machine

The broader human security concern with global health has triggered an explosion in the number of new governmental and non-governmental initiatives devoted to endemic diseases in the global South. Many of these are aimed at procuring new kinds of medical

interventions and distributing them to people living in developing countries. The Global Alliance for Vaccines and Immunization
(GAVI), launched in 2000, is a prominent case in point. As an international public–private health partnership, GAVI focuses on HIV/
AIDS, tuberculosis and malaria, as well as a range of other diseases,
in the developing world. The Geneva-based alliance consists of governments, research institutes, international organizations (such as
the WHO, UNICEF, the World Bank), as well as non-governmental
organizations, the Bill and Melinda Gates Foundation, and the
vaccine industry in both developed and developing countries.

The main purpose of GAVI is to extend the range of vaccines
that are available around the world. It does so both by developing
new vaccines and by increasing access to immunization around the
world. The alliance points out that it has already widened the availability of vaccines to many children in developing countries. It claims
that GAVI programmes have protected 26 million children against
diphtheria, tetanus and pertussis, as well as having immunized a
further 123 million children against hepatitis B. GAVI also seeks to
shorten the time lag between the development of new vaccines and
their introduction in developing countries – something it has already
done for pneumococcal vaccine and rotavirus vaccine through its
Accelerated Development and Introduction plans.

As of September 2007 GAVI had received US$298 million in
funding from government and private sources, with a donor list
including the governments of Australia, Canada, Denmark, France,
Germany, Ireland, Luxembourg, the Netherlands, Norway, Sweden,
the United Kingdom and the United States. It also receives funds
from the European Commission, the Gates Foundation and other
private contributors. However, GAVI only represents the tip of the
iceberg when it comes to what is now a long list of new international
initiatives that have emerged since the 1990s and that seek to pioneer
a range of medical interventions for alleviating the burden of endemic
diseases in the global South.

Today there are also a plethora of other organizations devoted to
specific diseases that are similarly trying to develop new vaccines and
treatments, or making existing ones more widely available around
the world. Beginning with HIV/AIDS, the organizations devoted

specifically to addressing the AIDS pandemic alone are already too numerous to list. The most prominent of these is undoubtedly UNAIDS – the specialized United Nations agency tasked with addressing the international spread of HIV/AIDS. Established in 1995, UNAIDS is located at the centre of a complex network of various UN programmes and affiliated organizations, including the World Health Organization and the World Bank.

The political objectives of UNAIDS are to mobilize leadership for effective action against the spread of HIV/AIDS, to monitor and evaluate the spread of the disease, and to support an effective response to it. As part of that remit, UNAIDS has also been making the case for viewing HIV/AIDS as a great human security threat. 'As a global issue', Peter Piot (2001) argued, in his capacity as Director of UNAIDS, 'we must pay attention to AIDS as a threat to human security, and redouble our efforts against the epidemic and its impact'. One of the principal goals of the UNAIDS leadership has thus been to increase the international funding available for extending access to medical treatment with anti-retrovirals for people living with HIV/AIDS. Indeed, it has stated that its desired aim is ultimately to achieve universal access to medical treatment.

The International HIV/AIDS Alliance and the International AIDS Vaccine Initiative (IAVI) are two further organizations created in the spirit of discovering and rolling out new medical treatments for people living with HIV/AIDS in developing countries. The International HIV/AIDS Alliance was established in 1993 by the governments of France, Sweden, the United States and the United Kingdom, the European Union and the Rockefeller Foundation. It works primarily through local organizations supporting community groups and other non-governmental organizations. To that end the International HIV/AIDS Alliance employs not only around 120 staff at its Brighton secretariat in the United Kingdom, but also a further 200 staff in country offices located in the Caribbean, China, India, Madagascar, Mozambique, Myanmar, South Sudan, Uganda, Ukraine and Zambia. In recent years its donor base has increased significantly and now includes thirteen governments, seventeen major trusts, and foundations, as well as corporate partners. Its income has tripled from US$20.6 million in 2003 to US$60.9 million in 2006, with the largest increase coming from the Global Fund to Fight HIV/ AIDS, Tuberculosis, and Malaria. However, 45 per cent of the total income of the alliance still comes from governments.

Although it takes a broad approach to its AIDS initiatives, securing access to medical treatment remains a priority for the alliance. Its primary objective in that respect is to ensure that local communities around the world are properly engaged in the process of rolling out anti-viral medications. It deems such community engagement vital not just for persuading local communities that the medicines are effective, but also for educating them about the importance of adhering to treatment regimens. The alliance thus works precisely at the interface of modern medicine and the community level, hoping thereby to enhance the coverage and efficacy of treatments in many developing countries.

The emphasis on medical interventions is even more pronounced in the case of the International AIDS Vaccine Initiative, set up in 1996. The specific goal of this non-profit international public–private partnership was to develop a safe, effective and accessible vaccine for HIV – a goal that has so far proved frustratingly elusive. To that end the initiative assembled a team of scientific researchers, largely drawn from the vaccine industry, which seeks to develop and trial vaccine candidates. Despite the well-known difficulties in producing a viable AIDS vaccine, annual global funding for vaccine research and development has tripled from US\$327 million in 2000 to US\$961 million in 2007 (IAVI 2008: 12). It continues to dedicate roughly three-quarters of its resources to AIDS vaccine research and development. Since the 1990s, the AIDS pandemic alone has thus prompted a mushrooming of new global health organizations and initiatives that are devoted to developing or rolling out medical treatments in the developing world.

Of course the AIDS 'industry' is often accused of attracting and absorbing a disproportionate amount of international health resources. In that respect, one might expect to find much more of a dearth in terms of initiatives concerned with other endemic diseases, such as tuberculosis and malaria. Nothing could be farther from the truth. Even more organizations have sprung up that are committed to developing new medical interventions for addressing the burden of malaria in the developing world. The Geneva-based Medicines for Malaria Venture was launched in this spirit in 1999. It is a non-profit organization devoted to finding new medicines for treating malaria, especially in order to deal with those types of malaria that have become resistant to inexpensive and widely used medicines such as chloroquine, sulfadoxine and pryimethamine.

The initial goal of the Medicines for Malaria Venture was to develop at least one new effective and affordable malaria drug by the end of the decade. The venture has thus been striving to bring together researchers and scientists from both the public and private sectors. It has four new medicines – artemisinin-based combination therapies (ACTs) – in the final stages of development. It is funded through contributions from governments (such as the British, Swiss, Dutch and American) and through private foundations (60 per cent of its US$273 million budget since 1999 has come from the Gates Foundation). Like the organizations devoted to HIV/AIDS, these initiatives have also seen considerable increases in funding. According to the 2007 annual report of the Medicines for Malaria Venture, 'funding for malaria from international donors has increased tenfold' over the course of the preceding decade (MMV 2007: 11).

Other initiatives devoted specifically to malaria try to combine such interest in new pharmacological responses with wider preventative measures. Additional organizations simultaneously pursuing both of these goals include the Rollback Malaria Partnership and the Malaria Consortium. The Roll Back Malaria Partnership was launched in 1998 by several United Nations programmes, including the World Health Organization, the United Nations Children's Fund (UNICEF), the United Nations Development Programme and the World Bank. In recent years, it has expanded to become one of the foremost public–private partnerships raising leadership and resources in order to reduce the burden of malaria. It brings together several actors and constituencies, including foundations; the private sector; the Global Fund to Fight AIDS, Tuberculosis and Malaria; malaria-endemic countries; researchers; non-governmental organizations; multilateral and development agencies; and OECD donor countries.

The Partnership also works toward achieving one of the Millennium

Development Goals, namely that, by 2015, malaria should no longer be a major cause of death and impediment to development. That is why it does not just want to achieve an increase in prevention strategies around the world where malaria is prevalent; it also wishes to procure some 228 million doses of ACTs every year. It similarly wishes to make available a further 19 million doses of chloroquine and primaquine every year (RBM 2009).

Established more recently, in 2003, the Malaria Consortium also strives to increase access to prevention, care and treatment for groups at risk from malaria (as well as other communicable diseases) in Africa and Asia. It works with a range of actors from local communities through to governmental and non-governmental organizations, as well as academics and international organizations. It has offices in Uganda, Mozambique, Sudan, Southern Sudan, Zambia, Nigeria, Ethiopia, Thailand and the United Kingdom. In addition to improving prevention, mobilizing leadership and increasing treatment capacity in partner countries, the Consortium again also wishes to increase access to effective treatment, especially in rural communities. It therefore works with ministries of health in partner countries to improve medicine acquisition policy, as well as engaging the private sector to deliver treatments directly to rural populations. These too are new initiatives that have been created since the turn of the century in the spirit of making a range of medical interventions more accessible internationally.

What, then, about tuberculosis? Here the picture is no different. More initiatives still have been created to address the plight of tuberculosis sufferers in low-income countries. Again the pattern in terms of an emphasis on medical treatments is quite similar. The Stop TB Partnership, for example, is a public–private partnership consisting of a complex network of donors: governmental and non-governmental agencies, individuals and international organizations. It was established in 2000, following a conference held in London in 1998, to stop the spread of tuberculosis. The aims of the initiative are ambitious in that it seeks to eradicate tuberculosis as a public health problem and ultimately to eradicate tuberculosis completely, much in the same way that smallpox has been eradicated. The Stop TB initiative also drafted the Amsterdam Declaration to Stop TB in March

2000, agreed by ministerial representatives from the twenty countries with the highest rates of tuberculosis, and calling for more concerted action.

The initiative now has seven working groups with different specializations including the expansion of directly observed therapies, the links between HIV and tuberculosis, the problems posed by MDR-TB, the development of new tuberculosis medicines and vaccines, and so forth. They have also launched the Global Plan to Stop TB (2006–15), which aims to save some 14 million lives, to treat some 50 million people (including 800,000 with MDR-TB) and to develop a safe, effective and affordable vaccine by 2015. Its cost over ten years would be close to US$56 billion.

Here too a strong interest in medical interventions is evident, which the Partnership pursues through the Global Drug Facility. The latter was created to tackle one of the main barriers to eliminating the global burden of tuberculosis, namely the unreliable availability and poor quality of drug supplies. The aim of the Global Drug Facility is thus to ensure a reliable and uninterrupted supply of high-quality medications that meet the quality standards of the World Health Organization. Amongst its successes, the Global Drug Facility counts sponsoring drugs for 644,000 patients in India, 220,000 patients in the Democratic Republic of Congo, and a further 200,000 in Bangladesh (Stop TB 2009). The activities of the Stop TB Partnership have been complemented since the late 1990s by two further prominent organizations focusing on tuberculosis: Target TB established in 2003, and TB Alert created in 1999.

It should be evident by now that this list of new global health initiatives could be extended considerably. However, the fundamental observation would not change: since the 1990s the broad human security concern with global health issues has led to the creation of an extensive array of new international organizations and global health programmes. That explosion in the number of global health initiatives also constitutes further evidence of the medicalization of security in that many of these programmes and organizations are again staffed by medical professionals. That is to be expected, of course, but it also represents yet another increase in the societal influence of many different types of medical professionals. They now have many new platforms at their disposal, from which they can also carry out their activities internationally. To varying degrees, moreover, all of these initiatives again also place a strong emphasis on eradicating or minimizing these human insecurities through better, newer or cheaper medical interventions, like vaccines and treatments. Human security too will therefore only be achieved by greater recourse to medical interventions.

Healthy Spending: New Funding Streams for Global Health

Where is the money coming from to fund the medical researchers and practitioners who are engaging in all of these international activities? Since the 1990s the heightened concern with global health issues has freed up substantial levels of funding for addressing these concerns. Development assistance for health issues alone has increased from US$2.5 billion in 1990 to almost US$14 billion in 2005 (GHW 2008: 211). The World Bank notes quite candidly that 'never before has so much attention – or money – been devoted to improving the health of the world's poor' (World Bank 2007: 149). The majority of this increase is from donor-country aid, which is channelled through the Development Assistance Committee (DAC) of the Organization for Economic Cooperation and Development (OECD). In 2006, member countries dispersed more than US$10 billion in such aid, with some significant non-DAC countries also increasing their funding (such as China) – although reliable information is not available for these countries (GHW 2008: 211). That, however, is only part of the story.

The recent expansion of funding for global health has also been driven by the use of new financing mechanisms and the entry of an important set of private foundations into the sector. In 2002, the Global Fund to Fight AIDS, Tuberculosis and Malaria was set up as a new funding mechanism for addressing health issues in the developing world. It was created following a commitment by the Group of Eight (G8) in July 2000 to address the plight of people with HIV/AIDS, tuberculosis, and malaria in low-income countries. This G8 meeting was followed, in 2001, by a summit of the Organization of African Unity at which Kofi Annan, in his capacity as Secretary General of the United Nations, called for the creation of a 'war chest' of US$10 billion per annum to address these three diseases. This 'war chest' eventually became the Global Fund, which approved its first grants in April 2002 (GHW 2008: 261).

The Global Fund is not a classic inter-state organization, in that it was not established by an international treaty. Another rare feature is that non-governmental organizations also enjoy voting rights in the Fund (Fidler 2004: 55). The Global Fund is not even an implementing agency, but 'merely' a financing mechanism. Technically the fund is thus an international public–private partnership that is primarily aimed at raising and distributing funds for programmes addressing AIDS, tuberculosis and malaria around the world. So far, the Global Fund has secured approved funding of US$10.1 billion, and funds over 500 programmes in more than 130 countries (House of Lords 2008: 34).

The Global Fund works largely on the basis of 'performance-based funding'. This means that grants are distributed incrementally, with programmes having to demonstrate results in order to receive continued funding. The Fund claims that more than 1.8 million people had been 'saved' by programmes sponsored through the Fund up to May 2007. By that same time, it claims to have placed more than 1 million people on ARV treatment, treated 2.8 million people with tuberculosis through DOTS, and distributed approximately 30 million insecticide-treated mosquito nets (Global Fund 2008: 23). Like the World Health Organization, the Global Fund too has been pushing the security debates on health, noting how these three diseases not only cause millions of deaths annually, but also produce 'measurable' economic loss, as well as 'in the worst-affected countries also increas[ing] the risk of social disintegration and political instability' (Global Fund 2008: 5).

Although the Global Fund is undoubtedly the most prominent international financing mechanism to emerge since the 1990s, it is not the only one. UNITAID is another new financing initiative created principally in response to HIV/AIDS, tuberculosis and malaria. It was founded in 2006 by the governments of Chile, France, Norway and the UK. Since that time it has already expanded to more than twenty-seven participating countries plus the Gates Foundation. Its purpose is to create stable and sustainable sources of funding for essential medicines, especially for HIV/AIDS, tuberculosis and malaria, in developing countries.

UNITAID principally tries to make treatment a more viable policy option by adopting a longer time horizon, and making more sustained purchasing commitments. This also allows the organization to secure lower prices from manufacturers. UNITAID's activities include expanding HIV/AIDS treatment and care for children, reducing prices for second-line medicines, accelerating the prevention of mother-to-child transmissions, and also increasing the availability of artemisinin-based combination therapy (ACT) and first-line tuberculosis treatments. Through the World Health Organization, it also supports activities to bring medicines onto the market faster by supporting the prequalification process of drugs and medicines.

UNITAID also employs a very innovative financing mechanism in that it raises most of its funding through a new solidarity tax which is placed on some airline tickets. The organization thus claims to have created a genuinely novel source of additional funding available for global public health. In those countries operating the tax regime, it applies to all airlines departing from that country. In France, the tax has been in effect since 1 July 2006 and it is presently also in operation in a number of other countries located in Latin America, Africa and Asia. Additional countries are planning to implement the tax. Just over 80 per cent of UNITAID's budget currently comes from that tax, with donors making up the rest. Its budget has been rising in recent years, with a US$389 million budget for 2008 (UNITAID 2008).

Further funding for global health issues has flowed from private foundations. The most prominent and significant of these is the Bill and Melinda Gates Foundation, established in January 2000. Although it is a charitable foundation, its annual resources are larger than the World Health Organization's core budget. Its portfolio covers three core areas: Global Development, Global Health and the United States (focusing on education, emergency relief and housing issues within that country). In 2007 the Gates Foundation paid out around US$916 million in its Global Health programmes (House of Lords 2008: 37). Its funding is heavily geared toward new technologies and new medical solutions to health issues. The Gates Foundation is also a significant donor to a variety of international health programmes. Indeed, its representatives sit on the board of most of the global health partnerships, including many of those discussed above.

Like many non-governmental organizations, however, the Gates Foundation is, strictly speaking, only accountable to its membership. In the case of the Gates Foundation, this means that it is essentially a family foundation driven by the interests of the Gates family. The Foundation operates with little or no scrutiny by governments or civil society. By 2005, it had amassed an endowment of US$29 billion, and in 2006 received a further US$31 billion donation from the investor Warren Buffet, enabling it to spend more than US$3 billion in 2008 (GHW 2008: 241). It is now the biggest foundation in the United States.

That is also the most significant difference between the Gates Foundation and the Clinton Foundation, which was established in 2002. The foundation of President William Jefferson Clinton has a much narrower remit, focusing much of its work on HIV/AIDS. In particular, the Clinton Foundation has sought to negotiate lower prices for ARVs and to help governments to improve their health delivery systems. It subsequently expanded its scope to cover access to diagnostic equipment and medicines for malaria as well. Increasingly, these private foundations too are part of the patchwork of new organizations and initiatives that have mushroomed in the field of health and human security since the end of the last century. They also illustrate how the growing human security concern with global health issues has created new funding streams for medical professionals and researchers.

Conclusion

Human security activities devoted to global health mark another instance in contemporary world politics where insecurity is becoming construed as a medical problem caused by the onset of disease. Yet, because human security entails a much wider health agenda, it also expands the scope of the medicalization of security further still. Human security activities in relation to global health span a much larger geographical domain than other health security agendas. As we have seen, pandemic preparedness and biosecurity discussions have been held predominantly amongst Western governments anxious about their inability to contain emerging infectious diseases outside of their borders, or indeed the spectre of a terrorist attack on their populations. Although these strategies possess international dimensions as well, human security debates have tended to concern themselves much more directly with low-income countries in the global South. They focus on diseases that affect those countries but which may, by and large, be contained outside the borders of the West. That wider geographic breadth of the human security agenda extends the medicalization of security beyond the borders of the West and makes its presence felt in most other regions of the world as well.

Human security activities also extend the scope of the medicalization of security by focusing on endemic diseases that are already claiming many lives around the world every day. In contrast, pandemic preparedness and biosecurity discussions dealt – strictly speaking – with phenomena that have not yet occurred. Although a new human H1N1 influenza pandemic did emerge in 2009, that difference between pandemic preparedness measures and human security activities is very striking when considering the case of H5N1 avian influenza. Although there have been isolated cases of human H5N1 infection, so far there has been no pandemic occurring in the human population, and it could be years before such an H5N1 pandemic emerges – assuming that it ever does. Pandemic preparedness measures for H5N1 are thus ostensibly oriented toward an unknown future.

The same is true in relation to policy initiatives on biological terrorism where (with the exception of the mysterious and unresolved case of the anthrax letters and other minor incidents) such a large-scale attack has also not yet occurred. Both of these debates on health security are thus concerned with the possibility of a catastrophic future. Human security deliberations, in comparison, address diseases that are already causing significant morbidity and mortality on a daily basis. That lengthens the list of diseases that can be considered as security threats. We need not wait for a catastrophic event or a new outbreak to occur. There is already much that needs be done in the present to alleviate the threat posed by disease.

Finally, human security debates also widen the scope of the medicalization of security by shifting the referent object of security to the individual. That inflates the list of possible medical threats to security further still. Virtually any disease that causes premature mortality can now legitimately be considered as a human security threat. Here, then, the medicalization of security is also amplified without actually making any novel claims about the level of threat that diseases pose. We have seen that pandemic preparedness discussions expand our definition of security to include diseases because, it is argued, we are now more vulnerable to an infectious disease outbreak in light of the increasingly globalized nature of our transport systems and the world economy. Biosecurity analysts voice concern that our vulnerability to an attack using an infectious disease has increased, given that recent scientific advances make the threat from biological weapons more severe, and given the increased threat such weapons pose when a state is engaged in a protracted conflict with a non-state enemy such as a terrorist movement.

Yet in the case of human security, no such novel claims about an increase in our vulnerability are being advanced. The elevation of global health issues to security threats, and the concomitant redefinition of insecurity as a medical problem, occur mostly through definitional fiat. They emerge as a consequence of the simple but far-reaching decision to privilege the individual as the referent object of security. That decisive gesture allows the human security framework to incorporate a much longer list of diseases on its agenda, and to cast its net of operations much more widely to the global South. That also makes the human security framework an even more sweeping attempt to medicalize security in the twenty-first century.

5

The Lifestyle Timebombs: Panics about Cigarettes, Fat and Alcohol

There is one further domain in world politics where the medicalization of security is unfolding today – and one that is frequently overlooked. Although this final instance of the medicalization of security is initially much more difficult to detect, it actually represents the most radical attempt yet to medicalize security in the twenty-first century. It can be found at play in the growing concerns expressed about the epidemic of non-communicable 'lifestyle' afflictions such as smoking, obesity and alcoholism that are now seen to threaten populations – especially in comparatively wealthy societies. The reason this medical redefinition of insecurity is harder to spot is that these debates hardly ever invoke the word 'security' directly. In fact, they are not normally seen to represent a formal part of the health security agenda. This stands in sharp contrast to the previous three cases.

Yet, increasingly, phenomena such as smoking, obesity and alcoholism are becoming perceived as something more than just routine public health issues; they are also considered to be graver and deeper threats to the population. That shift in perception is accomplished not through claims that these phenomena constitute direct security threats, but – more subtly – by frequently invoking the language and metaphors of security when discussing them. Smoking, obesity and alcoholism are now ubiquitously described in policy settings and the public media as representing deeper social 'crises' and indeed pernicious population 'timebombs'. As in the previous three cases, these occasionally frenzied discussions about the threat posed by a range of unhealthy lifestyles thus also begin to construe insecurity as being a phenomenon caused by the onset and spread of disease. The only – but crucial – difference is that they focus on 'lifestyle' diseases rather than infectious diseases.

Whilst the perception that these lifestyle conditions pose serious threats to populations may not have encouraged medical experts to become more closely involved in the formulation of security policy, the 'wars' waged on these phenomena have certainly prompted a further expansion in the societal jurisdiction of a wide range of medical professionals. Governments anxious about the threat posed by these conditions are turning to doctors, nutritionists and public health experts for detailed advice about which policies they can introduce in order to avert these urgent threats. They are asking how the patterns in which people consume food and drink, as well as the personal habits they adopt, can be readjusted in line with medical norms regarding what is considered to be healthy living?

In this process the medicalization of security reaches its highest amplitude yet. That is because securing populations against these threats will not only require the treatment of medical conditions that meet the classical definition of disease. It will also require the regulation of wider personal habits that have emerged in recent decades and that can eventually lead to disease. Discussions about the threat posed to populations by smoking, obesity and alcohol consumption thus radically inflate the scope of medicalization beyond the classical diseases to include our 'lifestyles' too and to consider them as diseases as well. These discussions imply that a secure society ultimately also requires citizens to engage in healthy behaviours.

Smoking out the Smokers: Confronting the Tobacco 'Epidemic'

Public health officials working in the field of tobacco regulation like to point out that cigarettes are one of the few legally sold products that will kill up to half of their consumers when used as intended by the manufacturers. When Christopher Columbus first encountered what he referred to as those 'strange' leaves in the New World (probably the nicotiana tobacum plant), he could hardly have imagined the fierce political debates that would unfold centuries later. At that time in human history, of course, cigarettes had not yet established themselves as the main form of tobacco consumption. As late as the eighteenth century, tobacco was still consumed mostly in snuff form, allowing it to be inhaled or 'snorted' through the nose. The nineteenth century then witnessed the rise of the cigar as the preferred mode of tobacco consumption. The cigar was displaced by the modern cigarette only in the course of the twentieth century, and the latter continues to represent the main form of tobacco consumption today. However, there are also popular forms of smokeless chewing tobacco, and outside of the West (especially in India and other South-East Asian countries) tobacco is frequently smoked in small hand-rolled bidis that produce even more tar, nicotine and carbon monoxide than standard cigarettes.

It is estimated that today more than 5 trillion cigarettes are sold annually, the vast majority of which are produced by companies such as Philip Morris (now part of Altria), British American Tobacco, Japan Tobacco / JR Reynolds and the China National Tobacco Corporation (WHO 2002: 30). At best, those cigarettes have to be considered very distant relatives of the tobacco plants encountered by Columbus, because tobacco is only one ingredient that makes up today's popular cigarette brands. Modern cigarettes are in fact highly complex and artificially manufactured products containing hundreds of additives that release thousands of different chemical compounds when lit. Astonishingly, that list includes hazardous chemicals otherwise used for a range of industrial purposes, such as acetone, ammonia, arsenic, benzene, cadmium and formaldehyde (Hoffmann and Hoffmann 2004). As is widely recognized today, smoking cigarettes is a known risk factor associated with several cancers, heart disease, strokes, emphysema and other diseases (WHO 2008b: 11).

Notwithstanding those ill-health effects, several developments since the turn of the century have favoured the global expansion of the tobacco market. International trade liberalization, which has reduced trade restrictions on tobacco products, has removed barriers to the global sale and distribution of these products (Taylor et al. 2000). The increased use of international media outlets for advertising has also facilitated that international expansion, allowing new markets in the developing world to be established (Tye et al. 1987; Amos and Mackay 2004). Another key driver of the tobacco 'epidemic' is undoubtedly the fact that many find smoking to be an enjoyable activity, despite the potentially negative long-term health consequences.

Yet others see smoking as a social activity, or as a way of coping with stress and anxiety (Kouvonen et al. 2005). Some even attempt to use smoking as a way of controlling their weight (Strauss and Mir 2001). Perhaps the most important factor underpinning the continuing demand for tobacco, however, rests in the addictive properties of nicotine itself. As many regular smokers attempting to quit their habit will have experienced, prolonged absence of nicotine exposure can produce a variety of unpleasant symptoms, such as cravings, restlessness and anxiety – making it more difficult to stop smoking.

Today, the scale of smoking has reached levels sufficiently high for the World Health Organization to describe the situation not just as a public health issue but as a deeper global crisis. The World Health Organization thus characterizes the contemporary international situation as a tobacco 'epidemic', and has declared a 'war' on 'the global tobacco crisis' (WHO 2008a: 14). Its most recent report on the tobacco industry warns unequivocally that 'the tobacco epidemic is devastating' and that 'the fight against tobacco must be engaged forcefully and quickly – with no less urgency than battles against life-threatening infectious diseases' (WHO 2008a: 8).

The war on tobacco is thus a paradigmatic case of taking a public health issue and construing it as a deeper source of insecurity. That process of framing smoking as a threat to the population further contributes to the medical redefinition of insecurity. Here too insecurity becomes understood as a phenomenon that is caused by the spread of disease within the population rather than stemming solely from the military capabilities and hostile political intentions of other states. If societies are to be healthy and secure, rates of smoking in the population will thus have to be substantially diminished around the world.

Why does the personal decision of millions of people around the world to adopt smoking as a habit now merit the designation of a 'crisis', 'threat' and 'timebomb'? Beyond using security metaphors as a strategy of risk communication, two factors are frequently invoked as a justification for viewing smoking as a deeper source of insecurity for populations that needs to be addressed through public health and medical measures. First, there is the significant scale of mortality caused by the use of these products. The World Health Organization estimates that there are approximately 1 billion people smoking tobacco in the world today, the majority of whom are men (although, in many parts of the world, smoking rates amongst women are on the rise). It is further estimated that every year smoking-related illnesses cause around 5.4 million deaths – a figure which is similar to the estimated number of deaths caused by AIDS, tuberculosis and malaria combined (WHO 2008b: 6).

The estimates of the World Health Organization also reveal that the burden of smoking-related morbidity and mortality is progressively shifting toward the developing world, where consumption is increasing at far greater levels than in the developed world (WHO 2008b: 16). It would thus be mistaken to view the smoking phenomenon as something solely affecting the affluent countries of the West. Rates of smoking are today increasing in low- and middle-income countries, due in part to the growing size of their populations in general. Yet smoking rates are also rising because those populations are being deliberately targeted by the tobacco industry through advertising campaigns. The tobacco industry is in the midst of shifting its focus from the older markets in high-income countries in the West to new and emerging markets in low- and middle-income countries. Faced with diminishing markets in the former, tobacco companies are trying to find new 'demand' in the latter (Amos and Mackay 2004). This means that concerns about the social effects of smoking are not confined to the comparatively wealthy countries of the West, but increasingly are registering amongst developing-country governments as well.

This trend also suggests that the global tobacco 'crisis' is likely to become worse before it gets better. Indeed, the World Health Organization paints a bleak picture for the future. One of its reports anticipates that by 2030 there will be more than 8 million deaths per year, more than 80 per cent of which will occur in developing countries. Unless urgent action is taken, smoking-related illnesses could kill 1 billion in the twenty-first century (WHO 2008b: 6). The report further points out that tobacco kills between a third and a half of all people who use it – on average, fifteen years prematurely (WHO 2008b: 14). Yet, in principle, those deaths are entirely preventable, making tobacco-smoking 'the single most preventable cause of death in the world today' (WHO 2008b: 8). Those 'unnecessary' deaths mark the first reason why smoking is deemed to be a serious threat to the population.

Smoking is also seen to represent a deeper crisis for a second reason: it is thought to have a range of negative economic effects. Of course, representatives of the tobacco industry point out that cigarette manufacturing leads to job creation, to profits for businesses, and also to substantial tax revenues for local and national governments. Significant tobacco business sectors do indeed exist in countries such as China, India, Indonesia, Thailand, Turkey, Egypt, Bangladesh and the Philippines. Countries like Malawi and Zimbabwe are also heavily dependent on the export of tobacco leaves.

Yet the World Health Organization counters tersely from a public health perspective that:

> the industry's overriding contribution to any country is suffering, disease, death – and economic losses. Tobacco use currently costs the world hundreds of billions of dollars each year. Tobacco-related deaths result in lost economic opportunities. In the United States, these losses are estimated at US$ 92 billion a year. Lost economic opportunities in highly populated, developing countries – many of which are manufacturing centres of the global economy – will be severe as the tobacco epidemic worsens, because half of all tobacco-related deaths occur during the prime productive years. The economic cost of tobacco-related deaths imposes a particular burden on the developing world, where four out of five tobacco deaths will occur by 2030. Data on tobacco's impact on global health-care costs are incomplete, but it is known to be high. In the United States, annual tobacco-related health-care costs are US$ 81 billion, in Germany nearly US$ 7 billion and in Australia US$ 1 billion. The net economic effect of tobacco is to deepen poverty. (WHO 2008b: 18–20)

Overall the World Health Organization thus prefers to think of the tobacco industry not as a job creator or useful tax revenue vehicle, but as a 'disease vector', because of its active role in promoting the consumption of cigarettes (WHO 2008b: 21). Earlier, the World Bank had come to a similar conclusion in its influential report entitled *Curbing the Epidemic: Governments and the Economics of Tobacco Control* (World Bank 1999). Smoking has thus become perceived as a wider and deeper threat to populations because of the direct toll of human lives in conjunction with wider economic costs. Here the construal of insecurity as something caused by the spread of diseases has therefore also unfolded for much the same reason as it has done in relation to the rapid spread of lethal infectious diseases.

As in the previous three case studies, the perception that smoking constitutes such a wider threat to the welfare and prosperity of populations has again also augmented the societal jurisdiction of a wide range of medical professionals. It has done so by making an additional form of human behaviour – smoking – amenable to much stronger regulatory intervention. In light of the advice of a raft of medical experts, many different policy measures have been developed and introduced by governments in the past few years to persuade people around the world to re-adjust their lifestyles in accordance with healthier norms. As we will see below, these measures have not restricted themselves to protecting individuals from the harmful effects of second-hand smoke; they have also attempted to persuade and encourage smokers to cease this unhealthy habit altogether.

The World Health Organization has been at the forefront of many of these efforts. Following a series of non-mandatory resolutions which it had been pursuing since the 1970s, and which did not have a strong impact, the organization turned toward a different tactic of using its treaty-making power to develop a framework convention on tobacco control. A framework convention is a binding international legal instrument that establishes broad commitments and a general system of governance for an issue area. The framework convention on tobacco control was negotiated under the auspices of the World Health Organization between 1999 and 2003.

In these negotiations, member states from regions likely to experience the majority burden in the next century – such as Africa, South-East Asia, the Caribbean, and Pacific Island countries – pushed for a strong treaty. But some countries hosting large tobacco production sectors also resisted any obligatory measures. A total ban on advertising was opposed by the United States, Japan and Germany, with a final compromise only being worked out in the final hours of the negotiations (GHW 2008: 354). Those differences notwithstanding, the framework convention was unanimously adopted by 192 states in May 2003, before coming into force on 27 February 2005.

The convention tries to reduce global rates of smoking through a combination of demand-side and supply-side measures. On the demand side, the convention made recommendations, for example, for annual tax increases on tobacco products of at least 5 per cent above inflation, and for further reducing the availability of international duty-free tobacco. Besides price measures to reduce demand, the convention also required states to protect persons from the effects of second-hand smoke in enclosed working spaces, public transport and public buildings – effectively placing restrictions on the number of places where people can smoke.

Tobacco companies in turn are urged to make more detailed and frequent disclosures of what is contained in cigarettes, to make half of the display area on cigarette packaging the standard size for health warnings, and in no case have those warnings take up less than 30 per cent. The convention also urges member states to undertake education and raise public awareness about the dangers of tobacco, as well as benefits of adopting a non-smoking lifestyle. Finally, the convention encourages member states to implement a comprehensive ban on tobacco advertising (to the extent that it is compatible with their respective legal constitutions). People around the world are thus to be put off the consumption of cigarettes by providing more information about their health effects, by making them more expensive and by reducing the extent of their marketing.

These attempts to stifle demand for tobacco products would have to be complemented by robust supply-side measures which are similarly intended to alter lifestyle choices. The framework convention thus also asks member states to commit themselves to making greater efforts to curb the illicit trade in tobacco products. The convention further imposes obligations on member states to ban and restrict the sale of tobacco to minors through making such sales illegal. That should also be further encouraged by ensuring that cigarettes are not available to young people on store shelves, by not selling candies that resemble cigarettes, and by preventing the use of cigarette vending machines that young people can access. Finally, the convention even urges member states to encourage agricultural diversification in order to promote alternative livelihoods to decrease dependence on tobacco revenues.

In light of the considerable commercial interests at stake, it is not surprising that the tobacco industry came out fighting hard against the framework. Historically the industry has a record of using a wide range of tactics for protecting its commercial interests. This has included becoming actively involved in tobacco smuggling (Gilmore and McKee 2004; Saloojee 2004: 273). This was intended to persuade governments that the introduction of more stringent taxation measures would simply lead to a loss of revenue for them, as people would increasingly resort to consuming smuggled, and therefore untaxed, cigarettes (Collin 2003: 78). The industry has in the past also paid scientists to produce research questioning the scientific links between smoking and ill-health, and has drawn up plans to actively undermine the World Health Organization's tobacco control programme (Yach and Bialous 2001: 1745).

More details of such activities have begun to emerge as a result of the Minnesota Settlement Agreement. This required major tobacco companies to make over 40 million pages of documents publicly accessible in a Minneapolis depository, whilst British American Tobacco was similarly required to make around 8 million pages of documents accessible in Guildford, England (Collin 2003: 62). Despite efforts by the industry to undermine the negotiations, the World Health Organization was nevertheless able to obtain sufficient consensus to get the framework convention agreed (Mamudu et al. 2008).

The World Health Organization has hailed the framework convention as a significant success, pointing out that it marks the first global public health treaty it has negotiated (FCTC 2009). The framework convention thus represents a tangible instance in which the World Health Organization actively encouraged the creation of new international law, and that saw an international organization encourage a new regulatory framework that could be perceived as threatening by large multi-national corporations with powerful commercial interests. From the perspective of those wishing to curb tobacco consumption, the convention has indeed had several positive effects. It raised the profile of tobacco control efforts so as to expose many states which had hitherto ignored the issue to considering directly the scientific evidence surrounding the health consequences of tobacco use. It also helped with the creation of international coalitions of non-governmental organizations, such as the Network for Accountability of Tobacco Transnationals. The convention even prompted the creation of an intergovernmental body – the Conference of the Parties – to oversee it.

Furthermore, given the convention's success in bringing about agreement on minimum international standards in relation to tobacco control, and in accordance with the convention's spirit of stronger regulation in this area, other countries have since also felt justified in introducing additional national policy measures that go beyond the recommendations of the convention itself. In 2000 Canada became the first country to introduce picture-based warning on tobacco packaging, a move again followed by other countries such as Australia, Belgium, Canada, Chile, Hong Kong, India, Jordan, New Zealand, Romania, Singapore, Switzerland, Thailand, the United Kingdom, Uruguay and Venezuela. In 2004 Ireland then became the first country to ban indoor smoking in all workplaces (including restaurants and bars), a move which several countries have again followed (including England, Estonia, France, Iran, Italy, Montenegro, the Netherlands, New Zealand, Norway, Scotland, Spain, Sweden and Venezuela) (GHW 2008: 356).

In order to provide further guidelines under the convention, the Conference of the Parties also met in Bangkok in July 2007. The conference recommended that parties to the convention should follow Ireland's precedent and ban all indoor workplace smoking within five years. The recommendations it issued also included developing; (1) a protocol to deal with the problem of the illicit trade in tobacco smuggling; (2) guidelines for eliminating tobacco advertising and promotion; (3) guidelines on monitoring the tobacco industry; and (4) research into tobacco product-testing standards, as well as finding economically viable alternatives to tobacco cultivation (FCTC 2007).

Despite these apparent successes, the framework convention also contains some limitations from the point of view of comprehensively addressing the health effects of tobacco consumption. It does not adequately address the issue of smokeless tobacco, which is not covered by the convention. That is a major omission, given that some studies have found that the rates of non-smoking tobacco use amongst adolescents, for example, are often as high as those of cigarette-smoking in many countries (Warren et al. 2006).

The treaty also has not been ratified by the United States, where it needs a two-thirds majority in the Senate to pass. The commitment of the United States government to the convention remains tenuous. Successive administrations in the United States have instead sought to use trade legislation to open up overseas markets, especially in Asia, to the export of American cigarettes (Chaloupka and Laixuthai 1996). Moreover, in the negotiations on the framework convention, the Bush administration sought to protect US cigarette manufacturers by opposing compulsory tobacco taxes, seeking as well to weaken several other provisions relating to advertising and second-hand smoke (Waxman 2002). The lack of greater support from one of the most important countries involved in the production and marketing of tobacco is a serious shortcoming, albeit one that the World Health Organization can do very little about.

A further limitation of the framework convention is that it contains no enforcement mechanisms other than relying on states to fulfill their obligations under the treaty. Beyond the public monitoring envisioned in the treaty, there are no penalties for countries who fail to implement the various aspects of the convention. Without additional protocols that toughen specific areas, the convention thus lacks teeth. This is compounded by a final and related problem, namely a lack of funding for implementing the measures demanded by the framework convention. Government representatives of many low-income countries claim that they lack both the expertise and financial resources to implement the convention properly. For this reason, low-income countries also pushed for a global fund to provide financial assistance, but this was rejected by the high-income countries in favour of more bi-lateral approaches (GHW 2008: 357).

These limitations notwithstanding, the swath of demand- and supply-side measures contained in the framework convention implies that, in order to meet the latter's ambitions in relation to reducing global smoking patterns, it will also be necessary to regulate and transform much wider aspects of society. Such measures will have to range from pursuing criminal activities such as smuggling, through to fundamental changes in how commercial and agricultural production are carried out in many countries. Of course, the wider regulation of society for the purposes of reducing the prevalence of disease is nothing new per se and has always been the ambition of 'social' medicine and public health. However, in targeting global smoking patterns, the framework convention adds yet another significant domain of social life to the list of issues that need to be realigned with medical norms regarding healthy living. The convention has also introduced stronger regulation to this effect.

What is more, these measures do not just target disease in the narrow sense. They aim to change wider lifestyle choices that are unhealthy in the sense that they too can eventually lead to disease. That, to be clear, is not to deny that such measures yield many important health benefits. Yet it is to show how the construal of smoking as a deeper and more pervasive threat to populations has again created a political environment that is conducive to extending the societal jurisdiction of medical professionals such as physicians and public health experts who are trying to curb smoking rates.

In the end, the extensive 'war' on 'the global tobacco crisis' waged since the 1990s by the World Health Organization and many other institutions thus emerges as another important manifestation of the medicalization of security. It is another of the sites in contemporary world politics where – for a complex set of different reasons – diseases are being articulated as a deeper and more pervasive threat to populations. From the medicalization perspective, that 'war' on smoking and tobacco similarly begins to construe insecurity implicitly as a medical problem caused by the onset and spread of disease. Once more, a significant effect of this medical redefinition of insecurity is that, beyond the public health benefits that the 'war' on tobacco yields, it also creates a wider social climate in which the societal jurisdiction of medical professionals expands further. It does so by opening up yet another domain of social life to stronger regulation in accordance with medical norms regarding healthy living. Smoking is not the only 'lifestyle' disease in relation to which that is happening today.

Drowning in Fat? The War on the Obesity Epidemic

A very similar pattern has been unfolding in relation to the problem of obesity. Obesity is usually understood as an abnormal or excessive accumulation of body fat at such levels that it presents significant risks to people's health. That renders the 'war' on obesity a war on excessive body fat. One does not need to look very far for examples of that 'war'. 'Obesity "equal to terror threat"' is the title of a news story reported by the internationally respected British Broadcasting Corporation in 2008 (BBC 2008). The article quotes a public health scholar who warns that 'the threat to our future health is just as significant as the current security threat'.

According to this view, obesity too is more than just an important public health issue; it is in fact a serious 'threat' to the welfare of the population, demanding urgent action. 'The government [of the United Kingdom] was quick to move for things like ID cards or 42–day detention without trial [after the London bombings in July 2005]', the expert insists, 'now it needs to show similar leadership in public health'. In practice, this would entail a more direct approach with less public consultation, larger warning labels on food, possible tax measures, and include new regulations that compel manufacturers to reduce the salt, fat and sugar contents of their products.

The BBC news story is representative of the many concerns that have been voiced by public health officials about rising obesity rates, not just in the United Kingdom but also in many other European and North American countries (see Gard and Wright 2005: 16–19). Though it would be tempting to dismiss such headlines as the mere hyperbole generated by media organizations bent on increasing their share of viewers and readers, such pronouncements go far beyond media outlets, emanating from senior levels of governments as well.

In the United States, the Surgeon General, Richard Carmon, has claimed that obesity was a bigger threat to the American population than terrorism, while the Secretary of State for Health and Human Services, Tommy Thompson, publicly called obesity a 'crisis' (Oliver 2006: 1). 'We consider this a major threat and will fight it', the Director of the National Institutes for Health echoed (Leonard 2004). Medical scholars similarly do not shy away from such designations, warning that in the United Kingdom obesity 'is out of control', that measures to stem this 'epidemic' are not working, and that it is 'time to wake up' because there is only a 'limited time to act' (Haslam, Sattar and Lean 2007: 1). By portraying obesity as a pervasive threat to society, such arguments too animate the redefinition of insecurity as something that is also brought about by the onset and spread of disease. Therefore they must also be considered further manifestations of the medicalization of security.

Why exactly are rising rates of obesity in many countries deemed a crisis and a source of insecurity? Obesity is perceived to be a threat to the population for at least two reasons. First, obesity generates premature mortality as individuals can die from the health complications it causes. Obesity is widely considered to represent a risk factor for several chronic and non-communicable conditions, including diabetes, cardiovascular disease (such as heart attacks and strokes), cancer (endometrial, breast and colon), some musculoskeletal disorders (such as osteoarthritis) and also some sleeping disorders (e.g. sleep apnoea) (McLannahan and Clifton 2008). Second, obesity is also thought to have a range of wider economic repercussions, not least for health care systems. The expert quoted above went on to speculate that obesity could literally 'overwhelm' the British National Health Service, with some predicting the doubling of people suffering from Type II diabetes by 2025. Others point out that obesity already costs the UK economy £3.5 billion every year and threatens to 'bankrupt the healthcare system' (Haslam, Sattar and Lean 2007: 2, 3).

How big a 'timebomb' is the obesity threat? According to influential estimates published by the head of the Centers for Disease Control and Prevention in the prestigious *Journal of the American Medical Association* in 2004, in the United States alone there are some 400,000 Americans dying because of obesity every year. 'Alarming' rising rates of obesity have also been found in the United Kingdom. The Health Survey of England – a survey conducted with a random sample of the population – found that, in 1993, 13.4 per cent of adult males and 17.8 per cent of adult females were obese, and 44.4 per cent of adult males and 32.2 per cent of adult females were overweight. The same survey carried out in 2005 showed substantial increases over the twelve-year period: 23.5 per cent of adult males and 24.8 per cent of adult females in England were obese; 43.4 per cent of adult males and 32.9 per cent of adult females were overweight (Crichton and Mulhall 2008: 100). These statistics show a sharp increase in obesity levels and make worrying reading indeed.

Yet some of the estimates of how many people are dying of obesity are based on science that is shakier than appears at first sight. For example, despite the US figures from the Center for Disease Control and Prevention (CDC) being widely circulated in policy reports and the public media at the time, subsequent analysis revealed that the data on which they were based was thirty years old, and that the estimates made fairly crude calculations that simply compared death rates amongst heavier persons with those who weighed less. Crucially, the calculations did not check to see whether the increased weight was a contributing factor in the cause of death. A congressional investigation was later held, and the CDC had to amend the report. Another study published the following year by different researchers at CDC then showed that people moderately 'overweight' actually live longer than those with a 'normal' weight. The study also found that, rather than 400,000 Americans dying because of obesity, the annual figure was actually closer to 26,000. That, incidentally, is less than the number of people dying as a result of being underweight (Oliver 2006: 3–4). Some obesity statistics are not as firmly grounded as they initially appear.

In part that is also due to the fact that overall levels of body fat in the population are usually tracked by a fairly crude measure – the Body Mass Index (BMI). The BMI is the most widely used anthropometric measure and is calculated by simply taking a person's weight (in kilogrammes or pounds) and dividing it by the square of the person's height (in feet or metres). Most human bodies fall somewhere within the index's spectrum, ranging from a BMI of around 15 (near starvation) to a BMI of over 40 (morbidly obese). A person with a BMI of 25 or more is today usually classified as being 'overweight', and those with a BMI of more than 30 are classified as being 'obese'. A person with a BMI under 18.5 is considered to be 'underweight'. The BMI thus is the key measure used to gauge the extent of today's obesity crisis.

Yet the BMI is an overly simplistic measure in at least three respects. First, in measuring the weight-to-height ratio, the BMI does not actually measure fat per se. It was never designed to fulfil that function. Tracing the historical origins of the BMI, as Eric Oliver (2006) has done, reveals why this is the case. The precursor to the BMI was first developed in the early nineteenth century by the Belgian astronomer, mathematician and sociologist Adolphe Quetelet, who was gathering data about French and Scottish army conscripts. Quetelet believed that mathematical laws governed not just the natural world but human societies as well. In order to prove his theory, he set out to detect mathematical and statistical regularities in a range of human phenomena. His measurements of heights and weights of the French and Scottish recruits formed an important part of this effort. It also means that the first application of this measure was to military populations.

Quetelet went on to plot the height and weight data along an axis, which generated a 'normal' weight distribution for each height (much like a bell curve). Playing with the numbers, Quetelet discovered that the weight of those toward the middle of the distribution curve (the 'normal') was exactly proportional to the square of their height – giving birth to the notion of the BMI, or the Quetelet Index as it was initially known. Quetelet had finally found the neat mathematical principle he was looking for, reaffirming his deeper conviction that human societies too were governed by neat mathematical relationships. Crucially, Quetelet then jumped to the conclusion that – because of this neat symmetry – that particular relationship between height and weight must also be the 'ideal' one. He therefore began to view those individuals who deviated from the statistical ideal as either 'underweight' or 'overweight' (Oliver 2006: 16–18). This means that the historical origins of the BMI actually have almost nothing to do with body fat per se.

Over a century later, the notion of the BMI was then picked up by the insurance industry. The latter was looking for a simple and reliable proxy measure to help it predict who would die early. Actuaries thus wanted to know the precise extent to which increased weight also elevated the probability of an early death, as that knowledge would allow them to set life insurance premiums more accurately. In the 1940s a statistician working for the Metropolitan Life Insurance

Company thus began to chart the death rates of its policy-holders using Quetelet's height-to-weight index. He found that those people who lived longest were those whose weight was closest to that of an average person of the age of twenty-five. Those tables, which had been developed for insurance purposes, subsequently became widely used by the government and health professionals for analysing the health of populations (Bray 2001).

Although the BMI remains the key measure used to gauge levels of obesity amongst individuals and populations today, it does not actually directly measure body fat per se. This can lead to a situation in which people with the same BMI are actually quite different in terms of their physical composition. Not only does the measure not work well at extremes of height (such as very short people or very tall people), but it is possible that a bodybuilder could have the same BMI as a sedentary or obese individual, because developed muscle can substantially contribute to a person's overall weight. Technically, many professional athletes are thus obese according to the BMI, even though they do not have large amounts of body fat. For that reason, the BMI only works well as an obesity measure in populations that are mostly sedentary. That is one limitation of the measure.

The history of the BMI is also directly implicated in a second of its shortcomings. There is nothing inherent in the BMI as a statistical indicator to tell us at what level we should think of people as being 'overweight' or 'obese'. There is no a-priori reason why the neat mathematical symmetry detected by Quetelet should be related to the health effects of accumulating body fact. Anthropologists note how evaluations about what weight and body shape are desirable have fluctuated over time and between cultures (Brown and Konner 1987). Setting the levels for what weight should be considered 'excessive' is not an exact science. In the United States, for instance, there was considerable controversy when a report by the National Institutes of Health recommended that the threshold for being overweight should be set at a lower BMI of 25, and for being obese at a lower BMI of 30 or more (the same level as that used by the World Health Organization). Simply changing the range of these categories not only 'produced' 37 million overweight Americans overnight, it also was something pushed for by the International Obesity Task Force in 1995 – an organization substantially funded by companies such as Hoffman-La Roche and Abbott Laboratories who produce weight-loss drugs such as Xenical and Meridia (Oliver 2006: 22, 29).

A final problem with the BMI is that, conversely, it may also create a false sense of being healthy in people with a bodyweight otherwise classified as 'normal' under the BMI categories. Yet there is some evidence to suggest that negative health effects can also emerge at BMI levels below 25 (Gill 2005: 431). The BMI can thus encourage a mistaken sense of being healthy when people begin to equate lack of excess body fat with a healthy body, which is often not the case. There are, for instance, many 'thin' people who never exercise or who consume many unhealthy foods. They believe that they are healthy simply because they are not fat, even though many medical professionals would disagree with that conclusion. All of these factors reveal the core measure used to gauge the obesity 'crisis' in most populations to be fairly crude.

Other measures for establishing the extent of the obesity 'crisis' have been developed in response to these problems. A different measure, for example, uses hip circumference ratios instead, which are designed to measure how much fat is carried around the stomach rather than the hips and thighs. That is because stomach fat is thought to pose the greatest health risk. It is a more precise measure of body fat than the BMI, but can easily generate measurement errors if not carried out carefully in practice. Another measure that has been developed is the percentage of a person's overall weight made up of body fat, which is called 'densitometry'. According to that measure, men are defined as obese if more than 25 per cent of their body weight is fat, and women if more than 30 per cent of their bodyweight is made up of fat. A person's percentage of body fat can in turn be measured either through underwater weighing or through skin fold testing. However, both of these alternative measures are more complicated and costly to assess, and therefore not as readily usable as the BMI, which only relies upon the accurate measurement of weight and height (Cedar 2008: 42).

The BMI thus remains the most widely used measure for tracking the obesity 'crisis', if only for the sake of cost and convenience, and despite its considerable limitations. Using those BMI ranges, the latest available figures compiled by the World Health Organization estimate that there are approximately 1.6 billion overweight adults (over the age of fifteen) in the world, and that there are more than 400 million obese adults. There were also 20 million overweight children in 2005. At the aggregate population level, obesity rates range internationally from below 5 per cent in China, Japan and some African nations, to over 75 per cent in urban Samoa (Pacific Island Group). But even in relatively low-prevalence countries like China, rates are approaching 20 per cent in some cities. Generally speaking, adult mean BMI levels of 22–3 kg/m2 predominate in Africa and Asia. Higher levels of 25–7 kg/m2 are prevalent across Europe and North America. Again, the World Health Organization anticipated a bleak future, projecting that by 2015 these figures would rise to 2.3 billion overweight adults, and to 700 million obese adults (WHO 2006). These estimates are sufficiently high to compel the World Health Organization to regard obesity not just as an important public health issue, but as a deeper crisis.

As in the case of smoking, moreover, that obesity 'crisis' is not confined to the affluent societies of the West. According to the World Health Organization, obesity is becoming a global crisis because obesity levels are rising in many developing countries as well, particularly in urban areas. That can generate the paradoxical situation in which some developing countries simultaneously experience a double burden, with over-nutrition and under-nutrition co-existing side by side. As Roy Smith has shown, examples of this phenomenon can be found in the Marshall Islands, where there are growing signs of obesity amongst some population groups (Smith 2003). The Marshall Islands have a population of around 65,000 people scattered across a number of islands and coral atolls (Smith 2003: 87). A nutrition survey carried out there in 1991 showed that older Marshallese people had increased incidence of obesity, with its associated problems of diabetes, hypertension, cardiac problems and so forth (Smith 2003: 88).

Beyond enabling the World Health Organization to consider obesity a global crisis, cases like the Marshall Islands also show just how complex the problem of accumulating excessive body fat is. For instance, interviews carried out there revealed that, within these societies, obesity was not viewed as a sign of health. Neither were the inhabitants uneducated about health. Nor did genetic factors appear to play a significant role. Rather, Smith found that there were a range of larger structural forces at play (Smith 2003: 90–6). Key drivers behind the accumulation of body fat in the Marshall Islands included low income, which meant that people could only afford to purchase cheap food, such as polished white rice or white bread, low-grade and fatty meats, foods high in fat such as chips, and sugary drinks. 'Healthier' foods such as fruit and vegetables tended to be imported there, and because of that were both perishable and often more expensive (Smith 2003: 97). Urbanization was another factor, meaning that there was no possibility of low-income populations supplementing those foods with locally grown produce. That urban environment also produced stress for people exposed to economic insecurity and cramped housing conditions, which for some was also a reason to find an outlet for their dissatisfaction in the consumption of food (Smith 2003: 97–8).

The promotion of imported foods was yet another important factor driving rising rates of obesity in the Marshall Islands. Many sugary and fatty foods were introduced to the island during the American military presence there, as a way of catering for the tastes of the US military, but the local population also began to acquire a taste for these goods. Food aid delivered by the Americans, which did not contain local foods, may also have played a role in changing nutritional preferences (Smith 2003: 100). Over the past decades, the diet on the islands has thus changed in a way that has encouraged increased levels of body fat.

At the micro-level, the case of the Marshall Islands thus illustrates very well the underlying complexity of the obesity problem, and in a way that is not always acknowledged by the World Health Organization. According to the latter, obesity is primarily the result of a simple caloric imbalance that arises when the amount of calories consumed exceeds those that are expended. The World Health Organization singles out two factors in particular: (1) a global shift toward consuming more energy-dense foods with high sugar and fat contents; and (2) decreased levels of physical activity associated with urbanization, new forms of transport and the sedentary nature of work (WHO 2006). The simplicity of that definition risks obscuring as much as it explains. In fact, obesity is a much more complex phenomenon, with researchers now turning their attention to a range of possible factors behind rising rates of obesity.

In countries such as the United States, an important factor being analysed is the growing proportion of food consumed away from home, with a higher percentage of the food budget spent on such food since the late 1990s. In part this is due to the rise in the number of two-income households, where both parents work on a daily basis. In the United States there are also more than 170,000 fast-food restaurants, and 3 million soft-drink vending machines (Chopra and Darnton-Hill 2004: 1558). Many of these fast food restaurants, in turn, offer large portion sizes, and deploy strategies for encouraging consumers to choose larger and more expensive serving sizes. Several of these companies have since also urged Congress to pass the Personal Responsibility in Food Consumption Act (known affectionately as the 'Cheeseburger bill'), which would protect them against future lawsuits. So far the bill has been passed twice by the House of Representatives, but has failed to become law due to not receiving Senate approval.

Other researchers have focused on the underlying economic factors that are at play in the rise of obesity rates, such as the general lowering in the cost of food in many North American and European countries. Some research has also been devoted to ascertaining whether agricultural subsidies, such as those going, for example, to the production of sugar and corn syrup in the United States, play a role – although the evidence remains disputed (Alston et al. 2008). Trade liberalization in turn has helped the formation of transnational food corporations and has also had effects on people's diets (Hawkes 2006), and has allowed food prices to drop. For example, innovations in intensive livestock production allow meats (such as chicken) to be produced faster and cheaper. Since the 1960s, the time needed to raise a broiler chicken has halved, from eighty-four days to between forty and fifty (Lee 2003: 114).

Technological innovations in the home are also attracting the attention of researchers – to ascertain, for example, how the invention of the microwave has affected the number of convenience foods and ready-meals purchased and consumed. The television set is yet another widely postulated 'culprit' in the rise of obesity (Gortmaker et al. 1996; Blass et al. 2006). The proliferation of television has also allowed food advertising to target children – most restrictions on which being abolished in the United States by the Reagan administration in the 1980s. That has spurred further debate about the role of such advertising in rising rates of obesity (Story and French 2004). Finally, the increased use of automated transport, especially the car, is also widely thought to be another technological factor contributing to an energy imbalance, along with the changing patterns of physically less demanding work in many developed economies, which encourage less 'burning' of calories.

Although the exact extent and drivers of the obesity crisis thus remain to be established, the growing concern surrounding obesity has already enabled a plethora of national and international public health institutions to adopt a strategy of pre-emption and to try defusing the 'timebomb' before it is too late. Here too the alarm surrounding rising rates of obesity has created a political environment amenable to increasing the societal jurisdiction of a range of medical and health professionals. Their expertise is now also required to shape behaviours related to dietary choice and patterns of physical exercise – things which used to be seen as essentially private matters.

Increasingly, these additional aspects of social life are therefore also becoming subjected to much more concerted efforts to realign them with medical norms regarding healthy living. Indeed, medical experts are now being actively invited by governments to draw up a range of possible interventions which will influence the lifestyle choices and consumption patters of individuals in a way that is conducive to reducing the prevalence of obesity amongst the world's populations. Again, this is not to dispute the possible health benefits of such interventions, but it shows how the construal of obesity as a deeper threat to the population also opens yet another domain of social life to more intensive forms of regulation.

Analysts examining the consumption behaviour of individuals find that food choices consist of a complex array of factors. These include the taste of the food, economic considerations around the price of the food, the convenience of obtaining it, its health aspects, and also considerations of variety. Many public health interventions

that are being explored therefore try to target one of these variables. For instance, some interventions simply consist of providing
more information about the health aspects of various foods. Others
look at pricing mechanisms and so forth. Much in this vein, the
World Health Organization, together with the Food and Agriculture
Organization of the United Nations, also led an international expert
consultation on diet and nutrition. That consultation culminated in
the World Health Organization's Global Strategy on Diet, Physical
Activity and Health, which was endorsed by the World Health
Assembly in May 2004.

The strategy's overall goal is 'to promote and protect health by
guiding the development of an enabling environment for sustainable
actions at individual, community, national and global levels that,
when taken together, will lead to reduced disease and death rates
related to unhealthy diet and physical inactivity' (WHO 2004c: 3).
In short, the strategy wishes to realign not only the eating behaviour
of individuals around the world in accordance with healthy norms,
but also patterns and levels of physical exercise, in order to restore an
energy balance. As in the case of smoking, defusing the obesity timebomb will require behavioural change, and will again require people
to turn toward the medical professions for guidance on the optimal
way of configuring their diets and eating habits.

The WHO strategy thus wishes to encourage a wholesale mobilization of society around that quest, and makes a long series of recommendations to that effect. Beginning with individuals themselves, the
strategy urges them to maintain a healthy weight by limiting their
intake of salt, sugar and fat (especially saturated fats and trans-fatty
acids), whilst increasing their consumption of fruits, vegetables,
grains, nuts and legumes (WHO 2004c: 4). Governments, in turn, are
asked to improve the surveillance of non-communicable diseases and
to draw up national strategies that include guidelines about nutrition and physical exercise. Governments are also urged to make balanced nutritional information more widely available, to discourage
the advertisement of unhealthy foods, and to consider introducing
food labelling mechanisms that provide more accurate information
to consumers as well as addressing misleading claims that some food
manufacturers make about the health properties of their products.

The strategy further urges governments to consider measures for reducing the use of salt, hydrogenated oils, and sugar in foods and beverages, including the use of taxation measures, subsidies and agricultural policies to encourage healthier diets. Such potential taxation measures have proved particularly controversial because of the difficulties in differentiating between healthy and unhealthy foods, and concerns that the lowest-income groups may end up paying the majority of the tax burden. Finally, governments are also asked to intervene on the physical activity side of the equation. They should develop policies that provide incentives for walking, cycling and other non-motorized forms of transport, as well as issuing clear messages about the health benefits of regular physical activity.

The WHO strategy would not be complete without also reaching out to the private sector, to see how it too can support the war on obesity – especially the transnational food industry. In 2005 the world's largest packaged-food manufacturers were Nestlé (Switzerland), Kraft (USA), Unilever (UK/Netherlands), PepsiCo (USA) and Danone (France). In turn the largest retailers by sales in 2006 were Wal-Mart (USA), Carrefour (France), Tesco (UK), Metro Group (Germany) and Kroger (USA) (GHW 2008: 132). These companies will need to be brought on-board if the strategy is to be successful. The strategy recommends that the food industry too should promote healthy diets in accordance with national guidelines, and that it should limit the levels of saturated fats, trans-fatty acids, free sugars and salts contained in foods. It should also make healthy foods more available at affordable prices, and provide consumers with more nutritional information.

Food manufacturers and retailers are not the only elements of the private sector that are relevant here. That list of commercial actors must also include the media and advertisers, employers, insurance companies, pharmaceutical companies, sporting-goods manufacturers and so forth. The strategy therefore makes recommendations for these groups as well. Employers, to cite but one example, are asked to ensure that workers have healthy choices available whilst in the workplace. All key actors within society are thus urged to come together in the war on obesity and to push those healthier norms deeper into societies around the world.

Yet, despite the harmonious picture of social mobilization painted by the strategy in terms of a coordinated multi-sector response, the realities on the ground have turned out to be quite different. In light of the substantial commercial interests at stake in this sector as well, it is perhaps not surprising that – as in the prior case of tobacco regulation – elements of the food industry too have proved resistant to international attempts at greater regulation. In the United States, for instance, the sugar growers represent a powerful constituency in the state of Florida, as well as in other key southern states where sugar cane is cultivated. When a World Health Organization study from 2003 suggested that sugar additives should represent no more than 10 per cent of a person's daily caloric intake, the sugar industry quickly mobilized and threatened to lobby Congress to hold back US funding for the World Health Organization as a way of compelling the latter to cease promoting the report (Hagmann 2003). The sugar industry argued that the conclusions were insufficiently grounded in scientific evidence, and that the selection of experts had been biased. They have every reason to cast doubt, because if the recommendation were to be lowered to 10 per cent, rather than the 25 five per cent more common in many countries today, it would come as a considerable shock to the demand for sugar.

In fact the food industry has tried countering these calls for more regulation through a variety of arguments. Representatives of the food industry often counter that, strictly speaking, there is no such thing as an unhealthy food, only an unhealthy diet (see also Feldman and Marks 2006). This shifts the responsibility for obesity from the food producers to the individual consumer, who is seen to be making unhealthy choices in their consumption of food. The food industry also tried to shift the blame for obesity to the other side of the obesity equation – the lack of physical exercise. The real blame for the rise in obesity rates lies in the decrease in the amount of physical exercise that is undertaken, so they argue. Of course, both of those arguments are strongly disputed by those campaigning for greater regulation.

Overall, the World Health Organization has thus been less successful in regulating the international food industry than it was in achieving consensus on minimum standards of tobacco regulation. Yet that does not detract from the underlying fact that – much like tobacco before it – obesity too has become an issue of heightened and urgent concern for many governments and public health advocates. As in the case of tobacco, moreover, the reasons for that change in perceptions are multiple and complex; and, as in the case of tobacco, the social effects of that elevation of obesity to a more serious threat to populations are essentially the same. The 'war' on obesity too encourages a partial redefinition of insecurity as something brought about by the onset of disease. It has similarly facilitated an expansion in the societal jurisdiction of medical professionals in that they are now called upon also to guide citizens in their choice of food, nourishment and levels of physical activity. Thus, the 'rise of obesity' crisis identifies yet further domains of social life – our consumption of food and levels of physical activity – that need to be controlled more closely and in accordance with what medical professionals determine to be healthy norms.

Going against the Grain: Curbing Excessive Alcohol Consumption and Binge Drinking

Warnings have also been issued more recently in relation to international levels of alcohol consumption – albeit so far to a comparatively lesser extent. Alcohol has been produced and consumed for thousands of years, and has historically even been used as a medicine (Anderson and Baumberg 2006: 1). Throughout that history, laws pertaining to alcohol have been designed and passed, often motivated by considerations of public order and market regulation. But it was not until the nineteenth century, after industrialization and the advent of highly distilled drinks, that 'alcoholism' emerged as a 'disease' and that laws and regulations were also drafted with a public health rationale (Anderson and Baumberg 2006: 1).

That quest to address alcohol abuse was revitalized in January 2008. At that point the World Health Organization's executive board agreed a plan to launch a global strategy to combat the damage inflicted by alcohol. It also considered launching a wider 'global war on alcohol' (Coghlan 2008). Ministers at national levels have since echoed that call, insisting that 'now is the time for action to defuse

the health time-bomb alcohol misuse is storing up for the future'
(Sturgeon 2008).

Why is alcohol consumption too becoming increasingly construed
as a 'crisis' that demands closer surveillance – much like smoking
and obesity? The reasons are essentially the same as in the case of
obesity. First, there is again the mortality caused by excessive alcohol
consumption. The World Health Organization estimates that, of
the 2 billion people who consume alcoholic beverages in the world,
around 76 million people are diagnosed with alcohol use disorders
(WHO 2004d: 1). It further estimates that around 1.8 million lives are
lost annually due to alcohol. Alcohol consumption is associated with
more than sixty different diseases and injuries – including cancers of
the oesophagus and liver, cirrhosis of the liver, automobile accidents
and even murders (WHO 2004d: 1).

The ill-health effects of alcohol are complex and, crucially, depend
not just on the average volume consumed, but also on the underlying
patterns of drinking. Moreover, the biochemical effects of alcohol
can also be beneficial, in that moderate alcohol consumption can, for
example, protect against the formation of blood clots. But alcohol
consumption can also have adverse effects for health, for example
when it triggers pancreatic damage. If the pattern of drinking is such
that it leads to intoxication, this can also lead to accidents, intentional
injury (including domestic violence) and death. Moreover, when the
pattern of consumption is indicative of alcohol dependence, this can
lead to a variety of further chronic conditions (WHO 2004d: 35–6).

There are also wider economic costs associated with alcohol consumption, although these have so far proved much more difficult to
quantify. Only a few studies have been conducted. Those that have
been carried out so far have used a variety of methods, so cannot be
compared directly with one another. Such studies indicate that the
social and economic costs of alcohol abuse in several Western countries range between an estimated 1 and 6 per cent of Gross Domestic
Product (GDP) (WHO 2004d: 66). Alcohol is argued to have a negative impact on labour and productivity, as well as generating costs
related to health care, health insurance, law enforcement and workplaces (EC 2006: 6).

A report by the European Commission entitled *Alcohol in Europe:*

A Public Health Perspective (Anderson and Baumberg 2006: v) estimates that alcohol-attributable diseases, injuries and violence cost the
health, welfare, employment and criminal justice sectors €125 billion
(€79–220 billion) per year in the European Union. That is equivalent
to 1.3 per cent of GDP. The report also found that harmful alcohol
consumption reduces the competitiveness of European business by
lowering productivity (Anderson and Baumberg 2006: 2). What is
more, with an estimated 23 million Europeans being dependent on
alcohol in any one year:

> Seven million adults report being in fights when drinking over the
> past year and (based on a review of a small number of national
> costing studies) the economic cost of alcohol-attributable crime
> has been estimated to be €33bn in the EU for 2003. This cost is
> split between police, courts and prisons (€15bn), crime prevention
> expenditure and insurance administration (€12bn) and property
> damage (€6bn). Property damage due to drink-driving has also
> been estimated at €10bn, while the intangible cost of the physical
> and psychological effects of crime has been valued at €9bn–€37bn.
> (Anderson and Baumberg 2006: 5)

As with the earlier case of tobacco, there is of course also an economic contribution from the alcohol industry. In the EU15 countries
(Austria, Belgium, Denmark, France, Finland, Germany, Greece,
Ireland, Italy, Luxembourg, Netherlands, Portugal, Spain, Sweden
and the United Kingdom), the alcohol trade generated €25 billion in
tax revenue in 2001 alone, and that is excluding sales tax and other
taxes within the supply chain (Anderson and Baumberg 2006: 2).
It also provides more than 750,000 jobs in drinks production, plus
further jobs in pubs, restaurants, shops and so forth (Anderson and
Baumberg 2006: 2). Nevertheless, arguments about the wider economic costs of alcohol consumption have similarly driven the construal of use of alcohol as a deeper crisis afflicting societies.

  In terms of geographic extent, this 'crisis' appears to have a strong
European dimension. Data about levels of alcohol consumption
around the world are gathered by the World Health Organization
– even at the level of particular types of beverages. Those data show
that in 2004, for example, the five countries with the highest adult
per capita consumption of beer in the world are the Czech Republic,

Ireland, Swaziland, Germany and Austria. Turning to wine, they were Luxembourg, France, Portugal, Italy and Croatia; and in terms of the spirits, the five countries with the highest adult per capita consumption in the world were the Republic of Moldova, Réunion, the Russian Federation, Saint Lucia and Dominica (WHO 2004d: 13).

Although problems with excessive alcohol consumption clearly exist in other countries as well, Europe thus remains the heaviest drinking region in the world today, with an estimated 11 litres of pure alcohol drunk per adult per year (Anderson and Baumberg 2006: 2). Yet the issue of alcohol again also takes on a more global dimension when focusing specifically on the problem of alcohol dependence. Rates of alcohol dependence range from around 5 per cent of the population or less in countries such as Argentina, Colombia, Japan, the Netherlands, Slovakia and the United Kingdom, to around 10 per cent of the population or more in Brazil, Peru and Poland (WHO 2004d: 30).

As in the case of smoking and obesity, the anxieties surrounding rising rates of alcohol consumption have widened the societal jurisdiction of the medical professions through the drafting of new policies aimed at influencing the rate at which people consume alcoholic beverages, as well as the manner in which they consume them. So far, public health experts have come up with several ways of addressing the issue. There are policies aimed at the population as a whole. These policies use regulatory mechanisms to govern more closely the sale and consumption of alcohol (such as number of stores selling alcohol, minimum drinking ages), public health campaigns and taxation measures. Other policies focus on specific behaviours related to alcohol consumption, such as drink-driving. Some interventions also target affected individuals directly through the primary health care system (Anderson 2004).

To date, however, the World Health Organization has encountered protracted difficulties in showing leadership when it comes to alcohol consumption. In part this is due to the fact that there is insufficient funding for their programme, especially a lack of continuous contributions coming from the regular budget. Moreover, alcohol producers have been accused of protecting their considerable commercial interests by attempting to influence national and international alcohol policy through setting up wider, industry-funded 'social aspects' organizations – such as the Amsterdam Group and the International Centre on Alcohol Policy (Anderson 2003). The World Health Organization is nevertheless in the process of developing a draft global strategy on reducing the harmful use of alcohol for 2010.

The difficulties they will encounter in establishing and implementing such a strategy may well be foreshadowed by similar efforts already undertaken in recent years by the European Commission. It released its 'EU strategy to support Member States in reducing alcohol related harm' (EC 2006) in 2006. The need for action is again justified by reference to both the health effects of harmful alcohol consumption, and the related social and economic consequences (EC 2006: 4). In terms of the health consequences, the strategy points out that studies show alcohol is the net cause of 7.4 per cent of all ill-health and early death in the European Union (EC 2006: 6). There are also links drawn to road accidents – with estimates of 10,000 people being killed by alcohol-related road accidents every year in the European Union – as well as to the long-term effects of 'binge-drinking' amongst young people, and excessive consumption of alcohol during pregnancy (EC 2006: 7).

In a way that reveals just how carefully politicians are treading in these waters, the European strategy goes out of its way to make clear that it is not opposed to alcohol consumption as such. It is principally concerned with misuse and its harmful consequences, particularly 'preventing and cutting back heavy and extreme drinking patterns, as well as under-age drinking, and some of their most harmful consequences such as alcohol-related road accidents and Foetal Alcohol Syndrome' (EC 2006: 4). The strategy also makes it clear that it is not even seeking a European harmonization of legislation in this field. Instead it will defer to national policies of member states. Mindful of those caveats, the European strategy ended up focusing on several key themes intended to align patterns of alcohol consumption along more healthy norms.

First, the European strategy aims to protect young people and children by curbing under-age drinking, and reducing the harm to children growing up in families suffering from alcohol-related problems.

That protection will also need to extend to the unborn child by reducing exposure of unborn children to alcohol during pregnancy. Second, the strategy seeks to reduce injuries and death from alcohol-related road accidents by focusing particularly on the age group of eighteen to twenty-four. In this age group, 35 to 45 per cent of fatalities are due to traffic accidents (EC 2006: 9).

The strategy further emphasizes preventing alcohol-related harm among adults and reducing the negative impact on the workplace by tackling alcohol-related chronic disorders, promoting workplace-related measures and providing better information to consumers. The strategy also encourages greater efforts to inform, educate and raise awareness on the impact of harmful and hazardous alcohol consumption and on appropriate consumption patterns, by educating EU citizens about the impact of alcohol on health, on the fetus, on under-age drinkers and on driving performance. Finally, the European Strategy hopes to develop and maintain a common evidence base at EU level that generates comparable information on alcohol consumption, on standard definitions of harmful alcohol consumption, on drinking patterns and so forth. That should put the European Union in a better position to evaluate the effectiveness of policies addressing these issues.

These are ambitious goals. Yet one cannot fail to notice that, in terms of the concrete measures proposed by the Commission, the strategy is actually rather weak. In the end, the European strategy is really much more about identifying a problem than about taking concerted action at this stage. Part of the reason for this was, again, an aggressive lobbying campaign which led to the dilution of earlier versions of the strategy which called for stronger action. The Institute of Alcohol Studies, which was tasked with providing the evidence base for this strategy, faced a sustained lobbying campaign by the industry for two years. This campaign culminated in the Commission agreeing to undertake an unprecedented peer-review of the report, with the industry nominating half of the scientists to be invited to review it (Baumberg and Anderson 2007: 1). When the reviewers then found that the report was comprehensive and accurate, Brewers of Europe paid for another report to be undertaken (Baumberg and Anderson 2007: 1–2).

Nevertheless, a growing problematization of the 'crisis' of alcohol consumption and binge drinking is now emerging. Increasingly, it looks as though many countries will, in the years ahead, be waging a 'war' on alcoholism as well. If they do, then this will become yet another area of world politics where insecurity is being implicitly construed as something caused by the onset of disease. In that case, this 'war' will probably also lead to a further augmentation in the societal jurisdiction of medical professionals, as patterns of alcohol consumption too become aligned more closely with norms regarding what constitutes a healthy lifestyle. Such a 'war' on alcohol, in short, would emerge as yet another manifestation of the medicalization of security.

Conclusion

Stark warnings issued about the threat posed by smoking, obesity and alcohol all too easily fail to be identified as a contemporary manifestation of the medicalization of security. It is true that, unlike the previous three case studies, these discussions do not explicitly identify their areas of concern as security threats. Yet they frequently mobilize the language and metaphors of security in order to construe those phenomena as threatening 'crises' and 'timebombs'. That use of security language elevates the significance of so-called 'lifestyle' diseases beyond the realm of routine public health concerns. These are also becoming perceived as deeper and more serious threats to the population. In suggesting that some of the gravest threats to the population emanate today from the phenomena of smoking, obesity and alcohol abuse, these discussions similarly begin subtly to redefine our understanding of insecurity as a medical problem caused by the spread of disease within the population. Therefore, these policy debates too must be considered as contemporary instances of the medicalization of security.

Ironically, such arguments about the threat posed by lifestyle conditions rest themselves upon a prior and even deeper process of medicalization, in which complex social phenomena like smoking, obesity and alcoholism first become construed as 'diseases'. These phenomena are not classical diseases in the sense that they do not constitute a direct disturbance, dysfunction or abnormality in the function of cells, tissues and organs. Thus they are considered 'diseases' metaphorically by virtue of the fact that they can cause death and disease. Yet, strictly speaking, that does not actually make them a disease any more than say traffic accidents, which also cause significant levels of morbidity and mortality around the world every year. In the cases of smoking, obesity and alcoholism, the medicalization of security thus rests on not a singular, but what is in fact a double, process of medicalization.

Precisely that 'double' medicalization also decisively widens the societal jurisdiction of the health professionals and renders these policy debates the most radical attempts yet to medicalize security. It pushes the logic of medicalization beyond the direct medical treatment of diseases within the human body, and extends it into the broader social realm by also allowing an array of medical professionals to reshape the lifestyle choices and behaviours of citizens in accordance with healthier norms. Being allowed – and indeed being invited – to readjust behaviours that increase the risk of acquiring disease in the future, opens up whole new areas of social life to the jurisdiction of the medical professions. Today, medical professionals no longer restrict themselves to 'fixing' bodies, but also actively encourage us to live more 'healthy' lives. They not only treat those people who are already ill, but also begin to treat those who may become ill. That ultimately renders the alarm expressed about a range of contemporary lifestyle 'diseases' one of the most radical attempts yet to medicalize the practice of security in contemporary world politics – even if it remains the most difficult one to detect and unearth.

6

Bodies as Battlefields: Medicalization and the Future of Health Security

At the outset of the new millennium deliberations about health security are not just changing the way particular diseases are governed in international relations. These discussions are also beginning subtly to medicalize the practice of security in contemporary world politics. Evaluating the wider ramifications of the rise of health security will therefore require that we look beyond the kinds of issues already identified by the 'securitization of health' perspective. There the focus has been on ascertaining whether the security framing of a range of international health issues is helpful for attempts to manage those diseases within the international system, or whether it is counter-productive and may ultimately even detract from such efforts. That question remains pertinent, to be sure. It must not, however, obscure the wider social and political effects engendered by the medicalization of security. The other side of the health–security equation matters just as much.

Thus we also need to discern how the practice of security changes when it becomes infused with the logic of medicalization. How, in other words, does the rise of health security transform the underlying security compact between the individual and the state? How, furthermore, does the medicalization of security compel governments to secure their populations differently? Today the medicalization of security is ultimately demanding of citizens that, in order to be secure, they must also allow security to be practised through their bodies. The provision of that security further requires of governments that they undertake a broad range of diverse medical functions in relation to their populations. Neither of these changes, in turn, will be accomplished without first subjecting populations to much more intensive and wider forms of medical surveillance.

From Battlefields to Bodies: Somatic Security and the Human Organism

One upshot of the medicalization of security is that the provision of security increasingly functions through intervening medically in the human organism. Security becomes somatic. Health security thus extends the range of sites and locations where security is practised in international relations. It takes the provision of security beyond the battlefield and brings it to bear directly on the individual human body as well. Or, to put it more succinctly, with the rise of health security the body becomes the new battlefield of the twenty-first century.

Peter Conrad (2007: 152–3) notes how in medicalization processes 'the focus on the individual has reinforced the proclivity of treating complex social problems with technological fixes (e.g., a medical, surgical, or pharmaceutical intervention), rather than by changing the social structure'. That is also true with regard to the medicalization of security. Here security becomes practised through the use of medical interventions introduced into the human body, rather than through the traditional means of foreign policy, diplomacy or military deployments – and often at the expense of addressing some of the wider social and economic forces at play in a range of contemporary insecurities. That shift toward practising security by intervening in the human organism is evident in all of the four cases that were analysed.

The first case study of pandemic preparedness is exemplary in this regard. Most of the health security debates about pandemic preparedness have focused on technological or medical interventions that are applied at the level of the individual body. This has taken the shape, for instance, of developing new vaccines, which the World Health Organization still considers as the most important medical intervention against human influenza pandemics. One of the first responses to the outbreak of the new pandemic H1N1 influenza virus in 2009 was thus immediately to start an international race to develop a new vaccine.

In the case of H5N1, which has not yet taken pandemic form, such a vaccine cannot be produced in advance. This is because influenza vaccines have to be strain-specific and no one can predict exactly what form a new pandemic H5N1 human influenza virus would take. That, however, has not stopped countries from prophylactically acquiring 'pre-pandemic' vaccines. Such pre-pandemic vaccines are based on a currently circulating strand of the H5N1 avian influenza virus. They will, therefore, not be an exact match to a future virus with more sustained human-to-human transmission characteristics. Yet they are likely to be close enough to offer the population at least some increased protection against such a virus. In the event of a new H5N1 pandemic, the exact level of protection would then depend on how far apart the future and current strains of H5N1 are in terms of their genetic make-up.

Not to be caught off guard, countries with the requisite resources have in the meantime also been quietly signing advance purchase orders with pharmaceutical companies to secure access to the first supplies of virus-specific H5N1 vaccines in the event of a pandemic. The UK government alone has set order levels for such a vaccine to cover the entire UK population (Batty 2007). Not surprisingly, significant international political battles have emerged around the procurement of these medicines, as developing countries fear they will not have access to such interventions in the case of a new outbreak.

Even where vaccines have not been available, governments have been able to turn toward other kinds of pharmacological interventions instead. For example, they have acquired stockpiles of anti-viral medications such as Tamiflu and Relenza. Although not a cure, Tamiflu could (if rolled out rapidly) reduce symptoms and the length of infection, and thus also reduce the impact of any future pandemic. The United States aims to maintain a stockpile of 81 million anti-viral drug regimens (HHS 2008: 1). In the United Kingdom, stockpiles for Tamiflu have been set at a level covering half of the UK population. Beyond anti-virals, these governments are also stockpiling millions of courses of antibiotics to treat complications that might arise from the pandemic, as well as respirators and face masks (Batty 2007). In retrospect, these stockpiles have also proved useful in the case of the pandemic influenza H1N1 2009 virus which initially proved susceptible to Tamiflu, although resistant strains began to emerge as early as the summer of 2009.

Whilst certainly understandable, this intensive focus on medical interventions contains a problematic aspect as well. It means that pandemic preparedness debates rarely interrogate or address a range of wider global developments that are contributing to the increased threat of an influenza pandemic. Such structural factors too play an important role, even if they are considerably more difficult to address. For example, Mike Davis argues passionately that, when it comes to the threat of a human H5N1 pandemic, the primary culprit is not so much the influenza virus itself, but the 'destiny' that mankind has forced upon the virus through 'overseas tourism, wetland destruction, a corporate "Livestock Revolution", and Third World urbanization with the attendant growth of megaslums'. To cite but one example, changes in food and agricultural production have led to unprecedented levels of livestock concentration, and the location of such 'megafarms' close to densely populated human dwellings, as in Hong Kong, creates nodes between the circulation of humans and birds that viruses can exploit in terms of jumping the species barrier (Davis 2005: 8). 'The essence of the avian flu threat', Davis (2005: 8) thus argues, 'is that mutant influenza of nightmarish virulence – evolved and now entrenched in ecological niches created by global agro-capitalism – is searching for a new gene or two that will enable it to travel at pandemic velocity through a densely urbanized and mostly poor humanity'.

Reading between the lines, the threat of a human H5N1 pandemic results from a capitalist world economy and the international circulation of tourists, labour, food products, livestock and capital that it encourages. To this list he adds a healthy dose of corporate greed and the corruption of political elites. Indeed, Davis (2005: 97–101) traces the clandestine involvement of the Bangkok-based company Charoen Pokphand (Asia's largest agricultural export conglomerate) in US politics, including its ties with the Democratic Party (to which it made an illegal US$250,000 donation in 1996), as well as the Bush family and the Carlyle Group in the United States.

Irrespective of whether we agree with Davis's account (and some would certainly question the emphasis on structural factors given the longer history of such pandemics occurring, as well as the role of wild birds in the spread of the virus), the more fundamental point still applies: the kinds of measures advocated in health security debates about pandemic influenza rarely engage with those structural factors.

Instead, the focus is predominantly on medical interventions that – in the event of a pandemic – will operate through and at the level of the individual human body. The logical endpoint of such an approach can be seen in the 'self-care' model pioneered by the British authorities in July 2009. Faced with an unexpected surge in human H1N1 infections, which placed a heavy burden on the National Health Service, they set up an internet-based national pandemic influenza service. This allowed individuals to obtain Tamiflu prescriptions simply by going through a quick online self-assessment questionnaire.

This same emphasis on medical interventions is also evident in the other manifestations of health security. Biosecurity debates have similarly emphasized medical interventions in the human organism. In the United States, as we have seen, the primary focus of Project BioShield has been to develop a range of 'medical countermeasures' that can be rapidly deployed in the event of a bioterrorist attack, or perhaps even taken as a precaution prior to any such outbreak occurring. Describing the activities of the National Institute of Allergy and Infectious Diseases, its Director testified before the Committee on Homeland Security that its achievements in this area included a research initiative:

> focused on the human innate immune system, which is comprised of broadly active 'first responder' cells and other non-specific mechanisms that are the body's first line of defense against infection. The delineation of methods to boost innate immune responses could lead to the development of fast-acting countermeasures that would be effective against a wide variety of pathogens or toxins that might be used in an attack. (Fauci 2005: 2)

Here the human immune system emerges as the new Maginot Line in the War on Terror.

Related achievements by the researchers at the National Institute of Allergy and Infectious Diseases reportedly include the discovery that anti-cancer drugs can help arrest poxviruses like smallpox, and the discovery of the minimum dose needed for a smallpox vaccine. This last discovery facilitated the acquisition of 300 million doses of smallpox vaccine for the US Strategic National Stockpile. Researchers at the National Institute of Allergy and Infectious Diseases have also been working on next-generation smallpox and anthrax vaccines that are less dangerous and have fewer side-effects (Fauci 2005: 3). They have even made some headway with a DNA-based vaccine against haemorrhagic fevers, such as Ebola.

In the case of bioterrorism policy, the emphasis has thus been on developing medical interventions that can be rapidly deployed in the event of such an attack taking place. As a result, all too few participants in biosecurity debates reflect on the wider international political factors that are driving the formation of terrorist groups, or the reasons why these groups wish to attack populations in the West. Instead, the focus quickly shifts toward overcoming more technical and logistical difficulties associated with developing and stockpiling medical countermeasures to deal with the problem. This is not to imply that the grievances of those terror groups, or their choice of means, are justified. Nor is it to deny that wider, structural factors can be much more difficult to transform, especially in the short term. It is, however, to reiterate the more fundamental point that the strategy for managing or responding to this source of insecurity again is located not at the wider social or political level, but in developing medical 'counter-measures' to that threat that will operate in and through the human body.

This is also the case when it comes to human security debates about health. Managing HIV/AIDS, malaria and tuberculosis in low-income countries has also seen a huge push toward new medical solutions. These efforts include the development of new medicines and vaccines to treat those diseases. In the case of the AIDS pandemic, where a vaccine has proved so elusive, there has been an increase in the number of people receiving treatment through life-prolonging anti-retroviral therapies (ARVs) to just under 2 million people in middle- and low-income countries in 2007 – although this still falls short of the 7.1 million people estimated to be in urgent need of ARVs in these countries (WHO 2007d: 5). Indeed, the Global Fund to Fight AIDS, Tuberculosis and Malaria boasts on its website that, as of December 2008, and with the help of its resources, more than 2 million are receiving anti-retroviral treatment for AIDS. What is more, 74 million anti-malaria drug treatments have been delivered, and a further 4.6 million cases of infectious tuberculosis have been detected and treated. Undoubtedly these interventions are medically beneficial for those who receive them. Indeed they are saving and prolonging lives. Yet, at a deeper level, it also means that here too the emphasis is again on medical interventions, rather than on the underlying economic, geographical, social or cultural drivers of these endemic diseases.

Finally, this quest for medical interventions targeting the human body is also evident in the case of public health 'timebombs' like smoking, obesity and alcoholism. Here, too, only very few questions are asked about the wider social conditions, and responsibility is often delegated to the individual. As former US Surgeon General David Satcher lamented in his foreword to a 2001 report on the issue of obesity:

> When there are no safe places for children to play, or for adults to walk, jog, or ride a bike, that's a community responsibility. When school lunchrooms or workplace cafeterias don't offer healthy and appealing food choices, that is a community responsibility. . . . And when we don't require daily physical education in our schools, that is also a community responsibility. (HHS 2001: xiii–xiv)

Although his insights into some of these wider structural forces at play is laudable, in practice the route increasingly pursued in relation to obesity has again been one of intervention in the human body.

In the case of preventative measures, this has taken the form of trying to influence what foods and nutrients people 'put' into their bodies, and trying to increase the time people spend exercising their bodies. In more drastic cases, it has also led to medical interventions in the form of diet pills, and even stomach-reduction surgery. In the United Kingdom, figures released by the Information Centre of the National Health Service reveal a 40 per cent increase in the number of obesity-related surgeries in 2008 alone. In total, there were 2,724 operations such as gastric bypasses to reduce the stomach size and stomach stapling, and the NHS is reportedly struggling to cope with rising demand. The Information Centre also revealed a 16 per cent increase in 2008 in the number of obesity medications that were reportedly prescribed, raising the total to 1.23 million (BBC 2009). These include medications such as orlistat which prevents the absorption of dietary fat and the appetite-suppressant sibutramine.

The smoking 'timebomb' is no different in this respect. In addition to a range of wider public health measures that ultimately try to prevent cigarette smoke from passing through the lungs of more and more people around the world, pharmacological products are again also being resorted to. Here the interventions of choice are nicotine patches, which reduce the craving associated with smoking. In the years 2007 and 2008, more than 2.5 million prescriptions were issued to assist people to stop smoking in the United Kingdom alone. Of these prescriptions, 1.8 million were for Nicotine Replacement Therapy (NHS 2008b: 88). In May 2009, the World Health Organization even managed to place two forms of Nicotine Replacement Therapy on the organization's model list of essential medicines, which is a list of those medicines that should be available at all times and at affordable prices in all functioning health systems (WHO 2009b). NHS figures further indicate that there were also 112,267 drug items for the treatment of alcohol dependency prescribed in primary care settings in England in 2007 – an increase of 20 per cent since 2003 (NHS 2008a).

In all of these cases, the human body marks an entry point for providing security. One of the principal effects of health security is therefore that it moves the human body to the foreground of contemporary security practices. Health security transforms the human body into the new battlefield of security, as the latter becomes ever more somatic. That is one crucial ramification of health security – and one that accrues irrespective of any other attendant medical or social benefits. Thus the medicalization of security ultimately demands of citizens that, in order to be secure, they must first become patients.

Nations as Hospitals: The Rise of Epidemiological Sovereignty

The medicalization of security also has a further ramification. It calls upon governments wishing to enhance the security of their populations to perform an ever growing range of public health functions. Health security, in short, also requires governments to practise what Foucault called 'social' medicine. Collectively, health security debates have already begun to encourage a subtle but important transformation in the nature of contemporary sovereignty since the last century. Being considered a proper state in international society increasingly depends not just upon the possession of formal, legal sovereignty, but also upon the ability of the government to monitor, manage and contain properly the spread of disease within their populations – much in the way Western societies have been doing for nearly two centuries.

In the European context, this crucial function was added to the list of responsibilities entailed by statehood as early as the eighteenth century. Beyond dealing with issues of war and peace, and organizing the material enrichment of societies, politics became more directly concerned with managing the population 'as a milieu of physical well-being, health and optimal longevity' (Foucault 2000a: 94). At that point in history the population's health and well-being were transformed from being random factors of human existence to become objects of overall and concerted policy interventions. In eighteenth-century Europe, sovereignty became epidemiological.

Today, international debates on health security extend and intensify this notion of epidemiological sovereignty beyond the borders of the West. This has certainly been the case in relation to international pandemic preparedness measures, which require states around the world to undertake a wider range of public health activities. The revised International Health Regulations are one significant case in point. As we have seen, they now legally require states to adopt a range of public health responsibilities relating to disease surveillance and reporting. Beyond the new requirements of the International Health Regulations, international organizations and national governments in the West have also pressured states around the world to draw up comprehensive pandemic response plans. At country level, 96 per cent of national authorities (140/146) now report having drafted national avian influenza preparedness plans that cover both human and animal populations – although many of these remain untested (World Bank 2008: 26).

Bioterrorism policies too have created new international responsibilities for states with respect to the management of disease. Again we have seen how, for example, Security Council Resolution 1540 now legally requires states to 'refrain from providing any form of support to non-State actors that attempt to develop, acquire, manufacture, possess, transport, transfer or use nuclear, chemical or biological weapons and their means of delivery'. Given that the resolution was passed by the Security Council, it now legally binds states to prevent the proliferation of biological weapons materials to non-state actors, and to prevent anyone assisting the latter in the development thereof. Here, too, being a 'good citizen' in international society and adhering to international law requires not only greater medical surveillance of naturally occurring infectious diseases, but also actively working against the proliferation of biological agents causing infectious disease to non-state parties.

That requirement for states to adopt stronger public health programmes is further evident in debates on human security. From the perspective of the human security framework, being a proper, well-run and legitimate state in the international system similarly requires governments actively to manage the health of their populations. Debates on human health security effectively mark a call to extend medical treatments that are widely available in high-income countries to a greater number of low- and middle-income countries around the world. This is part of a wider tendency within the human security agenda, whereby the ideal of a well-run society which it advocates closely resembles the society of the wealthy citizens of the developed world who have access to food in plentiful supply, good wages and, indeed, affordable health care (Duffield and Waddell 2004; MacFarlane and Khong 2006).

Thus the human security agenda seeks to highlight how, in many countries, governments are unwilling or simply unable to ensure the health of their populations, and to try to compel such governments to do more to improve the health of their citizens. To that end, the 2005 *Human Security Report* (HSR 2005: 92) drew upon existing data-sets in order to undertake a 'Human Security Audit' which identified the world's thirty 'least-secure' countries. Here, states are being pushed into undertaking more activities to manage the health of their populations not by making it a legal requirement, but effectively through a strategy of very public naming and shaming. In this way the human security framework also seeks to expose as inadequate those states that are unwilling or unable to provide properly for the health needs of their populations.

This linking of proper statehood to a range of public health activities can, finally, also be found in policy discussions about a range of lifestyle illnesses. Countries outside of the West are today being urged to manage not just infectious disease threats, but also non-communicable diseases linked with the consumption of tobacco, energy-rich foods, and alcohol. Here states are being urged to monitor and shape the levels of cigarette consumption through using their powers – be it by developing national guidelines, funding public health campaigns or using taxation measures to curb demand. Some of these activities, too, have become a legal requirement because of the binding nature of the Framework Convention on Tobacco Control. These activities are also being extended to the management of the population's waistline, as well as its drinking culture – although responding to these phenomena has not yet become a legal requirement for states.

The overall effects of the medicalization of security are thus to compel states to become more active managers of the health of their populations, and to endow sovereignty with a more explicit epidemiological dimension. This push toward epidemiological (rather than merely juridical) sovereignty has not gone uncontested in the international system. Traditionally, this system has been based on the legal equality of states. Under international law, states are thus seen to be sovereign in relation to internal and domestic matters. According to Article 2(7) of the United Nations Charter, 'nothing contained in the present Charter shall authorize the United Nations to intervene in matters which are essentially within the domestic jurisdiction of any state'. Health issues were traditionally seen as 'internal' matters and thus were to be managed according to the priorities of national governments. Making various public health activities a legal requirement for states thus begins to encroach upon issues traditionally considered to be matters of internal sovereignty and has left many developing countries feeling uneasy. Not surprisingly, the rise of epidemiological sovereignty has thus also generated new tensions in the international system.

The Indonesian government has been at the forefront of the resistance to this development. Confronted with an ever growing array of demands from the West in relation to H5N1 pandemic preparedness measures, Indonesia decided to remind Western governments of its sovereignty under international law, asserting what it called its 'viral sovereignty'. Indonesia's role in international H5N1 pandemic preparedness efforts is crucial because many of the recent avian influenza outbreaks have occurred within that country. Yet since 2005 the Indonesian government has only shared with the World Health Organization samples taken from less than a handful of the more than 100 people who are known to have died from avian influenza in that country. Furthermore, Indonesia is no longer notifying the World Health Organization of outbreaks of avian or human forms of influenza.

In March 2007 the Indonesian Health Ministry then announced that it would also cease to provide avian influenza viral material to the Global Influenza Surveillance Network (GISN) run by the World Health Organization for the purposes of surveillance and vaccine development. That network consists of four collaborating centres: the Centers for Disease Control in Atlanta (USA), the National Institute for Medical Research in London, the National Institute of Infectious Diseases (Japan) and a laboratory in Melbourne, Australia. The network analyses material every year in order to identify the most likely strains that manufacturers should use when making vaccines for seasonal influenza viruses. To that end, the network remains dependent on samples of viral material being submitted from various governments through their national influenza centres – including Indonesia.

The justification advanced by the Indonesian government for this decision to cease sharing its viral samples was that, because the viruses originated in Indonesia, that country should be entitled to control the information obtained therefrom, and the commercial uses to which it is put. The viruses, in other words, are a matter that fall within its internal sovereign jurisdiction. However, it is impossible to know exactly why the Indonesian government is concerned about sharing this information about influenza viruses with the wider international community. Publicly, the Indonesian government cites at least two different sets of concerns behind their stance.

First, it is worried about the security implications of virus sharing. The Indonesian government already became concerned in 2006 when they saw that virus sequences had been sent to the Los Alamos National Laboratory in the United States – which is a national security rather than public health laboratory. At times, the Indonesian Health Minister, Siti Fadilah Supari, has come close to accusing the United States government of trying to develop a biological weapon based on the virulent strain of bird flu found in Indonesia. In part for this reason, the Indonesian government is also threatening to shut down a public health laboratory in Jakarta, jointly staffed by Indonesian and US military scientists, that engages in disease surveillance in Indonesia – the National Medical Research Unit 2 (NAMRU- 2).

Second, and perhaps the more likely cause of the dispute, the Indonesian government cites commercial justifications. The Indonesian government appears concerned about the prospect of freely sharing such virus samples, only to be charged later high prices for products developed on the basis of information they provided. All the while, pharmaceutical companies are profiting from the products developed from the viral samples of Indonesia and other countries. The Indonesian government, for example, discovered that viral material it was forwarding to the World Health Organization network was being passed on – without its permission – to pharmaceutical companies in Australia, and possibly elsewhere, in order to develop new vaccines. This was contrary to World Health Organization guidelines, which require explicit permission from the donor government. Faced with these charges, the World Health Organization then removed the guidelines from its website and issued different 'best practice' guidelines for sharing viral material.

The Indonesian government is thus concerned that the developed world will continue to benefit from such information- and virus-sharing arrangements, as they will have the resources to produce and purchase new pharmacological products. In contrast to the push for epidemiological sovereignty whereby governments around the world are to have 'epidemiological' responsibilities to the international community at large, Indonesia has instead asserted its 'viral sovereignty' – reminding the international community that, as a legally sovereign state, it has no duty to share such virus samples with other states. Indonesia has even argued that the Convention on Biological Diversity explicitly grants countries such as Indonesia sovereignty over their biological resources, and that viruses constitute such biological resources.

Indonesia's actions have understandably caused considerable consternation and alarm in the international public health community. The latter relies on such viral materials to track the evolution of the H5N1 virus, to develop new vaccines and so forth. And yet increasingly Indonesia is not alone in its position. Thailand has begun to voice similar concerns. Indeed, the notion of 'viral sovereignty' has even been adopted by the Indian government in a dispute with Bangladesh, and the 112 members of the non-aligned movement have also considered endorsing the idea as well (Holbrooke and Garrett 2008). The old notion of legal sovereignty has thus reared its head once more, giving rise to a contest over whether the future of the international order will remain based primarily on the legal notion of sovereignty, or whether state sovereignty will progressively become conditional upon fulfilling a range of epidemiological responsibilities – including the sharing of virus samples.

Western governments certainly have no interest in laying the matter to rest, and have led the way in countering Indonesia's challenge. US representatives have charged that Indonesia's invocation of sovereignty over viral material poses a risk to global health security, and that, although such sharing was not a technical violation of the International Health Regulations, it violated the spirit of that agreement. The Indonesian government has also been put under growing pressure by the United States and is being labelled a rogue state in relation to international health security. The stern commentary by Richard Holbrooke and Laurie Garrett in the pages of the *Washington Post* is illustrative in this respect:

> In this age of globalization, failure to make viral samples open-source risks allowing the emergence of a new strain of influenza that could go unnoticed until it is capable of exacting the sort of toll taken by the pandemic that killed tens of millions in 1918. . . . The failure to share potentially pandemic viral strains with world health agencies is morally reprehensible. Allowing Indonesia and other countries to turn this issue into another rich–poor, Islamic–Western dispute would be tragic – and could lead to a devastating health crisis anywhere, at any time. (Holbrooke and Garrett 2008)

Such gestures are intended to increase the pressure on the Indonesian government to integrate itself into the structures of international disease surveillance.

The entire notion of global health security is thus also a site in contemporary world politics where a new norm of epidemiological sovereignty is being articulated in a gradual, if also heavily contested, manner. In order to fulfil the mandate of health security, states will increasingly have to carry out a growing range of medical functions at both the individual and collective levels – such as diagnosing disease outbreaks, sharing information on viruses and other biological materials, stockpiling medicines, creating surge capacity for responding to pandemics or bioterrorist attacks, regulating tobacco consumption and so forth. In the era of epidemiological sovereignty, in short, states will – metaphorically speaking – have ever more to resemble enormous hospitals. That too is a crucial ramification of the rise of health security.

Toward a Medical Panopticon? Security as a Conduit of Medical Control

The medicalization of security also has one final consequence. Neither of the above two transformations envisioned by health security will be accomplished without first subjecting populations to much more intensive and wider forms of medical surveillance. Thus the medicalization of security ultimately also turns the provision of security into a conduit for intensifying the medical control of populations – both within and beyond the borders of the West.

Medical control is different from direct coercion in that it marks a more subtle way of regulating society. It entails a process whereby more and more elements of the population become subjected to various forms of medical surveillance, are made aware of their health status, and are encouraged (rather than compelled) by doctors and public health campaigns to take greater efforts to modify their behaviour around a set of norms identified as healthy. In this regard, modern medicine has come to rely not just on diagnostic technologies, but also on systems tracking more generic risk factors for a variety of health conditions. The medical 'gaze' has thus expanded considerably to include large numbers of people in the population who are monitored not because they are already ill, but because they may become ill in the future.

Health security debates intensify such forms of medical control by arguing that the task of securing individuals and populations against these health threats can only be accomplished through implementing more extensive medical surveillance of the population. In the West that can be seen in the United States: the National Strategy for Pandemic Influenza launched on 1 November 2005 included the improvement of surveillance and early warning systems as one of its three key components. For example, this plan included increasing the number of the members of the Sentinel Provider Network (SPN) to 1 or more per 250,000 members of the population. Members of that network report the number of weekly outpatient visits related to influenza-like illness and submit specimens for laboratory testing (HHS 2006). This has created a denser surveillance network around the US population for the purposes of detecting pandemic threats.

The Homeland Security Presidential Directive 21 issued by the White House in October 2007, which established the National Strategy for Public Health and Medical Preparedness, similarly contained increased surveillance and early warning measures as one of its four key components. It further called upon the Secretary of Health and Human Services to establish an operational national epidemiological surveillance system for human health. In the West, the quest for greater security against a future pandemic has thus been accompanied by the development of new medical surveillance systems, as well as the intensification of existing ones.

Such pandemic preparedness measures have also increased the medical surveillance of populations beyond the borders of the West. Aline Leboeuf notes in her analysis of international efforts to address avian influenza how interviewees from many different countries felt that infectious disease surveillance has improved as a result of pandemic preparedness efforts and that 'there are now more and more surveillance systems at the global level' (Leboeuf 2009: 29). Several examples from Asia, where it is feared a new pandemic is most likely to emerge, can be cited to illustrate her point. In Cambodia, for instance, the response to highly pathogenic avian influenza was initially hampered by the lack of a proper surveillance system to track the unfolding of the disease. Outside support was thus provided to pioneer different forms of surveillance to compensate for national surveillance weaknesses, including monitoring markets and creating a sentinel villages network (Desvaux et al. 2006).

In Thailand too, the arrival of avian influenza prompted the use of new surveillance mechanisms. There the government launched the 'X-Ray' campaign – a huge cross-sectional disease surveillance campaign covering the entire population (Safman 2009: 17–18). The name of the campaign was metaphorical rather than literal as it did not rely on the actual use of X-ray technology. Rather, the campaign was more low-tech and consisted of village health volunteers actively seeking out cases of disease in villages. This process is now carried out twice a year, and aims to cover every household in the country simultaneously. In these instances too, medical surveillance is being pushed deeper into Asian societies (even though by means that are not necessarily very complex or sophisticated technologically), and there is an attempt to extend geographically some minimal forms of medical control that have already been instantiated in the West for a long time.

The medical surveillance of populations has also been augmented through less direct means in the context of pandemic prepared-ness. We have seen how the recently revised International Health Regulations, for instance, have granted the World Health Organization the ability to draw on information stemming from non-official sources rather than just relying on official notifications by the states concerned. Whereas the World Health Organization could previously only act officially on information that member states volunteered, it can now also use non-official sources like the Global Public Health Intelligence Network (GPHIN) and Pro-MED mail internet-based systems scanning a range of electronic sources for information on disease outbreaks. This multiplies the sources of surveillance informa-tion available to international organizations, enabling them to obtain a better picture of disease developments in a range of developing countries. It also increases the incentives for member states to share information as the World Health Organization is likely to acquire that information through other channels. As a result of such pandemic preparedness efforts, a growing proportion of the world's population is thus becoming subjected to indirect forms of medical surveillance and control.

Bioterror initiatives have increased the medical surveillance of populations further still. In the United States, Project BioWatch pushed the surveillance of populations to new levels with the creation of a network of air samplers around major US cities in order to detect an environmental release of biological agents. That and other biosecurity programmes also encouraged the greater use of information technology to monitor the population for symptoms of an outbreak of infectious disease. In New York City, a new surveillance system was designed to provide an early warning of a gastrointestinal epidemic that worked not by testing members of the population directly, but by monitoring aggregated data from three different sources, such as diarrhoea cases at sentinel nursing homes, submissions of diarrhoea stools to laboratories for analysis, and over-the-counter sales of diarrhoea medications (Fearnley 2008: 68). Here medical surveillance works not by direct clinical diagnosis, but by detecting wider clusters of symptoms in the population that may otherwise appear random.

Crucially, this idea of 'syndromic' surveillance was subsequently incorporated into Project BioSense. Under the auspices of the Centers for Disease Control and Prevention, BioSense gathers real-time data from a variety of national sources (including military ones), such as the sales data of a large pharmaceutical chain, and submissions to a private laboratory service (Fearnley 2008: 77). Following some teething problems, the Centers for Disease Control and Prevention then created a centralized office for analysing BioSense alerts at the BioIntelligence Office (Fearnley 2008: 78). More recently, efforts have also been undertaken, in collaboration between the Centers for Disease Control and Prevention and the DHS, to integrate BioSense and BioWatch data into a single, seamless surveillance system. Syndromic surveillance too has thus enabled the intensification of the medical surveillance of populations by pioneering new systems of which most members of the population will not even be aware, given they never come into direct contact with them.

The increased medical surveillance of populations has also resulted from human security debates about health – especially outside of the West. This was already evident in the policy recommendations that came of out the Commission on Human Security. These recommendations again pointed to the need to increase national disease surveillance, and to integrate such systems at the global level (Commission on Human Security 2003: 108–10). Human security debates thus frequently advocate improvements of the medical surveillance of populations in the global South. In the case of HIV/AIDS, for example, international institutions which collect data on HIV prevalence amongst the world's populations, such as UNAIDS, have in the past argued strongly in favour of a human rights approach to testing, i.e. insisting that people should have access to voluntary counselling and testing (VCT). In this model, individuals chose whether or not to undertake an HIV test and, if they wished to do so, had to present at local medical facilities, often returning on a separate occasion to receive the result. Here the human right to choose whether or not to take an HIV test is deemed more important than the imperatives of medical surveillance.

Yet, recently, critics of voluntary counselling and testing have become louder, and increasingly counter that knowing one's HIV status is a necessary first step in seeking treatment. In many developing countries, the vast majority of those living with HIV are not even aware of it. Despite years of education campaigns, many still do not seek voluntary testing. Because they do not even know that they are HIV-positive, many people also will not seek treatment as a result, nor will they take measures to prevent the spread of HIV to others.

In a co-authored article published in the influential British medical journal the *Lancet*, Kevin de Cock, who has since become the Director of the World Health Organization's Department of HIV/AIDS, decided to breach the earlier consensus by arguing that:

> We think that the emphasis on human rights in HIV/AIDS prevention has reduced the importance of public health and social justice, which offer a framework for prevention efforts in Africa that might be more relevant to people's daily lives and more likely to be effective. . . . [O]n the basis of epidemiological data, we think that HIV/AIDS is the greatest threat to life, liberty, and the pursuit of happiness and prosperity in many African countries.

> Interventions, therefore, must be quantitatively and qualitatively commensurate with the magnitude of the threat posed by the disease. (de Cock et al. 2002: 68)

If the disease had reached a similar magnitude in, say, New York or Geneva, he chided, there would be an overwhelming emergency response based on regular testing, diagnosis, prevention and treatment, and so forth. Here the human security concern with the AIDS pandemic ends up leading to calls for introducing much more robust HIV-testing and surveillance of populations in the global South. In order to save lives, the ill must first be identified.

Indeed, as it became clear that international initiatives to roll out access to treatment in developing countries were encountering difficulties in meeting their targets, pressure for greater amounts of testing increased much more universally. Some developing countries have thus already begun to change their testing practices in favour of 'routine' testing, whereby all patients within a clinical setting will be informed that they will be tested for HIV as a matter of course, unless they deliberately opt out of doing so.

In January 2004 Botswana changed its policy to a routine 'opt-out' testing policy in antenatal clinics and other medical facilities. In Uganda, too, the parliamentary committee on HIV/AIDS has called for compulsory testing of pregnant women, with others already calling for such compulsory testing to apply to the population at large because 'one of the impediments to the anti-HIV/AIDS campaign in the country is the defective data collection methodology' (Monitor 2007). In quite different ways, human security debates about health thus similarly encourage the extension of the medical surveillance of populations, especially in low-income countries.

Finally, the medical control of populations is also driven deeper into societies through the public health panics surrounding smoking, obesity and alcoholism. Here the calls for biomedical surveillance are less explicit than in the previous three cases. However, the increasingly ubiquitous demands for 'evidence-based' policy require that when frameworks on tobacco or obesity are drawn up by international organizations and national governments, background information on these phenomena is compiled and made available. In the case of smoking, the Framework Convention has thus been accompanied by the compilation of national trends, often broken down by age, gender, nationality and so forth, in terms of smoking habits, morbidity and mortality rates. Similar data are now also being gathered on obesity trends through the Body Mass Index, with the creation of ranking lists of the most obese populations being created at international organizations, whilst others also track levels of physical exercise undertaken in populations.

The European Commission's activities on alcohol similarly entailed, in the first instance, commissioning a comprehensive report tracking data on alcohol consumption, again focusing on different national levels of per-capita consumption, broken down by various age groups. As we saw, the report even broke the data down to the level of different types of alcoholic beverages (beer, wine, spirits, etc.). In the United Kingdom, trends in alcohol consumption are also monitored by the National Health Service. The latter tracks the number of people reporting that they consume more than the recommended allowance of alcohol, and collates these figures according to gender and age (especially amongst children). The National Health Service further tracks the links between alcohol consumption, morbidity and mortality, as well as the costs of these to the health service.

In all of these cases, a growing proportion of the human population is becoming traversed by a much denser network of medical surveillance. That deeper penetration and geographic expansion of medical control, driven by the imperatives of health security, is another crucial, and wider, effect of the medicalization of security. It means that, both within and beyond the West, the quest for health security is also turning security into a technology for intensifying the medical control of populations at the outset of the twenty-first century. Thus the medicalization of security turns the pursuit of security into a tool for advancing the dream of a universal and global system of medical surveillance.

Conclusion

If the thesis about the medicalization of security defended in this book is correct, then the ramifications of the rise of health security are not limited to the ways in which concerns about a diverse range of health issues might render the contemporary international security agenda unmanageable. Nor are they restricted to the ways in which health security initiatives could distort wider public health and humanitarian objectives. As important as those considerations are, there are deeper consequences attending the medicalization of social and political life that is being accelerated and intensified today through a range of ongoing health security initiatives. At the outset of the twenty-first century, practising security increasingly demands that citizens become patients, that states resemble huge hospitals, and that security itself becomes a technology of medical control.

How are we to respond to this further medicalization of society – a medicalization that has also penetrated the domain of politics and even the practice of security? Several decades ago, Ivan Illich mounted a passionate plea to resist the medicalization of life. He pursued the medicalization critique to its limit by suggesting that medicine has actually done more harm than good in modern societies (Illich 1975). The real improvements in health over the past century, he argued, have less to do with doctors, and more to do with adjustments in the wider social environment – such as better nutrition, clean water, sanitation, housing and so on. Critics of Illich retort that this claim still needs to be verified empirically (Daykin and Jones 2008: 127). They also point to the many benefits of medicalization, especially in terms of developing new therapies, as well as dealing with deviant behaviour in a less overtly moralistic fashion. Some have even charged that many medicalization critiques are themselves self-interested, and amount to their own form of 'sociological imperialism' (Strong 1979).

Yet we do not have to go to the extreme lengths of Illich to appreciate a more fundamental point: the principal effect of the recent rise of health security is to infuse the logic of medicalization much more deeply into the domains of national and international politics, and indeed into the practice of security. That makes health security another significant element in the wider medicalization of society (and indeed of life itself) that Illich and others have tried to chronicle. Today, medicine is not only defining who we are and how we relate to one another; it is beginning to shape our assessments of whether or not our existence is deemed to be secure.

In this respect, health security debates are also testament to the very failure of Illich's campaign. Despite several decades of critiquing the medicalization of society, that trajectory of medicalization shows few signs of abating and remains in full swing. If anything, it has today moved beyond the confines of the clinical setting where so many sociologists have traditionally looked for clues to its nature. Today, the medicalization of social life has reached a stage where it can even begin to shape the highest and most sacrosanct domain of politics – the provision of security.

It appears, then, that our historical juncture at the outset of the new millennium is also no longer defined by any collective desire to resist this medicalization of life. On the contrary, it is marked by our very inability to conceive of any limits to the social application of medical reason. Can we still think of any meaningful principles to muster against this medicalization of life? Who – besides those who still benefit commercially from products that make people ill – will dare to raise their voice against the spirit of medicine and its attendant health benefits?

Here we begin to discover just how pervasively we now define ourselves, and our collective aspirations, in relation to health and medicine. In the aftermath of secularization and the 'death of God', it seems that we cannot dream of any greater human achievement than prolonging our corporal existence on planet Earth for as long as possible. Health has become one of the highest political imperatives – 'at once a duty for each and the objective of all' (Foucault 2000a: 94). To that end, we forge ahead with ever more sophisticated ways of manipulating the human organism. This quest has now been given a new lease of life by the decoding of the human genome. The medical imagination thus continues to pervade our cultural horizon today and, in no small measure, makes us who we are today.

This too has undoubtedly facilitated the rapid rise of health security ideas in recent years. For what does the concept of health security represent if not the political endpoint of medical reason – the latter now elevated to the highest and most desirable political good. If that political trajectory is sustained in the years ahead, the implications for the coming century could be profound. Perhaps the quest for health security will eventually even relegate the experience of insecurity, from being a defining element of the human condition to constituting merely another form of pathology to be remedied through pharmacological intervention. Mangling Clausewitz, security might simply become the continuation of medicine by other means. Then it will truly be the case, as the drafters of the constitution of the World Health Organization already argued more than fifty years ago, that international peace and security will only be attainable in the twenty-first century by first pursuing the imperative of health through the practice of medicine.

References

Abraham, Thomas. 2005. *Twenty-First-Century Plague: The Story of SARS*. Baltimore: The Johns Hopkins University Press.

Aldis, William. 2008. 'Health Security as a Public Health Concept: A Critical Analysis'. *Health Policy and Planning* 23: 369–75.

Alibek, Ken, and Charles Bailey. 2004. 'BioShield or Biogap?' *Biosecurity and Bioterrorism* 2(2): 132–3.

Al-Rodhan, N., Lyubov Nazaruk, Marc Finaud and Jenifer Mackby. 2008. *Global Biosecurity: Towards a New Governance Paradigm*. Geneva: Editions Slatkine.

Alston, Julian, Daniel A. Sumner and Stephen A. Vosti. 2008. 'Farm Subsidies and Obesity in the United States: Naonal Evidence and International Comparisons'. *Food Policy* 33(6): 470–9.

Altman, Sidney, Bonnie L. Bassler, Jon Beckwith et al. 2005. 'An Open Letter to Elias Zerhouni'. *Science* 307(5714): 1409–10.

Amos, Amanda, and Judith Mackay. 2004. 'Tobacco and Women' in Peter Boyle, Nigel Gray, Jack Henningfield, John Seffrin and Witold Zatonski (eds.) *Tobacco and Public Health: Science and Policy*. Oxford: Oxford University Press: 329–51.

Anderson, Peter. 2003. *The Beverage Alcohol Industry's Social Aspects Organisations – A Public Health Warning*. Brussels: Eurocare.

—— 2004. 'State of the World's Alcohol Policy'. *Addiction* 99: 1367–9.

Anderson, Peter and Ben Baumberg. 2006. *Alcohol in Europe: A Public Health Perspective*. London: Institute of Alcohol Studies.

Arnold, David, ed. 1988. *Imperial Medicine and Indigenous Societies*. Manchester: Manchester University Press.

Austin, John. 1962. *How to Do Things with Words*. Cambridge, Mass.: Harvard University Press.

Ban, Jonathan. 2001. *Health, Security, and U.S. Global Leadership*. Washington, DC: Chemical and Biological Arms Control Institute.

Barnett, Tony, and Alan Whiteside. 2006. *AIDS in the Twenty-First Century: Disease and Globalization*. 2nd edn. Basingstoke: Palgrave.

Bashford, Alison. 2004. *Imperial Hygiene: A Critical History of Colonialism, Nationalism and Public Health*. Basingstoke: Palgrave.

Batty, David. 2007. 'Government Unveils Plans to Fight Future Flu Pandemic'. *The Guardian*. 22 November.

Baumberg, Ben, and Peter Anderson. 2007. 'The European Strategy on Alcohol: A Landmark and a Lesson'. *Alcohol & Alcoholism* 42(1): 1–2.

BBC. 2007. 'Outcry at Tanzanian HIV Beating'. *BBC News*. 28 November. Available at: http://news.bbc.co.uk/1/hi/world/africa/7117184.stm.

—— 2008. 'Obesity "equal to terror threat"'. *BBC News*. 14 August. Available at: http://news.bbc.co.uk/1/hi/health/7559420.stm.

—— 2009. 'NHS Obesity Surgery "On the Rise"'. *BBC News*. 25 February 2009. Available at: http://news.bbc.co.uk/1/hi/health/7909865.stm.

Berry, F. Clifton, and John Greenwood. 2005. *Medics at War: Military Medicine from Colonial Times to the 21st Century*. Annapolis, Md.: Naval Institute Press.

Blass, Elliot, Daniel Anderson, Heather Kirkorian, Tiffany Pempek, Iris Price and Melanie F. Koleini. 2006. 'On the Road to Obesity: Television Viewing Increases Intake of High-Density Foods'. *Physiology & Behavior* 88(4–5): 597–604.

Booysen, F. and M. Bachmann. 2002. 'HIV/AIDS, Poverty and Growth: Evidence from a Household Impact Study Conducted in the Free State Province, South Africa'. Paper presented at the Annual Conference of the Centre for the Study of African Economies. Oxford. 18–19 March.

Bray, George. 2001. 'Anthropometric Assessment: Height, Weight, Body Mass Index' in Carolyn Berdanier (ed.) *Handbook of Nutrition and Health*. Boca Raton, Fla.: CRC Press: 695–708.

Brown, P., and M. Konner. 1987. 'An Anthropological Perspective on Obesity'. *Annals of the New York Academy of Sciences* 499: 29–46.

Brundtland, Gro Harlem. 2003. 'Global Health and International Security'. *Global Governance* 9(4): 417–23.

Buzan, Barry, Ole Wæver and Jaap de Wilde. 1998. *Security: A New Framework for Analysis*. Boulder, Colo.: Lynne Rienner.

BWC. 1972. Convention on the Prohibition of the Development, Production and Stockpiling of Bacteriological (Biological) and Toxin Weapons and on Their Destruction. Available at www.opbw.org.

Caballero-Anthony, Mely. 2005. 'SARS in Asia: Crisis, Vulnerabilities, and Regional Responses'. *Asian Survey* 45(3): 475–95.

—— 2006. 'Combating Infectious Diseases in East Asia: Securitization and Global Public Goods for Health and Human Security'. *Journal of International Affairs* 59(2): 105–27.

Cabinet Office. 2008. *The National Security Strategy of the United Kingdom: Security in an Interdependent World*. London: The Cabinet Office.

Cannon, Geoffrey. 2004. 'Why the Bush Administration and the Global Sugar Industry are Determined to Demolish the 2004 WHO Global Strategy on Diet, Physical Activity and Health'. *Public Health Nutrition* 7: 369–80.

CBACI. 2000. *Contagion and Conflict: Health as a Global Security Challenge*. Washington, DC: The Chemical and Biological Arms Control Institute and the Center for Strategic and International Studies.

Cedar, S. 2008. 'Human Biology and Health' in Jennie Naidoo and Jane Wills (eds.) *Health Studies: An Introduction*. 2nd edn. Basingstoke: Palgrave: 22–45.

Chaloupka, Frank, and Adit Laixuthai. 1996. *U.S. Trade Policy and Cigarette Smoking in Asia*. NBER Working Paper No. 5543. Cambridge, Mass.: National Bureau of Economic Research.

Cheluget Boaz, Caroline Ngare, Joseph Wahiu, Lawrence Mwikya, Stephen Kinoti, and Bannet Ndyanabangi. 2003. 'Impact of HIV/AIDS on Public Health Sector Personnel in Kenya'. Presentation to the ECSA Regional Health Ministers' Conference in Livingstone, Zambia. 17–21 November.

Chen, Lincoln, and Vasant Narasimhan. 2003. 'A Human Security Agenda for Global Health', in Lincoln Chen et al. (eds.) *Global Health Challenges for Human Security*. Cambridge, Mass.: Harvard University Press: 3–12.

Chin, James. 2007. *The AIDS Pandemic: The Collision of Epidemiology with Political Correctness*. Abingdon: Radcliffe.

Chopra, M., and I. Darnton-Hill. 2004. 'Tobacco and Obesity Epidemics: Not so Different after All?' *British Medical Journal* 328: 1558–60.

Coghlan, Andy. 2008. 'WHO Considers Global War on Alcohol Abuse'. *New Scientist*. 20 April.

Collin, Jeff. 2003. 'Think Global, Smoke Local: Transnational Tobacco Companies and Cognitive Globalization' in Kelley Lee (ed.) *Health*

Impacts of Globalization: Towards Global Governance. Basingstoke: Palgrave: 61–85.

Commission on Human Security. 2003. *Human Security Now.* www.humansecurity-chs.org/finalreport/FinalReport.pdf.

Commission on the Prevention of WMD Proliferation and Terrorism. 2008. *World at Risk: The Report of the Commission on the Prevention of WMD Proliferation and Terrorism.* New York: Random House.

Conrad, Peter. 1992. 'Medicalization and Social Control'. *Annual Review of Sociology* 18: 209–32.

—— 2007. *The Medicalization of Society: On the Transformation of Human Conditions into Treatable Disorders.* Baltimore: The Johns Hopkins University Press.

Conrad, Peter, and Joseph Schneider. 1992. *Deviance and Medicalization: From Badness to Sickness.* Expanded edn. Philadelphia: Temple University Press.

Crawford, Dorothy. 2000. *The Invisible Enemy: A Natural History of Viruses.* Oxford: Oxford University Press.

—— 2007. *Deadly Companions: How Microbes Shaped Our History.* Oxford: Oxford University Press.

Crichton, Nicola, and Anne Mulhall. 2008. 'Epidemiology and Health' in Jennie Naidoo and Jane Wills (eds.) *Health Studies: An Introduction.* 2nd edn. Basingstoke: Palgrave: 73–107.

CSIS. 2006. *Public Health and International Security: The Case of India.* Washington, DC: Center for Strategic and International Studies.

—— 2009. *U.S. National Security and Global Health: An Analysis of Global Health Engagement by the U.S. Department of Defense.* Washington, DC: Center for Strategic and International Studies.

Curtin, Philip. 1998. *Disease and Empire: The Health of European Troops in the Conquest of Africa.* Cambridge: Cambridge University Press.

Davies, Sara. 2008. 'Securitizing Infectious Disease'. *International Affairs* 84(2): 295–313.

Davis, Mike. 2005. *The Monster at Our Door: The Global Threat of Avian Flu.* New York and London: The New Press.

Daykin, Norma, and Mat Jones. 2008. 'Sociology and Health' in Jennie Naidoo and Jane Wills (eds.) *Health Studies: An Introduction.* 2nd edn. Basingstoke: Palgrave: 108–46.

de Cock, Kevin, Dorothy Mbori-Ngacha and Elizabeth Marum. 2002. 'Shadow on the Continent: Public Health and HIV/AIDS in Africa in the 21st Century'. *The Lancet* 360: 67–72.

Desvaux, S., S. Sorn, D. Holl, et al. 2006. 'HPAI Surveillance Programme in Cambodia'. *Developments in Biologicals* 124: 211–24.

de Waal, Alex. 2002. *'New-Variant' Famine: How Aids Has Changed the Hunger Equation.* Allafrica.com. Available at: http://allafrica.com/stories/200211200471.html.

—— 2006. *AIDS and Power: Why There Is No Political Crisis – Yet.* London: Zed Books.

DHS. 2007. *DHS' Management of BioWatch Program.* Washington, DC: Office of Inspector General. Department of Homeland Security.

Drimie, S. 2003. 'HIV/AIDS and Land: Case Studies from Kenya, Lesotho and South Africa'. *Development Southern Africa* 20(5): 647–58.

Dry, Sarah. 2008. *Epidemics for All? Governing Health in a Global Age.* Working Paper No. 9. Brighton: STEPS Centre.

Duffield, Mark, and Nicholas Waddell. 2004. 'Human Security and Global Danger: Exploring a Governmental Assemblage'. Department of Politics and International Relations. University of Lancaster. Available at: www.bond.org.uk/pubs/gsd/duffield.pdf.

Durodie, Bill. 2004. 'Facing the Possibility of Bioterrorism'. *Current Opinion in Biotechnology* 15: 264–8.

Ear, Sophal. 2009. *Cambodia's Victim Zero: Global and National Responses to Highly Pathogenic Avian Influenza.* STEPS Working Paper 16. Brighton: STEPS Centre.

EC. 2006. An EU Strategy to Support Member States in Reducing Alcohol-Related Harm. Communication from the Commission to the Council, the European Parliament, the European Economic and Social Committee and the Committee of the Regions. Brussels. 24 October.

ECDC. 2004. Regulation (EC) No 851/2004 of the European Parliament and of the Council of 21 April 2004 Establishing a European Centre for Disease Prevention and Control. Available at: http://ecdc.europa.eu/en/About_us/Key_documents/Documents/ecdc_regulations.pdf

Elbe, Stefan. 2002. HIV/AIDS and the Changing Landscape of War in Africa. *International Security* 27(2): 159–77.

—— 2003. *Strategic Implications of HIV/AIDS.* International Institute for Strategic Studies. Adelphi Paper No. 357. Oxford: Oxford University Press.

—— 2006. 'Should HIV/AIDS Be Securitized? The Ethical Dilemmas of Linking HIV/AIDS and Security'. *International Studies Quarterly* 50(1): 119–44.

—— 2009. *Virus Alert: Security, Governmentality and the AIDS Pandemic.* New York: Columbia University Press.

Enemark, Christian. 2007. *Disease and Security: Natural Plagues and Biological Weapons in East Asia.* London: Routledge.

Epstein, Gerald. 2007. 'Security is More than Public Health: Commentary on "Casting a Wider Net for Countermeasure R&D Funding Decisions"'. *Biosecurity and Bioterrorism* 5(4): 353–7.

Fan, E. 2003. *SARS: Economic Impact and Implications.* ERD Policy Brief No. 15. Manila: Economics and Research Department, Asian Development Bank.

FAO. 2003. *HIV/AIDS and Agriculture: Impacts and Responses – Case Studies from Namibia, Uganda and Zambia.* Rome: Food and Agricultural Organization.

Fauci, Anthony. 2005. 'Testimony Before the Committee on Homeland Security, Subcommittee on the Prevention of Nuclear and Biological Attack United States House of Representatives'. 28 July. Available at: http://www3.niaid.nih.gov/about/directors/pdf/7-28-2005_homeland_security_testimony.pdf.

FCTC. 2007. 'Conference of the Parties to the WHO Framework Convention on Tobacco Control. Second Session. Decisions and Ancillary Documents'. Geneva: World Health Organization. Available at: http://apps.who.int/gb/fctc/PDF/cop2/COP2_07_CDDecisions-en.pdf.

——2009. 'WHO Framework Convention on Tobacco Control'. Geneva: World Health Organization. Available at: www.who.int/fctc/en/.

Fearnley, Lyle. 2008. 'Redesigning Syndromic Surveillance for Biosecurity' in Andrew Lakoff and Stephen J. Collier (eds.) *Biosecurity Interventions: Global Health and Security in Question.* New York: Columbia University Press: 61–88.

Feldbaum, Harley. 2009. 'The HIV/AIDS – National Security Nexus: A History of Risks and Benefits'. Doctoral Thesis. London School of Hygiene and Tropical Medicine. University of London.

Feldbaum, Harley, P. Patel, E. Sondorp and K. Lee. 2006. 'Global Health and National Security: The Need for Critical Engagement'. *Medicine, Conflict and Survival* 22(3): 192–8.

Feldman, Stanley, and Vincent Marks. 2006. *Panic Nation: Unpicking the Myths We're Told about Food and Health.* London: John Blake.

Fidler, David. 2003. 'Public Health and National Security in the Global Age: Infectious Diseases, Bioterrorism, and Realpolitik'. *George Washington International Law Review* 35: 787–856.

—— 2004. *SARS: Governance and the Globalization of Disease.* New York: Palgrave.

—— 2007. 'A Pathology of Public Health Securitism: Approaching Pandemics as Security Threats' in Andrew F. Cooper, John J. Kirton and Ted Schrecker (eds.) *Governing Global Health: Challenge, Response, Innovation.* Aldershot: Ashgate: 41–64.

Fidler, David, and Lawrence Gostin. 2008. *Biosecurity in the Global Age: Biological Weapons, Public Health and the Rule of Law.* Palo Alto, Calif.: Stanford University Press.

Foucault, Michel. 2000a. 'The Politics of Health in the Eighteenth Century' in *Essential Works of Foucault*, Vol. III: *Power.* Trans. Robert Hurley and others. New York: The New Press: 90–105.

—— 2000b. 'The Birth of Social Medicine' in *Essential Works of Foucault*, Vol. III: *Power.* Trans. Robert Hurley and others. New York: The New Press: 134–56.

—— 2003. *Society Must Be Defended: Lectures at the Collège de France 1975–1976.* Trans. David Macy. New York: Picador.

Franco, Crystal. 2008. 'Billions for Biodefense: Federal Agency Biodefense Funding, Fy2008–Fy2009'. *Biosecurity and Bioterrorism* 6(2): 131–46.

Franco, Crystal, and Michael Mair. 2007. 'U.S. Senate Examines Anthrax Preparedness Efforts'. *Biosecurity and Bioterrorism* 5(4): 290–1.

FSA. 2007. *Financial Risk Outlook.* London: Financial Services Authority.

Gabriel, Richard, and Karen Metz, eds. 1992. *A History of Military Medicine*, Vol. I. Westport, Conn.: Greenwood.

Gale, Jason. 2008. 'Flu Pandemic May Cost World Economy up to $3 Trillion'. Bloomberg. 17 October. Available at: www.bloomberg.com/apps/news?pid=20601202&sid=ashmCPWATNwU&refer=healthcare.

GAO. 1999. *Combating Terrorism: Observations on the Threat of Chemical and Biological Terrorism.* Washington, DC: United States General Accounting Office.

—— 2001. *U.N. Peacekeeping: United Nations Faces Challenges in Responding to the Impact of HIV/AIDS on Peacekeeping Operations.* Washington, DC: United States Government Accountability Office.

—— 2007. *Project BioShield: Actions Needed to Avoid Repeating Past Problems with Procuring New Anthrax Vaccine and Managing the Stockpile of Licensed Vaccine.* GAO-08–88. Washington, DC: United States Government Accountability Office.

—— 2008. *Health Information Technology: More Detailed Plans Needed for the Centers for Disease Control and Prevention's Redesigned BioSense Program.* GAO-09–100. Washington, DC.: United States Government Accountability Office.

Gard, Michael, and Jan Wright. 2005. *The Obesity Epidemic: Science, Morality and Ideology.* London: Routledge.

Garrett, Laurie. 2005. *HIV and National Security: Where Are the Links?* New York: Council on Foreign Relations.

Gellman, Barton. 2000. 'The Belated Global Response to AIDS in Africa: World Shunned Signs of the Coming Plague'. *Washington Post.* 5 July.

GHSI. 2002. Ministerial Statement. London. March. Available at: http://ghsi.ca/english/statementlondonmar2002.asp.

GHW. 2008. *Global Health Watch 2: An Alternative World Health Report.* London: Zed Books.

Gill, Timothy. 2005. 'Obesity in Asian Populations' in Peter Kopelman, Ian Caterson and William Dietz (eds.) *Clinical Obesity in Adults and Children.* 2nd edn. Oxford: Blackwell: 431–9.

Gillespie, Stuart, ed. 2006. *AIDS, Poverty, and Hunger: Challenges and Responses.* Washington, DC: International Food Policy Research Institute.

Gilmore, A., and M. McKee. 2004. 'Moving East: How the Transnational Tobacco Industry Gained Entry to the Emerging Markets of the Former Soviet Union –part I: Establishing Cigarette Imports'. *Tobacco Control* 13: 143–50.

Global Fund. 2008. 'The Global Fund: Who We Are. What We Do'. Geneva: The Global Fund to Fight AIDS, Tuberculosis and Malaria.

Goddard, N., V. Delpech, J. Watson, M. Regan and A. Nicoll. 2006. 'Lessons Learned from SARS: The Experience of the Health Protection Agency, England'. *Public Health* 120: 27–32.

Gortmaker, Steven, Aviva Must, Arthur Sobol, Karen Peterson, Graham A. Colditz and William H. Dietz. 1996. 'Television Viewing as a Cause of Increasing Obesity among Children in the United States, 1986–1990'. *Archives of Pediatrics and Adolescent Medicine* 150(4): 356–62.

Grimard, Franque, and Guy Harling. 2004. 'The Impact of Tuberculosis on Economic Growth'. Montréal: Department of Economics, McGill University. Unpublished paper. Available at: http://neumann.hec.ca/neudc2004/fp/grimard_franque_aout_27.pdf.

Guillemin, Jeanne. 2005. *Biological Weapons: From the Invention of State-Sponsored Programs to Contemporary Bioterrorism*. New York: Columbia University Press.

Hagmann, Michael. 2003. 'Nutritionists Unimpressed by Sugar Lobby's Outcry'. *Bulletin of the World Health Organization* 81(6): 469–70.

Halle, Christian. 2002. 'HIV/AIDS as a Threat to Global Security'. Paper presented to conference, Yale University, 8–9 November. Conference Proceedings available at: www.yale.edu/icrg/ICRG_2002_POST-CONF_PROCEEDINGS_WO_SLEWIS.pdf.

Hanna, Donald, and Yiping Huang. 2004. 'The Impact of SARS on Asian Economies'. *Asian Economic Papers* 3(1): 102–12.

Haslam, David, Naveed Sattar and Mike Lean. 2007. 'Obesity – Time to Wake up' in Naveed Sattar and Mike Lean (eds.) *ABC of Obesity*. Oxford: Blackwell.

Hawkes, Corinna. 2006. 'Uneven Dietary Development: Linking the Policies and Processes of Globalization with the Nutrition Transition, Obesity and Diet-Related Chronic Diseases'. *Globalization and Health* 2(4). Published online. Available at: www.globalizationandhealth.com/content/pdf/1744-8603-2-4.pdf

Hei, Wen, Zhong Zhao, Jian Wang and Zhen-Gang Hou. 2004. 'The Short-Term Impact of SARS on the Chinese Economy'. *Asian Economic Papers* 3(1): 57–61.

HHS. 2001. *The Surgeon General's Call to Action to Prevent and Decrease Overweight and Obesity*. Washington, DC: The Department of Health and Human Services.

—— 2006. *National Strategy for Pandemic Influenza Implementation Plan: Summary of Progress*. Washington, DC: Department of Health and Human Services. Available at: www.pandemicflu.gov/plan/federal/strategyimplementationplan.html.

—— 2008. *Guidance on Antiviral Drug Use during an Influenza Pandemic*. Washington, DC: The Department of Health and Human Services.

Hoffmann, Ilse, and Dietrich Hoffmann. 2004. 'The Changing Cigarette: Chemical Studies and Bioassays' in Peter Boyle, Nigel Gray, Jack Henningfield, John Seffrin and Witold Zatonski (eds.)

Tobacco and Public Health: Science and Policy. Oxford: Oxford University Press.

Holbrooke, Richard. 2000. Comments on *Voice of America*. 8 June. Transcript available at: www.globalsecurity.org/military/library/news/2000/06/000608–aids1.htm.

Holbrooke, Richard, and Laurie Garrett. 2008. 'Sovereignty That Risks Global Health'. *Washington Post*. 10 April.

House of Lords. 2008. *Diseases Know No Frontiers: How Effective Are Intergovernmental Organisations in Controlling Their Spread?* Vol. I: *Report*. London: The Stationery Office.

HSR. 2005. *Human Security Report 2005: War and Peace in the 21st Century*. The University of British Columbia. Oxford: Oxford University Press.

Huang, Yanzhong. 2003. *Mortal Peril: Public Health in China and Its Security Implications*. Washington, DC: Chemical and Biological Arms Control Institute.

Human Rights Watch. 2003. *Just Die Quietly: Domestic Violence and Women's Vulnerability to HIV in Uganda*. New York: Human Rights Watch.

IAVI. 2008. *Sustaining the HIV Prevention Research Agenda: Funding for Research and Development of HIV Vaccines, Microbicides and Other New Prevention Options*. New York: International AIDS Vaccine Initiative. Available at: www.hivresourcetracking.org/content/RT_report_August2008.pdf.

ICG. 2001. *HIV/AIDS as a Security Issue*. Washington, DC, and Brussels: International Crisis Group.

Illich, Ivan. 1975. *Medical Nemesis*. London: Calder and Boyars.

Ingram, Alan. 2007. 'HIV/AIDS, Security and the Geopolitics of US–Nigerian Relations'. *Review of International Political Economy* 14(3): 510–34.

Interpol. 2007. *Bioterrorism Incident Pre-planning and Response Guide*. Lyon: ICPO-Interpol.

Kamolratanakul, P., H. Sawert, S. Kongsin, et al. 1999. 'Economic Impact of Tuberculosis at the Household Level'. *The International Journal of Tuberculosis and Lung Disease* 3(7): 596–602.

Kassalow, Jordan. 2001. *Why Health Is Important to US Foreign Policy*. Council on Foreign Relations. 19 April.

Kay, Adrian, and Owain Williams, eds. 2009. *Global Health Governance: Crisis, Institutions and Political Economy*. Basingstoke: Palgrave.

Kelle, Alexander. 2005a. *Securitization of International Public Health – Implications for Global Health Governance and the Biological Weapons Prohibition Regime.* Bradford Regime Review Paper No. 1. Bradford: University of Bradford.

—— 2005b. *Bioterrorism and the Securitization of Public Health in the United States of America – Implications for Public Health and Biological Weapons Arms Control.* Bradford Regime Review Paper No. 2. Bradford: University of Bradford.

—— 2007. 'Securitization of International Public Health: Implications for Global Health Governance and the Biological Weapons Prohibition Regime'. *Global Governance* 13(2): 217–35.

Kilbourne, Edwin. 2006. 'Influenza Pandemics of the 20th Century'. *Emerging Infectious Diseases* 12(1): 9–14.

Klotz, Lynn. 2008. 'Response to Epstein's Commentary'. *Biosecurity and Bioterrorism* 6(1): 108–13.

Kober, Katharina, and Wim van Damme. 2006. 'Public Sector Nurses in Swaziland: Can the Downturn Be Reversed? *Human Resources for Health* 4(13): 1–11.

Koch, Erin. 2008. 'Disease as Security Threat: Critical Reflections on the Global TB Emergency' in Andrew Lakoff and Stephen J. Collier (eds.) *Biosecurity Interventions: Global Health and Security in Question.* New York: Columbia University Press: 121–46.

Kouvonen, Anne, Mika Kivimaki, Marianna Virtanen, Jaana Pentti and Jussi Vahtera. 2005. 'Work Stress, Smoking Status, and Smoking Intensity: An Observational Study of 46,190 Employees'. *Journal of Epidemiology and Community Health* 59: 63–9.

Laxminarayan, Ramanan, Eili Klein, Christopher Dye, Katherine Floyd, Sarah Darley and Olusoji Adeyi. 2007. *Economic Benefit of Tuberculosis Control.* Policy Research Working Paper 4295. Washington, DC: The World Bank. Human Development Network. Available at: www-wds.worldbank.org/external/default/WDSContentServer/IW3P/IB/2007/08/01/000158349_20070801103922/Rendered/PDF/wps4295.pdf.

Lean, George. 2005. 'It Is a Bigger Threat than Terrorism'. *Independent on Sunday.* 16 October.

Leboeuf, Aline. 2009. *The Global Fight against Avian Influenza: Lessons for the Global Management of Health and Environmental Risks and Crises.* Health and Environment Reports No. 2. Paris: Institut Français des Relations Internationales.

Leboeuf, Aline, and Emma Broughton. 2008. *Securitization of Health and Environmental Issues: Process and Effects*. Working Paper. Paris: Institut Français des Relations Internationales.

Lederberg, Joshua, Robert E. Shope and Stanley C. Oaks, Jr (eds.) 1992. *Emerging Infections: Microbial Threats to Health in the United States*. Committee on Emerging Microbial Threats to Health. Institute of Medicine. Washington, DC: National Academy Press.

Lee, Kelley. 2003. *Globalization and Health: An Introduction*. Basingstoke: Palgrave.

Leonard, Mary. 2004. 'US Launches a Fight against Obesity'. *The Boston Globe*. 10 March. Available at: www.boston.com/news/ nation/articles/2004/03/10/us_launches_a_fight_against_obesity/.

Lupton, Deborah. 1997. 'Foucault and the Medicalization Critique' in Alan Petersen and Rubin Bunton (eds.) *Foucault, Health and Medicine*. London: Routledge: 94–110.

MacFarlane, Neil, and Yuen Foong Khong. 2006. *Human Security and the UN: A Critical History*. Bloomington and Indianapolis, Ind.: Indiana University Press.

Macleod, R., and M. Lewis, eds. 1988. *Disease, Medicine, and Empire: Perspectives on Western Medicine and the Experience of European Expansion*. London: Routledge.

Mair, Michael. 2006. 'Brief Report: Recent Progress in Biodefense Countermeasure Development'. *Biosecurity and Bioterrorism* 4(4): 325–43.

Mamudu, Hadii, R. Hammond and Stanton Glantz. 2008. 'Project Cerberus: Tobacco Industry Strategy to Create an Alternative to the Framework Convention on Tobacco Control'. *American Journal of Public Health* 98(9): 1630–42.

Matheny, Jason, Michael Mair, Andrew Mulcahy and Bradley T. Smith. 2007. 'Incentives for Biodefense Countermeasure Development'. *Biosecurity and Bioterrorism* 5(3): 228–38.

Mathers, Colin, and Dejan Loncar. 2006. 'Projections of Global Mortality and Burden of Disease from 2002 to 2030'. *PLos Medicine* 3(11): 2011–30.

McInnes, Colin. 2006a. 'HIV/AIDS and Security'. *International Affairs* 82(2): 315–26.

—— 2006b. 'Securitising Health'. Paper presented at the annual meeting of the International Studies Association. San Diego, Calif. 22 March.

McInnes, Colin, and Kelley Lee. 2006. 'Health, Security and Foreign Policy'. *Review of International Studies* 32(1): 5–23.

McLannahan, Heather, and Pete Clifton, eds. 2008. *Challenging Obesity: The Science behind the Issues*. Oxford: Oxford University Press.

Menon, K.. 2006. 'SARS Revisited: Managing "Outbreaks" with "Communications"'. *Annals of the Academy of Medicine* 35(5): 361–7.

Miller, Judith, Stephen Engelberg and William Broad. 2001. *Germs: Biological Weapons and America's Secret War*. New York: Simon & Schuster.

MMV. 2007. *Annual Report 2007*. Geneva: Medicines for Malaria Venture.

Mongoven, Ann. 2006. 'The War on Disease and the War on Terror: A Dangerous Metaphorical Nexus'. *Cambridge Quarterly of Healthcare Ethics* 15: 403–16.

Monitor. 2007. 'Compulsory HIV Testing: Right Move'. *The Monitor* (Kampala). 11 March.

NHS. 2008a. *Statistics on Alcohol: England, 2008*. National Health Service Information Centre. Available at: www.ic.nhs.uk/pubs/alcohol08.

—— 2008b. *Statistics on Smoking: England, 2008*. National Health Service Information Centre. Available at: www.ic.nhs.uk/pubs/smoking08.

NIC. 2000. *The Global Infectious Disease Threat and its Implications for the United States*. Available at: www.cia.gov/cia/reports/nie/report/nie99–17d.html.

—— 2003. *SARS: Down but Still a Threat*. National Intelligence Council: ICA 2003–09. Available at: www.dni.gov/nic/PDF_GIF_otherprod/sarsthreat/56797book.pdf.

NSS. 2006. *The National Security Strategy of the United States*. Washington, DC: The White House.

NYT. 2005. 'Grounding a Pandemic'. *New York Times*. 6 June.

Oliver, J. Eric. 2006. *Fat Politics: The Real Story behind America's Obesity Epidemic*. Oxford: Oxford University Press.

Oslo Ministerial Declaration. 2007. 'Oslo Ministerial Declaration – Global Health: A Pressing Foreign Policy Issue of Our Time'. *The Lancet* 369: 1373–8.

Ostergard, Robert L., Jr, ed. 2005. *HIV, AIDS and the Threat to National and International Security*. London: Palgrave.

Paris, Roland. 2001. 'Human Security: Paradigm Shift or Hot Air?' *International Security* 26(2): 87–102.

Parker, Elizabeth, and Bryan Pate. 2005. 'Implementing UN Security Council Resolution 1540 to Combat the Proliferation of Biological Weapons'. *Biosecurity and Bioterrorism* 3(2): 166–73.

PDD. 1996. Presidential Decision Directive NSTC-7. Washington, DC: The White House.

Pelletier, Marc. 2008. 'Letter to the Editor'. *Biosecurity and Bioterrorism* 6(1): 114–16.

Peterson, Susan. 2002/3. 'Epidemic Disease and National Security'. *Security Studies* 12(2): 43–81.

Petro, James B., Theodore R. Plasse and Jack A. McNulty. 2003. 'Biotechnology: Impact on Biological Warfare and Biodefense'. *Biosecurity and Bioterrorism* 1(3): 161–8.

Piot, Peter. 2001. AIDS and Human Security. Speech delivered at the United Nations University. Tokyo. 2 October. Available at: www. unaids.org/html/pub/media/speeches01/piot_tokyo_02oct01_en_ doc.htm

Pisani, Elizabeth. 2008. *The Wisdom of Whores: Bureaucrats, Brothels and the Business of AIDS*. London: Granta Books.

Price-Smith, Andrew. 2001. *The Health of Nations: Infectious Disease, Environmental Change, and Their Effects on National Security and Development*. Cambridge, Mass.: MIT Press.

—— 2009. *Contagion and Chaos: Disease, Ecology, and National Security in the Era of Globalization*. Cambridge, Mass.: MIT Press.

Rajeswari, R., R. Balasubramanian, M. Muniyandi, S. Geetharamani, X. Thresa and P. Venkatesan. 1999. 'Socio-economic Impact of Tuberculosis on Patients and Family in India'. *The International Journal of Tuberculosis and Lung Disease* 3(10): 869–77.

RBM. 2008. 'Economic Costs of Malaria'. Information Sheet. Geneva: Roll Back Malaria Partnership.

—— 2009. *Malaria Commodity Access*. Geneva: Roll Back Malaria Partnership. Available at: www.rollbackmalaria.org/psm/index. html.

Rose, Nikolas. 2007. 'Beyond Medicalization'. *The Lancet* 369: 700–2.

Rosenau, William. 2001. 'Aum Shinrikyo's Biological Weapons Program: Why Did It Fail?' *Studies in Conflict and Terrorism* 24: 289–301.

Rushton, Simon. 2007. 'Securitizing HIV/AIDS: Pandemics, Politics and SCR 1308'. Paper presented at the Annual Convention of the International Studies Association. Chicago.

Ryan, Jeffrey, and Jan Glarum. 2008. *Biosecurity and Bioterrorism: Containing and Preventing Biological Threats*. New York: Elsevier.

Safman, Rachel. 2009. *The Political Economy of Avian Influenza in Thailand*. STEPS Working Paper 18. Brighton: STEPS Centre.

Saloojee, Yussuf. 2004. 'Tobacco in Africa: More than a Health Threat' in Peter Boyle, Nigel Gray, Jack Henningfield, John Seffrin and Witold Zatonski (eds.) *Tobacco and Public Health: Science and Policy*. Oxford: Oxford University Press: 267–77.

Searle, John. 1969. *Speech Acts: An Essay in the Philosophy of Language*. Cambridge: Cambridge University Press.

Shah, M., N. Osborne, T. Mbilizi and G. Vilili.. 2002. *Impact of HIV/ AIDS on Agriculture Productivity and Rural Livelihoods in the Central Region of Malawi*. Lilongwe, Malawi: Care International in Malawi.

Shea, Dana, and Sarah Lister. 2003. *The BioWatch Program: Detection of Bioterrorism*. Congressional Research Service Report No. RL 32152. Washington, DC: Congressional Research Service.

Shinya, K., M. Ebina, S. Yamada, M. Ono, N. Kasai and Y. Kawaoka. 2006. 'Influenza Virus Receptors in the Human Airway: Avian and Human Flu Viruses Seem to Target Different Regions of a Patient's Respiratory Tract'. *Nature* 440(7083): 435–6.

Shisana, O., E. Hall, K. Maluleke et al. 2003. *The Impact of HIV/ AIDS on the Health Sector: National Survey of Health Personnel, Ambulatory and Hospitalized Patients and Health Facilities*. Pretoria: Human Sciences Research Council and the Medical Research Council.

Siu, Alan, and Y. C. Richard Wong. 2004. 'The Economic Impact of SARS: The Case of Hong Kong'. *Asian Economic Papers* 3(1): 62–83.

Smith, Roy. 2003. 'The Impact of Globalization on Nutrition Patterns: A Case Study of the Marshall Islands' in Kelley Lee (ed.) *Health Impacts of Globalization: Towards Global Governance*. Basingstoke: Palgrave.

Stop TB. 2009. *The GDF: A New Perspective on TB Procurement*. Geneva: Stop TB Partnership. Available at: www.stoptb.org/gdf/ whatis/what_is.asp.

Story, Mary, and Simone French. 2004. 'Food Advertising and Marketing Directed at Children and Adolescents in the US'. *International Journal of Behavioral Nutrition and Physical Activity* 1(3). Published online. Available at: www.ijbnpa.org/content/1/1/3.

Strauss, R, and H. Mir. 2001. 'Smoking and Weight Loss Attempts in Overweight and Normal-Weight Adolescents'. *International Journal of Obesity* 25(9): 1381–5.

Strong, P. 1979. 'Sociological Imperialism and the Profession of
    Medicine: A Critical Examination of the Thesis of Medical
    Imperialism'. *Social Science and Medicine* 13A: 199–215.
Sturgeon, Nicola. 2008. 'Action on Scotland's Drink "Time Bomb"'.
    News Release. Edinburgh: Scottish Government. 17. June. Available
    at: www.scotland.gov.uk/News/Releases/2008/06/17093834.
Szasz, Thomas. 2007. *The Medicalization of Everyday Life: Selected
    Essays*. Syracuse, NY: State University of Syracuse Press.
Takemi, Keizo, Masamine Jimba, Sumie Ishii, Yasushi Katsuma, and
    Yasuhide Nakamura. 2008a. 'Global Health, Human Security, and
    Japan's Contributions'. Paper presented at the international sympo-
    sium on 'From Okinawa to Toyako: Dealing with Communicable
    Diseases as Global Human Security Threats'. Tokyo. 23–24 May.
    Available at: www.jcie.org/researchpdfs/globalhealth/final_paper.pdf.
—— 2008b. 'Human Security Approach for Global Health'. *The Lancet*
    372: 13–14.
Taylor, Allyn, Frank J. Chaloupka, Emmanuel Guindon and Michaelyn
    Corbett. 2000. 'The Impact of Trade Liberalization on Tobacco
    Consumption' in Prabhat Jha and Frank Chaloupka (eds.) *Tobacco
    Control in Developing Countries*. Oxford: Oxford University Press:
    343–64.
Tye, Joe, Kenneth Warner and Stanton Glantz. 1987. 'Tobacco
    Advertising and Consumption: Evidence of a Causal Relationship'.
    Journal of Public Health Policy 8(4): 492–508.
UNAIDS. 2001. *AIDS Epidemic Update*. December. Geneva: UNAIDS.
—— 2003. *On the Front Line: A Review of Policies and Programmes to
    Address HIV/AIDS among Peacekeepers and Uniformed Services*.
    Geneva: UNAIDS.
—— 2008. *2008 Report on the Global AIDS Epidemic*. Geneva:
    UNAIDS.
UNDP. 1994. *Human Development Report, 1994: New Dimensions
    of Human Security*. New York: United Nations Development
    Program; Oxford: Oxford University Press.
UNITAID. 2008. 'UNITAID 2008 Budget'. Geneva: UNITAID.
    Available at: www.unitaid.eu/images/governance/EB6/eb6_
    budget2008.pdf.
UPMC. 2009. 'BioAgents and Epidemic Diseases Background
    Information'. Pittsburgh, PA: University of Pittsburgh Medical
    Center. Center for Biosecurity. Available at: www.upmc-
    biosecurity.org/website/focus/agents_diseases/background.html.

Wæver, Ole. 1995. 'Securitization and Desecuritization' in Ronnie Lipschutz. (ed.) *On Security*. New York: Columbia University Press: 46–86.

Warren, C., N. Jones, M. Eriksen and S. Asma. 2006. 'Patterns of Global Tobacco Use in Young People and Implications for Future Chronic Disease Burden in Adults'. *The Lancet* 367(9512): 749–53.

Waxman, Henry. 2002. 'The Future of the Global Tobacco Treaty Negotiations'. *New England Journal of Medicine* 346: 936–9.

WEF. 2006. *Global Risks 2006*. A World Economic Forum Report. Geneva: World Economic Forum.

WHA. 2001. 'Global Health Security – Epidemic Alert and Response'. Report by the Secretariat prepared for the Fifty-Fourth World Health Assembly. A54/9. Geneva: World Health Assembly.

WHO. 1946. *Constitution of the World Health Organization*. Geneva: World Health Organization. Available at: www.who.int/governance/eb/who_constitution_en.pdf.

—— 2002. *The Tobacco Atlas*. Geneva: World Health Organization.

—— 2003. *Severe Acute Respiratory Syndrome (SARS): Status of the Outbreak and Lessons for the Immediate Future*. Geneva: World Health Organization

—— 2004a. *World Health Report 2004*. Geneva: World Health Organization.

—— 2004b. *WHO Guidelines for the Global Surveillance of Severe Acute Respiratory Syndrome. SARS. Updated Recommendations*. October 2004. Geneva: World Health Organization.

—— 2004c. *Global Strategy on Diet, Physical Activity and Health*. Geneva: World Health Organization.

—— 2004d. *Global Status Report on Alcohol 2004*. Geneva: World Health Organization.

—— 2004e. 'Summary of Probable SARS Cases with Onset of Illness from 1 November 2002 to 31 July 2003'. Geneva: World Health Organization. Available at: www.who.int/csr/sars/country/table2004_04_21/en/index.html.

—— 2005. *Factsheet: Malaria in Africa*. Geneva: World Health Organization.

—— 2006. *Obesity and Overweight*. Fact Sheet No. 311. September. Geneva. World Health Organization.

—— 2007a. *A Safer Future: Global Public Health Security in the 21st Century. The World Health Report 2007*. Geneva: World Health Organization.

—— 2007b. *Malaria*. Fact Sheet No. 94. Geneva: World Health Organization.

—— 2007c. *Scale of Assessments 2008–2009*. Geneva: World Health Organization.

—— 2007d. *Towards Universal Access: Scaling Up Priority HIV/ AIDS Interventions in the Health Sector*. Geneva: World Health Organization.

—— 2008a. *Global Tuberculosis Control: Surveillance, Planning, Financing*. Geneva: World Health Organization.

—— 2008b. *WHO Report on the Global Tobacco Epidemic, 2008*. Geneva: World Health Organization.

—— 2008c. 'Cumulative Number of Confirmed Human Cases of Avian Influenza A/(H5N1) Reported to WHO'. 16 December. Geneva: World Health Organization. Available at: www.who.int/csr/disease/ avian_influenza/country/cases_table_2008_12_16/en/index.html.

—— 2009a. 'Safety of Pandemic Vaccines'. Geneva: World Health Organization. Available at: www.who.int/csr/disease/swineflu/ notes/h1n1_safety_vaccines_20090805/en/ index.html.

—— 2009b. 'Two Forms of Nicotine Replacement Therapy Chosen as WHO "Essential Medicines"'. Geneva: World Health Organization. Available at: www.who.int/tobacco/communications/highlights/ note_nrt_therapy/en/index.html.

Williams, Dylan. 2006. 'World Health: A Lethal Dose of US Politics'. *Asia Times*. 17 June. Available at: http://atimes.com/atimes/ Southeast_Asia/HF17Ae01.html.

Williams, Michael. 2003. 'Words, Images, Enemies: Securitization and International Politics'. *International Studies Quarterly* 47(4): 511–31.

Williams, Simon J., and Michael Calnan. 1996. 'The "Limits" of Medicalization?: Modern Medicine and the Lay Populace in "Late" Modernity'. *Social Science and Medicine* 42(12): 1609–20.

World Bank. 1999. *Curbing the Epidemic: Governments and the Economics of Tobacco Control*. Washington, DC: The World Bank.

—— 2005. *Program Framework Document for Proposed Loans/Credits/ Grants in the Amount of US$500 Million Equivalent for a Global Program for Avian Influenza Control and Human Pandemic Preparedness and Response*. Washington, DC: World Bank.

—— 2007. *Healthy Development. The World Bank Strategy for Health, Nutrition, and Population Results*. Washington, DC: World Bank.

—— 2008. *Responses to Avian Influenza and State of Pandemic Readiness Fourth Global Progress Report.* Washington, DC: World Bank.

Yach, Derek, and Stella Bialous. 2001. 'Junking Science to Promote Tobacco'. *American Journal of Public Health* 91(11): 1745–8.

Zelikow, Philip (2000) 'Review of The Global Infectious Disease Threat and Its Implications for the United States'. *Foreign Affairs* 74(4): 154.

Zola, I. 1972. 'Medicine as an Institution of Social Control'. *Sociological Review* 20: 487–503.

—— 1983. *Socio-Medical Inquiries.* Philadelphia: Temple University Press.

Zubay, Geoffrey, S. Touma, R. Balfour et al. 2005. *Agents of Bioterrorism: Pathogens and Their Weaponization.* New York: Columbia University Press.

Index

Page numbers followed by 't' refer to a table, eg. 103t

11 September 4, 8, 68, 77, 113

Abbott Laboratories 149
Abraham, Thomas 42
absenteeism 51, 109
accidents 96–7, 158, 161, 162, 163–4
addiction 16, 135
advertising 134, 136, 138, 139, 141, 142,
    153, 154, 155
aflatoxin 73
Africa 46, 111, 138, 150
    HIV/AIDS 34–5, 102–3, 109, 128, 183
    and malaria 107, 110, 124
agriculture 112, 139–40, 141, 143, 153,
    155, 168
AIDS see HIV/AIDS
air travel 31–2, 38–9, 44–5, 65, 128
alcohol and alcoholism 9–10, 16, 132–3,
    157–64, 171, 172, 175, 184–5
    alcohol industry 159, 160–1, 162
    and employment 158, 159, 162
    health benefits of alcohol 157, 158
Aldis, William 3, 58
Alibek, Ken 70, 92
Allen, Charles 80
Al-Rodhan, N. 69, 70, 76, 87, 88
Alston, Julian 152
Altman, Sidney 94
American Psychiatric Association 16
American War of Independence 68
Amherst, Sir Jeffrey 68
Amos, Amanda 134, 136
Amsterdam Declaration to Stop TB 124–5
Amsterdam Group 161
Anderson, Peter 157, 159, 160, 161, 162
Angola 34

Annan, Kofi 127
anthrax
    as biological weapon 8, 70, 73–4, 77–8,
        84, 85, 89, 96
    vaccination 89, 90, 170
antibiotics 4, 28, 74, 88, 167
anti-retroviral drugs (ARVs) 103, 127,
    129, 170
anti-toxins 88
anti-viral drugs 28, 63, 64, 88, 122, 167,
    169
    see also medical countermeasures
anxiety 43–4, 79–81, 135
arena viruses 84
Argentina 160
Armed Forces Medical Intelligence Center
    (AFMIC) 34
Arnold, David 31
artemisinin-based combination therapies
    (ACTs) 123, 124, 128
ASEAN (Association of South-East Asian
    Nations) 45
Asia 150, 180–1
    and HIV/AIDS 103t, 128
    and malaria 107, 124
    and SARS 38, 39, 42
    and smoking 134, 138, 142
Asian Development Bank 45
Assyrians 68
athletes 148
Atlanta 49
attention deficit disorder 22
Aum Shinrikyo cult 8, 78–80
Austin, J. L. 10–11
Australia 120, 137, 141, 176, 177
Austria 159, 160

avian flu *see* influenza, H5N1 (avian flu)
Azerbaijan 50

baldness 16, 22, 24
Bangladesh 105, 125, 137, 178
Bashford, Alison 31
Batty, David 167
Baumberg, Ben 157, 159, 160, 162
BBC 104, 144, 171
Beijing 39, 41, 44–5, 50
Belgium 141, 159
Bernard, Kenneth 55
Berry, F. Clifton 31
binge drinking 157–63
BioIntelligence Office 182
biological warfare 67–72
biological weapons 72–3, 81–2, 84–5,
    174, 177
Biological Weapons Convention (BWC)
    71, 72–4, 81
Biomedical Advanced Research and
    Development Authority (BARDA)
    63, 91–2
biomedical experts 83
biosecurity 7, 41, 66–98
    see also health security
bioterrorism 4–5, 6, 70, 74, 75–82,
    130–1
    and anthrax 8, 24, 70, 77–8, 96, 170
    Aum Shinrikyo cult 8, 78–80
    countermeasures 63, 66, 169–70, 173–4,
        179, 182
    post 11 September attacks 8, 68, 77–8
    and smallpox 4, 169–70
Blass, Elliot 153
Body Mass Index (BMI) 146–50, 185
Booysen, F. 110
Boston 85, 96
Botswana 184
botulinum toxin 70, 73, 78, 84, 89
Bray, George 148
Brazil 114, 160
Brewers of Europe 162
British American Tobacco 134, 140
British Civil Contingency Secretariat 47
Brown, P. 148
brucellosis 70, 73, 84, 85

Brunei 45
Bruntland, Gro Harlem 32
Buffett, Warren 129
Bush, George W. administration 62, 74,
    80–1, 88–9, 91, 93, 142
Bush family 168
Buzan, Barry 11

Caballero-Anthony, Mely 13, 42
Cabinet Office 32
Caffa 68
Cairo 117
Cambodia 45, 180–1
Camp Funston, Kansas 48
Canada 38, 39, 40, 41, 61, 117, 120, 141
cancer 134, 145, 158, 169
Cannon, Geoffrey 118
Canton Export Exhibition 44
Caribbean 103t, 121, 138
Carlyle Group 168
Carmon, Richard 144
casualties, civilian 67, 77, 92
CBACI 35
Cedar, S. 149
Center for Disease Control and Prevention
    26
Center for Strategic and International
    Studies, Global Health Policy
    Center 54
Centers for Disease Control and
    Prevention (CDC) 51, 56, 83, 86,
    88, 93, 145, 146, 176, 182
Central Intelligence Agency (CIA) 34,
    35, 73
cerebrovascular disease 103, 134, 145
Chaloupka, Frank 142
Charoen Pokphand, company 168
Cheluget, Boaz 109
Chemical and Biological Weapons
    Scientific Advisory Group 87
chemical weapons 67–8, 69, 79, 81–2, 87,
    174
Chen, Shaohua 9
Chicago 85
children 111, 119, 128
    and alcoholism 161, 162, 185
    mortality rates 102, 103, 107

children (*cont.*)
  and obesity 150, 153, 171
  and smoking 139, 142
Chile 127, 141
Chin, James 102
China 50, 105, 117, 121, 137, 150
  and biological attacks (deliberate) 70,
    71
  and SARS 37–8, 39, 41, 44–5, 61
chlorine gas 69
chloroquine 123, 124
cholera 8, 58, 59, 68, 70
Chopra, M. 152
cigarettes 133, 134, 139
Clinton administration 34, 55, 73–4
Clinton Foundation 129
Coghlan, Andy 157
Cold War 72, 73
College of American Pathologists 96
Collin, Jeff 140
Colombia 160
Commission on Human Security 101, 108,
    114, 183
Commission on the Prevention of WMD
    Proliferation and Terrorism 80
community security 100
Conference of the Parties 141
Congo-Brazzaville 34, 117
Congress, US 88
Conrad, Peter 15, 16, 19, 27, 28, 166
  and Schneider, Joseph 15, 16
consumption 3, 45, 51, 152, 153, 156
Convention on Biological Diversity
    177
Convention on the Prohibition of
    Development, Production,
    Stockpiling and Use of Chemical
    Weapons and on Their Destruction
    81
Convention on the Prohibition of the
    Development, Production and
    Stockpiling of Bacteriological
    (Biological) and Toxin Weapons
    and on Their Destruction 81
Copenhagen 117
corporate greed and corruption 168
Cote d'Ivoire 34

Council on Foreign Relations, Global
    Health Program 54
Crawford, Dorothy 48, 49, 68, 106, 107
Crichton, Nicola 146
crime 158, 159
Croatia 160
Crowe, Admiral William J., Jr 80
CSIS 14
Curtin, Philip 31
Czech Republic 159

Davies, Sara 10
Davis, Mike 168
Daykin, Norma 186
de Cock, Kevin 183–4
de Waal, Alex 35, 112
death, premature 101–2, 130, 145, 161
Defense Intelligence Agency 34
Democratic Party, US 168
Democratic Republic of Congo 34, 105, 125
Denmark 120, 159
densitometry 149
Department of Defense (DoD) 56
Department of Health and Human
    Services (HHS) 58–9, 83–4, 88, 89,
    90, 93–4, 167, 171, 180
Department of Homeland Security 56,
    86, 93
Desvaux, S. 181
developed world 6, 9–10
developing countries
  endemic disease 6, 9, 24, 99, 101–2, 109,
    112–13, 126, 128, 130
    see also HIV/AIDS; malaria;
      tuberculosis
  and lifestyle diseases 136, 142, 150
  medical intervention 115, 120, 167
DHS 84–6, 89, 182
diabetes 145, 150
diphtheria 1, 59, 120
Directly Observed Therapy - Short Course
    (DOTS) 106, 111, 127
disease 7–9, 74–5
  endemic 96, 99–131, 171
    developing countries 6, 9, 24, 99,
      101–2, 109, 112–13, 126, 128, 130
    gastrointestinal 182

infectious disease 3, 4, 30
  of lifestyle 9–10, 24, 132–64, 175, 184–5
  notifiable 59–60
disease management 1, 19–22, 23
Djibouti 50
Dlamini, Guga 104
Dominica 160
Drimie, S. 111
drink-driving 160
drug resistance 4, 8, 102, 105–6, 108, 123
Dry, Sarah 59
Durodie, Bill 95

East Timor 36
Ebola 8, 58, 59, 68, 78, 84, 170
economic impacts 43–6, 127, 137–8, 145
  alcoholism 158–9, 161, 185
  H1N5 (avian flu) 50, 51–2
  HIV/AIDS 110–11, 127
economic security 100, 108, 110–11
education 44, 108, 111, 162
Egypt 50, 137
Elbe, Stefan 10, 35
emphysema 134
employment 108, 111, 112, 137, 152, 155,
    158, 159, 162, 171
Endo, Seiichi 78
environmental issues 3, 100, 108
Environmental Protection Agency 86
epidemiology 54, 119, 172–9
Epstein, Gerald 94
Eritrea 34
Estonia 141
Ethiopia 105, 124
Europe 39, 103t, 107, 150, 160–2, 173
European Centre for Disease Prevention
    and Control (ECDC) 57
European Commission 5, 120, 158–9,
    161–2, 185
European Union (EU) 41, 57, 121, 159,
    161–2
exercise 149, 151, 153, 154, 155, 156, 157,
    171

face masks 44, 167
Fan, E. 45
fat 144, 147, 148, 149, 151, 154, 155

Fauci, Anthony 170
FBI (Federal Bureau of Investigation) 76
FCTC 140, 141
Fearnley, Lyle 182
Federation of American Scientists 61
Feldbaum, Harley 55
feminism 18
Fidler, David 10, 12, 39, 58, 127
  and Gostin, Lawrence 6, 13, 69, 70, 71,
    72, 74, 79, 89, 94–5, 96
Finland 159
First World War 48–9, 69
Florida 156
food
  advertising 153, 154, 155
  consumption 152, 153, 156
  contamination 67, 84, 93
Food and Agriculture Organization (FAO)
    112, 154
Food and Drug Administration 90, 92, 93
food industry 3, 144, 151, 152, 154, 155–6,
    168
food poisoning 84
food security 4, 100, 108–9, 111–13
  food aid 119, 151
foreign policy 54, 114–15
Foucault, Michel 19–21, 23, 26, 172, 173,
    187
Framework Convention on Tobacco
    Control 175, 185
France 41, 120, 141
  and alcoholism 159, 160
  and biological attacks (deliberate) 69,
    72
  and HIV/AIDS 120, 121, 127, 128
  and World Health Organization 114,
    117
Franco, Crystal 90, 93–4
Frankfurt 38
fruit and vegetables 151, 154
FSA (British Financial Services authority)
    51, 52
funding 93–4, 126–9, 142, 160

Gabriel, Richard 31
Gale, Jason 52
gambling 16

Gates Foundation 26, 120, 123, 128–9
GDP (gross domestic product) 110, 158, 159
Gellman, Barton 35
General Accounting Office, US 79
genetic engineering 74–5, 170, 187
Geneva 49, 117, 119
Geneva Protocol 69–70, 71, 72
Germany 41, 69, 117, 120, 137, 138, 159, 160
GHW 89, 117, 126, 127, 129, 138, 141, 142, 155
Gill, Timothy 149
Gillespie, Stuart 112
Gilmore, A. 140
glanders 84, 85
Global Alliance for Vaccines and Immunization (GAVI) 120
Global Fund to Fight HIV/AIDS, Tuberculosis and Malaria 122, 123, 125, 126–7, 170–1
'Global Health Security: Epidemic Alert and Response' resolution 3
Global Health Security Initiative (GHSI) 4–5, 26, 114
Global Influenza Surveillance Network 49, 176
global interdependence 8
Global Outbreak Alert and Response Network (GOARN) 57–8
Global Pandemic Influenza Action Plan to Increase Vaccine Supply 63–4
Global Plan to Stop TB 125
Global Public Health Intelligence Network (GPHIN) 61, 181
Global Strategy on Diet, Physical Activity and Health 118, 154
Goddard, N. 41
Gortmaker, Steven 153
Government Accountability Office (GAO) 36, 87, 90
Greece 159
Greeks, ancient 68
Grimard, Franque 111
Group of Eight (G8) 126
Guangdong province, China 37–8, 39, 45, 49

Guillemin, Jeanne 67, 68, 69, 73, 74, 78, 88, 89
Gulf War 73

H1N1 2009 (swine flu) *see* influenza
H2N2 influenza virus *see* influenza
H5N1 (avian flu) *see* influenza
Hagmann, Michael 118, 156
Halle, Christian 36
Hanna, Donald 44
Hanoi 39
hantavirus 84
Haslam, David 145
Hawkes, Corinna 152
health, global 1, 10, 113–29, 178
Health Canada 61
health care systems 9, 83, 87, 109–10, 119, 145, 160, 174–5
health care workers 39, 109
health inequalities 13, 108
Health Protection Agency 41, 58
helth security 1-29, 37, 42, 47, 54, 56-8, 88, 97, 100-1, 108, 109–10, 113–14, 130, 132, 165-6, 168-9, 172-4, 178-80, 185-7
'Health Security and Environment' Cluster 5
Health Security Committee 5
Health Survey of England 145–6
heart disease 103, 134, 145, 150
Hei, Wen 45
Henry L. Stimson Center, Global Health Security programme 54
hepatitis 8, 120
hip circumference ratios 149
HIV/AIDS 2, 8
  in developing countries 9, 99, 101–4, 170, 183–4
    Africa 13–14, 34–5, 102–3, 109, 128, 183
    Asia 103t, 128
  economic impacts 110–11, 127
  and food security 111, 112
  and France 120, 121, 127, 128
  medical interventions 28, 35, 62, 122, 128, 170, 183–4
  mortality rates 9, 41, 102–3, 105, 136

mother-to-child transmission 128, 184
and national security 13–14, 32, 33–7,
    43, 46, 56–7, 59
organizations involved in 54, 118,
    120–2, 126–7
    Global Fund to Fight HIV/AIDS,
        Tuberculosis and Malaria 122, 123,
        125, 126–7, 170–1
    United Nations Program on HIV/
        AIDS (UNAIDS) 34, 35, 36–7,
        56–7, 101–2
    and World Health Organization
        (WHO) 114, 121, 128, 170
pandemics 13–14, 101–2, 121
and tuberculosis 111, 124–5
and United States 121, 129
HIV/AIDS Task Force 54
Hoffman-La Roche, company 149
Hoffmann, Ilse 134
Holbrooke, Richard 36, 178
Homeland Security Presidential Directive
    21 63, 180
homosexuality 16
Hong Kong 38, 39, 40, 41, 42, 45, 50, 141,
    168
House of Lords 127, 129
housing 151, 186
Houston 85
HSR (*Human Security Report*) 174
Human Development Report 100
human rights 183
Human Rights Watch 104
Human Security Now 101
humanitarian action 13, 118
hyperactivity 16, 24

Illich, Ivan 186
income 111, 151, 152, 155, 174
India 105, 111, 121, 125, 134, 137, 141,
    178
individuals and security 100, 129–31, 166,
    169, 185–8
Indonesia 45, 50, 105, 114, 137, 175–9
influenza 5, 24, 47–8, 49, 59, 60, 166–8,
    173, 176, 180–1
    H1N1 2009 (swine flu) 1–2, 8, 32, 33,
        40, 64, 130, 166, 167

H2N2 influenza virus 96
H5N1 (avian flu) 2, 32, 33, 47–53, 130,
    173, 180–1
    and national security 8, 47, 51, 52, 53,
        60, 63, 166–7, 168, 176–9
    and United Kingdom 47, 48, 167
    and World Health Organization
        (WHO) 47, 52–3, 63–4, 176, 177
information dissemination 39, 40,
    43–4
injury 158, 159, 161, 162
Institute of Alcohol Studies 162
Institute of Medicine 7–8
insurance 51, 147–8, 155, 158
International AIDS Vaccine Initiative
    (IAVI) 121, 122
International Centre on Alcohol Policy
    161
International Health Regulations 3, 58,
    59–61, 173, 178, 181
International HIV/AIDS Alliance 121–2
International Obesity Task Force 148–9
international relations 14, 22–5, 30, 97,
    166
International Society for Infectious
    Diseases 61
Interpol 76
Iran 141
Iraq 42, 50, 73
Ireland 38, 41, 120, 141, 159, 160
Italy 41, 117, 141, 159, 160

Japan 40, 50, 70, 71, 78–9, 117, 138, 150,
    160, 176
Jianlun, Dr Liu 38
Jordan 141

Kamolratanakul, P. 111
Kenya 109
Kilbourne, Edwin 49
Klotz, Lynn 80, 91, 95
Kober, Katharina 109
Koch, Erin 68, 105
Korea 50
Kosovo 36
Kouvonen, Anne 135
Kowloon 40

laboratories 41
Laos 45
Latin America 103t, 107, 128
law enforcement 158
Laxminarayan, Ramanan 111
Lean, George 47
Leboeuf, Aline 12, 51, 180
Lederberg, Joshua 8
Lee, Kelley 152
Leonard, Mary 144
leprosy 68
lifestyle 24, 132–64, 175, 184–5
liver disease 8, 120, 158
London 49
Los Alamos National Laboratory 177
Los Angeles 85
luck 40, 42
Lugar, Richard 47
Lupton, Deborah 18, 19, 21
Luxembourg 120, 159, 160

McInnes, Colin 10
McLannahan, Heather 145
Macleod, R. 31
Madagascar 121
Mair, Michael 90, 92
malaria 8, 106–8
  in developing countries 9, 99, 101, 102,
    107, 110, 124, 170–1
  economic impact 109–10, 127
  medical countermeasures 28, 123, 170
  mortality rates 9, 107, 136
  organizations involved in 120, 123–4,
    129
    Global Fund to Fight HIV/AIDS,
      Tuberculosis and Malaria 122, 123,
      125, 126–7, 170–1
    World Health Organization (WHO)
      102, 107, 109–10, 123
  and United Kingdom 123, 127
Malaria Consortium 123, 124
Malawi 112, 137
Malaysia 45
Mamudu, Hadii 140
Manila 116
Marshall, George 1
Marshall Islands 150–1

Marxism 18
mass-casualty care system 63
masturbation 16
Material Threat Determination (MTD) 84
Matheny, Jason 91
Mathers, Colin 103
Matsumoto, Japan 78
Mbogela, Tumaini 104
Médecins Sans Frontières 26, 118, 119
media 155
medical countermeasures 30, 39–41, 62–4,
    65, 66, 88–97
medical equipment 28, 30
medical intervention 27-9, 31, 49, 52,
    119–26, 166–9, 170–1, 179-85
  developing countries 115, 120, 167
  malaria 28, 123, 170
  tuberculosis (TB) 28, 59, 128
medical professionals 17–19, 25–7, 65, 99,
    119, 138
  and alcoholism 160, 163
  and biological attacks (deliberate) 66,
    82–8, 98
  and global health 113–19, 125–6
  and lifestyle diseases 133, 164
  and national security 30, 54–62
  and obesity 154, 157
  and patients 17–18, 19–22, 26
medicalization 14–29, 72–5
  and lifestyle diseases 163-4, 171, 172
  and security 72, 165, 166, 185-8
    and health security 22–3, 97, 172–3
    and insecurity 23–5, 68–9, 97, 113
    and lifestyle diseases 143, 145, 163–4
    and national security 46, 53, 65
  and social issues 16–22, 26
medicalization theory 22–3, 29
medicines 118, 128
Medicines for Malaria Venture 123
Melbourne, Australia 49, 176
meliodosis 85
men 136, 145–6
Menon, K. 40
menopause 16, 22
Metropark Hotel, Hong Kong 38
Metropolitan Life Insurance Company
    147–8

Mexico 117
microbiology 54
Middle East 107
migration 3, 66
military capabilities 28, 31
military forces, HIV/AIDS prevalence
	rates 34–5
Millennium Development Goals 123–4
Miller, Judith 73
Minnesota Settlement Agreement
	140–2
Moldova, Republic of 160
Mongoven, Ann 42
Montenegro 141
morality 17
morbidity 83, 84, 130, 185
mortality 50–1, 130
	biological weapons 83, 84
	children 102, 103, 107
	HIV/AIDS 9, 41, 102–3, 105, 136
	and lifestyle diseases 135–8, 145–6, 158,
		185
	malaria 9, 107, 136
	SARS (severe acute respiratory
		syndrome) 41–2, 43, 46
	tuberculosis (TB) 9, 102, 104–5, 136
mosquitoes 106, 107–8, 110, 127
Mozambique 121, 124
Myanmar 45, 121

Namibia 112
nano-technologies 75
National Health Service (British) 145, 169,
	171, 172, 185
National Influenza Monitoring Laboratory
	49
National Institute for Medical Research
	176
National Institute of Allergy and Infectious
	Diseases (NIAID) 89, 93, 94,
	169–70
National Institute of Infectious Diseases
	(Japan) 176
National Institutes of Health 56, 93, 94,
	95, 148
National Intelligence Council (NIC) 8, 13,
	34, 35, 38, 39, 40, 41, 45

National Intelligence Estimate 34
National Medical Research Unit 2
	(NAMRU-2) 177
National Risk Register 47
National Security Council, US 73
National Security Strategy, US 32
National Strategy for Pandemic Influenza
	62, 180
National Strategy for Public Health and
	Medical Preparedness 63, 180
Netherlands 117, 120, 123, 141, 159, 160
Network for Accountability of Tobacco
	Transnationals 141
New Delhi 117
New York City 85, 182
New York Times 47
New Zealand 141
Nicotine Replacement Therapy 172
Nietzsche 25
Nigeria 34, 50, 105, 124
Nipah virus 8, 84
Nixon administration 71
non-governmental organizations 118, 120,
	123, 127, 141
North America 39, 103t, 150
Norway 114, 117, 120, 127, 141
Nuclear Threat Initiative, Global Health
	and Security Initiative 54
nuclear weapons 67–8, 72, 73, 81–2, 174
nutrition/diet 149, 153–4, 156, 171, 186

Obama, Barack 47
obesity 9–10, 16, 132–3, 144–57, 163–4,
	171, 175, 184–5
	and children 150, 153, 171
	and employment 152, 155, 171
	and United Kingdom 144, 145–6, 171
	and United States 144, 145, 148, 152,
		156
	and World Health Organization (WHO)
		148, 150, 151–2, 154, 156
Oceana 103t
OECD (Organization for Economic
	Cooperation and Development)
	123, 126
Oliver, J. Eric 144, 146, 147, 149
Organization of African Unity 126–7

Oslo Declaration 115
osteoarthritis 145
Ostergard, Robert L., Jr 34
Oxfam 118

Pacific Islands 138
Pakistan 50, 105
Pandemic and All Hazards Preparedness
        Act 63
pandemics 6
    HIV/AIDS 13–14, 101–2, 121
    and national security 30–65, 130–1
    surveillance systems 94–5, 166–9, 173,
        180–1
    and United Kingdom 32, 176
    and United States 167, 168, 176–7, 178,
        180
    and World Health Organization (WHO)
        166, 181–2
    see also influenza
Paris, Roland 113
Parker, Elizabeth 81–2
Pasteur, Louis 68
patients 17–18, 19–22, 26, 172, 186
peacekeepers 36
Pelletier, Marc 96
Personal Responsibility in Food
        Consumption Act ('Cheeseburger
        bill') 152
pertussis 120
Peru 160
Peterson, Susan 13–14
Petro, James B. 74–5
pharmaceutical industry 18, 25, 63, 90, 91,
        128, 155, 177, 187
Philadelphia 85
Philippines 42, 45, 105, 137
Piot, Peter 56, 121
Pisani, Elizabeth 102
plague 58, 59, 68, 70, 84, 85, 89, 96
pneumococcal vaccine 120
Poland 160
poliomyelitis 1, 60
political stability 34, 35, 127
politics 1, 2, 12, 13–14, 23, 25–7, 100,
        114–15, 173, 186–8
population 3, 19–22, 27–9, 179–85

Portugal 159, 160
post-traumatic stress disorder 16
poultry 51, 64, 168
poverty 108, 118, 137, 168
pregnancy 16, 18, 161, 162, 184
President's Plan for AIDS Relief (PEPFAR)
        62
Presidential Decision Directive on
        Emerging Infectious Diseases 1996
        (PDD) 55–6
prevention 19–22, 119, 136, 171
Price-Smith, Andrew 7
productivity levels 158, 159
profitability 137
Project BioSense 86–7, 93, 182
Project BioShield 89–93, 95, 169
Project BioWatch 85–6, 93, 182
Pro-MED-mail 61, 181
public health 7, 9-10, 12, 19–22, 26, 28–9,
        85
    systems 32, 83, 94–5, 172–5
Public Health Agency of Canada 61
Public Health Research Institute, New
        Jersey 96
Public Health Security and Bioterrorism
        Preparedness and Response Act 88

Q fever 70, 78, 84
quarantine 39–41, 58–9, 93
Quetelet, Adolphe 147

Rajeswari, R. 111
RAND Corporation 54
RBM 110
Reagan administration 153
recession 51
Red Cross, International Committee of
        118–19
Relenza 64, 167
Réunion 160
ricin 84
Rockefeller Foundation 121
Rollback Malaria Partnership 123–4
Romania 41, 50, 141
Romans 68
Rose, Nikolas 21
Rosenau, William 78, 80

rotavirus 120
Royal Institute of International Affairs 54
Rushton, Simon 36
Russia 50, 70, 71
Russian Federation 160
Ryan, Jeffrey 68, 70, 71, 77, 78, 85, 86, 87, 92

Safman, Rachel 181
Saint Lucia 160
Saloojee, Yussuf 140
salt 144, 154, 155
Samoa 150
San Diego 85
San Francisco 85
sanitation 118, 186
sarin gas 8, 78
SARS (severe acute respiratory syndrome) 2, 33, 37–46, 52, 58
  and national security 8, 53, 59, 60, 61
Satcher, David 171
Science, journal 94
Scotland 49, 141
Searle, John 11
Second World War 70, 71
securitization theory 14–15
security
  biosecurity 7, 41, 66–98
  health security 1, 2, 3–14, 26–7, 57–62, 100–1, 108, 113–14, 165–72
    and medicalization 22–3, 97, 172–3
    and politics 12, 13–14, 100, 173, 186–8
    and public health 7, 9–10
  and individuals 7, 9, 100, 129–31, 166, 169, 185–8
  insecurity 23–5, 30, 99–131, 151
    and biological attacks (deliberate) 68, 76, 87
    and medicalization 23–5, 43, 53, 68–9, 97, 113, 129, 132, 188
    pandemics 33, 37
  and lifestyle diseases 9–10, 135, 138, 145, 157, 163–4
  medicalization 14–29, 53, 185–8
    and biological attacks (deliberate) 68–9, 72–5

and lifestyle diseases 132, 143, 145, 163–4
and SARS 46, 53
and surveillance 165, 185
national 7–9, 13, 30–65, 130–1
  and H5N1 (avian flu) 8, 47, 51, 52, 53, 60, 63, 166–7, 168, 176–9
  and HIV/AIDS 13–14, 32, 33–7, 43, 46, 56–7, 59
  policy 30, 34, 54, 55–6
  and SARS 42–3, 46, 53
  and United States 7–9, 55–6
Senegal 114
Sentinel Provider Network (SPN) 180
Shah, M. 112
Shanxi province, China 39
Shea, Dana 85, 86
shellfish toxins 73
Shinya, K. 53
Shisana, O. 109
shyness 24
Singapore 38, 39, 40, 41, 45, 141
Singapore Straits Times 42
Siu, Alan 40, 45
sleep apnoea 145
Slovakia 160
smallpox 1, 4, 59, 60, 169–70
  as biological weapon 68, 73, 84, 85, 88–9, 92
Smith, Roy 150–1
smoking 9, 132, 133–43, 172
  and medicalization 163–4, 171, 172
  and mortality 135–8, 185
  research 140, 141
  second-hand smoke 138, 139, 141, 142
  surveillance systems 175, 179, 184–5
  and World Health Organization (WHO) 135–6, 138–41, 143, 156–7, 172
smuggling, tobacco industry 140, 141, 143
social impacts 18–19, 35, 51, 127, 161, 171, 186
social issues 15, 16–22, 26
social life 8, 17, 18–19, 21, 143, 153, 157, 164, 187
South Africa 104, 105, 109, 110, 114

South America 39
Southern Research Institute 96
Soviet Union 73, 92
Spain 41, 68, 141, 159
Spanish flu 48
speech act theory 10–12, 15
St. Louis 85
starvation 49, 112, 119, 150
stigma, social 103–4
stockpiling, medication and equipment 62,
    88, 89, 92, 167, 170, 179
    see also medical countermeasures
stockpiling, weapons 69
Stop TB Partnership 124–5
Story, Mary 153
Strategic Advisory Committee for Global
    Health Security 5
Strategic National Stockpile (SNS) 90,
    93, 169
Strauss, R. 135
stress 135, 151
Strong, P. 186
Sturgeon, Nicola 157
subsidies 152, 155
Sudan 121, 124
sugar, in diet 144, 151, 154, 155
sugar industry 118, 152, 156
suicide attacks 77
surveillance systems 5, 119, 165, 179–85
    biosurveillance 63, 173–4
    Global Influenza Surveillance Network
        49, 176
    and lifestyle diseases 175, 179, 184–5
    pandemics 94–5, 166–9, 173, 180–1
Swaziland 109, 160
Sweden 41, 120, 121, 141, 159
swine flu *see* influenza, H1N1 2009
Switzerland 41, 123, 141

Taipei 41
Taiwan 41
Takemi, Keizo 108, 115
Tamiflu 64, 167, 169
Tanzania 34, 104
Target TB 125
taxation 128, 137, 139, 140, 144, 155, 159,
    160, 175

Taylor, Allyn 134
TB Alert 125
technological innovation 152–3
television 152–3
terrorism 4, 5, 8, 42, 47, 52, 113, 130
    see also bioterrorism
tetanus 120
Texas A&M University 96
Thailand 45, 50, 111, 114, 118, 124, 137,
    141, 178, 181
thermal scanners 40–1
Thompson, Tommy 4, 144
tobacco, advertising 134, 136, 138, 139,
    141, 142
tobacco, smokeless 133–4, 141–2
tobacco industry 134, 136, 137, 138, 140,
    141, 142
Tokyo 8, 40, 49, 78
Toronto 39
tourism 3, 44–5, 51, 168
trade 8, 134, 142, 152
    illicit 139, 140, 141
transmission
    animals to humans 38, 64, 168
    human-to-human transmission 33, 51,
        52–3, 83, 167
transport 8, 32, 151, 153
travel *see* air travel 128
treatments *see individual diseases*; medical
    countermeasures
Treaty on the Non-Proliferation of Nuclear
    Weapons 81
tuberculosis (TB) 104–6, 111
    in developing countries 9, 99, 101,
        170–1
    and HIV/AIDS 111, 125
    MDR-TB and XDR-TB 105–6, 125
    medical countermeasures 28, 59,
        128
    mortality 9, 102, 104–5, 136
    organizations involved in 120, 122,
        124–5, 126–7
        and World Health Organization
            (WHO) 102, 105, 106, 125
    treatments 8, 105–6
tularaemia 70, 73, 84, 85, 89, 96
Turkey 50, 137

Tye, Joe 134
typhoid 1
typhus 59, 84
Tzasz, Thomas 25

Uganda 112, 121, 124, 184
Ukraine 121
UNITAID 127–8
United Kingdom 41, 127, 144, 169
  and biological attacks (deliberate) 68,
    70, 72
  and H5N1 (avian flu) 47, 48, 167
  and HIV/AIDS 121, 127
  and lifestyle diseases 141, 144, 145–6,
    159, 160, 171, 172, 185
  and malaria 123, 127
  organizations involved in 117, 120,
    124
  and pandemics 32, 176
United Nations 6, 36–7, 73, 87
United Nations Charter 81–2, 175
United Nations Children's Fund (UNICEF)
    120, 123
United Nations Development Program
    (UNDP) 100, 110, 111, 123
United Nations Program on HIV/AIDS
    (UNAIDS) 34, 35, 36–7, 56–7,
    101–2, 121, 183
United Nations Security Council 36, 56,
    81–2, 173–4
United States 34, 38, 47, 58–9, 121, 123,
    180
  and biological attacks (deliberate) 70,
    71, 72, 73–4, 76, 169, 182
  and lifestyle diseases 137, 138, 142, 144,
    145, 148, 152, 156
  and national security 7–9, 55–6
  and organizations involved in health
    security 117–18, 120
  and pandemics 167, 168, 176–7, 178,
    180
UPMC 84
urbanization 3, 151, 168
Uruguay 141

vaccination programmes 117, 119, 120,
    167

vaccines 4, 28, 30, 73, 92, 125
  biological weapons 83, 88
  HIV/AIDS 122, 170
  influenza 63–4, 166–7, 176
  see also medical countermeasures
VaxGen 90
Venezuela 141
Venezuelan equine encephalitis 70, 73
Vietnam 38, 41, 45, 50
violence 104, 108, 159
viral encephalitis 84
viral haemorrhagic fevers 59, 70, 84, 89,
    170
Virchow, Rudolf 62
voluntary counselling and testing (VCT)
    183

Wæver, Ole 12
war 24
war crimes 70
War on Terror 66, 82, 87–8, 93, 97–8,
    169
Warren, C. 142
Washington, DC 85, 117
water supply 4, 67, 68, 118, 119, 186
Waxman, Henry 142
weather conditions 77
weight control 135, 149, 171
wetland destruction 168
Williams, Dylan 118
Williams, Simon J. 17, 18
women 112, 136, 145–6, 161
Working Group on Civilian Biodefense
    83
World Bank 120, 123, 126, 137
  on H5N1 (avian flu) 47, 50, 51, 52, 53,
    64, 173
  on HIV/AIDS 111, 121
World Economic Forum (WEF) 52
World Health Assembly (WHA) 3, 5, 117,
    154
World Health Day 6
World Health Organization (WHO) 1, 2,
    59–61, 116–18, 129
  and biological attacks (deliberate)
    87–8
  and endemic disease 114

World Health Organization (WHO) (*cont.*)
    and HIV/AIDS 114, 121, 128, 170
    and malaria 102, 107, 109–10, 123
    and tuberculosis 102, 105, 106, 125
  and global health 5–6, 26, 28, 57–8,
    59–61, 87, 113–19, 120, 188
    Global Influenza Surveillance
      Network 49, 176
    Global Strategy on Diet, Physical
      Activity and Health 118, 154
  and lifestyle diseases 134
    and alcoholism 157, 158, 160–1
    and obesity 148, 150, 151–2, 154,
      156
    and smoking 135–6, 137, 138–41,
      143, 156–7, 172
  and pandemics 166, 181–2
    and H5N1 (avian flu) 47, 52–3, 63–4,
      176, 177
    and SARS 38, 39, 41
World Health Report 6, 102–3

'X-ray' campaign 181

Yach, Derek 140
yellow fever 58, 59

Zambia 112, 121, 124
Zelicow, Philip 13
Zimbabwe 137
Zola, Irving 17
Zubay, Geoffrey 48, 73, 79